YR HEN IAITH

Nyni, a wêl ei hurddas trwy niwl ei hadfyd,
Codwn, yma, yr hen feini annistryw.

Yr Heniaith, Waldo Williams

CELTIC STUDIES PUBLICATIONS VII

Yr Hen Iaith

Studies in early Welsh

edited by

PAUL RUSSELL

CELTIC STUDIES PUBLICATIONS

ABERYSTWYTH

2003

Celtic Studies Publications

for customers in North America:

Celtic Studies Publications
c/o The David Brown Book Co.
P. O. Box 511, 28 Main Street
Oakville, CT 06779
USA

editorial correspondence:

CSP-Cymru Cyf
Centre for Advanced Welsh and Celtic
Studies
National Library of Wales
Aberystwyth, Ceredigion sy23 3hh
Wales

Front cover illustration: Aberystwyth, National Library of Wales, Peniarth MS 1 (the Black Book of Carmarthen) folio 37 verso, showing part of the text of a praise poem of *c.* 1100 to the prince Hywel ap Goronwy.

CONTENTS

Preface   vii

PETER SCHRIJVER, The etymology of Welsh *chwith* and the semantics and morphology of PIE *$k^{(w)}sweib^h$-   I

PAUL RUSSELL, *Rowynniauc, Rhufoniog*: the orthography and phonology of /μ/ in Early Welsh   25

PETER KITSON, Old English literacy and the provenance of Welsh *y*   49

SIMON RODWAY, Two developments in medieval literary Welsh and their implications for dating texts   67

GRAHAM ISAAC, The structure and typology of prepositional relative clauses in Early Welsh   75

ALEXANDER FALILEYEV, PAUL RUSSELL, The dry-point glosses in Oxoniensis Posterior   95

PIERRE-YVES LAMBERT, The Old Welsh glosses on Weights and Measures   103

PETER BUSSE, Are there elements of non-standard language in the work of the Gogynfeirdd?   135

ERICH POPPE, The Progressive in *Ystorya Bown de Hamtwn*   145

JOHN T. KOCH, *Marwnad Cunedda* a diwedd y Brydain Rufeinig   171

Abbreviations   199

References   202

PREFACE

In April 1999 a week-end colloquium was held at Jesus College, Oxford on 'The History of Welsh before 1500' organised by Professor Thomas Charles-Edwards. The papers in this volume are part of the outcome of that Colloquium. We are grateful to the trustees of the Rhŷs Fund for their support and encouragement at the Colloquium.

Not all the papers in this volume were given at the Colloquium: some speakers had already committed their contribution elsewhere or their topic was part of a larger undertaking or pressure of other commitments prevented them from contributing to the volume. In some cases those speakers have made other contributions to this volume (Peter Schrijver and John Koch). In some cases, speakers had been invited to the Colloquium but had been unable to attend but were still invited to contribute papers to the volume (Alexander Falileyev). In one instance, a paper given at a subsequent conference seemed to the editor to be of such relevance as to be worth incorporating in the volume (Peter Kitson on Welsh *y*). There were eleven papers given at the Colloquium of which six are published here. All but two of the contributors to this volume gave papers at the Colloquium.

The ten studies in this volume cover a wide range of different fields from Indo-European etymology to detailed syntactic analysis of a single Middle Welsh text. Peter Schrijver pursues the etymology of Welsh *chwith* across the full range of Indo-European languages, concluding that it is related to a range of words meaning 'curved, curving' and that it had developed to the meaning 'left' by way of 'not straight, crooked, inappropriate'. Two studies focus on matters of orthography and phonology: Paul Russell considers possible spellings of /μ/ in Old and Middle Welsh and goes on to consider the phonological development of this and related troublesome segments; Peter Kitson, coming at Welsh from an Old English perspective, examines possible English origins for the use of *y* in Welsh. Simon Rodway makes another valuable contribution to our understanding of the verbal morphology of the Gogynfeirdd in analysing the different endings in use for the 3rd singular imperfect indicative and the 3rd singular present subjunctive. Graham Isaac looks at prepositional relative clauses and shows that they are more widespread in Celtic languages than had previously been thought; he argues that the prepositional relative structure, i.e. 'upon which he fell', was replaced by the resumptive pronoun pattern, i.e. 'which he fell upon (it)', within British. The remainder of the contributions consider linguistic features in relation to specific texts. Alexander Falileyev and Paul Russell re-examine the dry-point glosses in Oxoniensis Posterior (Oxford, Bodley MS, 572) and conclude that none is definitely Brittonic (contrary to Jackson's view) and therefore it need no longer be assumed that they presuppose a bilingual environment. Pierre-Yves Lambert provides a much-needed new edition of the text on weights and measures together with the Old Welsh glosses. Peter Busse discusses colloquial elements in the language of the Gogynfeirdd. Erich Poppe analyses the use of the progressive in a particular Middle Welsh text, *Ystorya Bown de Hamtwn*. John Koch re-edits *Marwnad Cunedda* and argues that linguistically it should be dated to the pre-Old Welsh period and that it may reflect conditions in North Britain at the end of the Roman occupation.

I am grateful to Thomas Charles-Edwards for reading drafts and making suggestions. This project would not have seen the light of day without the willingness of John Koch to publish the volume, and I note my thanks to him for his help in preparing the chapters for publication.

PAUL RUSSELL

The etymology of Welsh *chwith* and the semantics and morphology of PIE $*k^{(w)}sweib^{h}$-

Peter Schrijver

1. *chwith*: SEMANTICS

GPC s.v. provides the following array of translations of Welsh *chwith*: 'left; left-handed; awkward, bungling, uncouth; unfortunate, sinister, sad; strange, unaccustomed, unusual; wrong, amiss'. The systematic connection between these glosses is not immediately evident, nor is it clear which are the earliest attested meanings. Is one to think of a primary early meaning 'left', whence on the one hand 'left-handed', 'bungling, awkward, uncouth' and, on the other, 'opposite to right', which then develops into 'unfavourable, sinister, wrong, amiss', and 'not as it should be', which leads to 'strange, unaccustomed, unusual'? This is certainly conceivable, and it seems to be more or less what the Welsh glosses to *chwith* imply.[1] The problem is, however, that the Middle and Early Modern Welsh attestations by GPC do not support this view of things. None of the MW attestations mentioned by GPC can be translated with 'left, left-handed'. It seems that *chwith* rather describes wrongness, the absence of established order, of how things should be.

The earliest attestation of *chwith* is in one of Llywarch ap Llywelyn's poems in praise of Rhodri ab Owain o Wynedd, which dates from between 1175 and 1195 (CBT V, 7). The earliest manuscript version is in hand **α** of H (dated to around 1300 by Huws NLWJ xxii (= MWM 193-226)). Lines 9–10 of that poem in fo. 104b.41 read: *Teyrnas yth law lid Gereint nyd chwith / yr chwydad esgereint* 'Lordship in

---

[1] 'Aswy, yn perthyn i'r ochr honno i'r corff dynol sydd fel rheol yn wannach na'r llall, gwrthwyneb i'r dde' (i.e. 'left, pertaining to that side of the human body which as a rule is weaker than the other, opposite to the right'). Abbreviations of texts in this section are those of GPC.

your hand, o wrath of Gereint, is not *chwith* because you disgorged enemies'.[2] The context would seem to allow a translation 'unfortunate' (*anffodus*, Jones CBT V, p. 75), 'unfitting' (TYP[2] 360), as well as various other glosses, such as 'awkward, disarrayed', which appear in later attestations. All one can say with certainty that *chwith* cannot possibly mean 'left, left-handed'. I would subscribe to Bromwich's interpretation and translate 'unfitting, amiss, wrong, not as it should be', being the opposite of 'in order, right, fitting, as it should be', as this fits in better with the other attestations of the word.

Wrongness with respect to how things should be is a semantic feature present in two Early Modern Welsh examples where *chwith* refers specifically to clothing. In BBCS xvii.81 (15–16th c.), someone 'without new clothes' is *hwidd* (with a note-worthy spelling). Similarly in the Welsh translation of the First Book of Samuel (I Sam. xxiv.6, 1588), *chwîth fu gan Ddafydd o herwydd iddo dorri cwrr y fantell* 'David felt *chwith* after he had torn the edge of his mantle'. In the latter example it is not so much disarray as the feeling of impropriety this brings about that is being described by *chwith*. This fits in with the following passage from TN xxvi: *Chwîth oedd can y Brytaniait welet cymysciat* 'The Britons felt awkward when they saw the confusion'.

The element of impropriety and awkwardness bridges the gap between the examples and the semantics of Early Mod.W derivatives such as *chwitho* 'to stand aghast, be dismayed, astonished' and *chwithder* 'amazement at something un-expected happening'. The idea of *chwith* denoting an aberration from how something should be also agrees with the highly specific meaning of Mod.W *chwithnod*, which is not a 'left mark' but 'reversed mark' (GPC: 'sheep's ear-mark whose pattern is the opposite or reverse of another'). Similarly, Mod.W *o chwith* means 'wrongly, the wrong way about'.

Other MW examples can now be tackled more easily. In BY 20, *y Othoniel y bu vab a elwit Aioth, a hwnnw a vv chwith* 'Othoniel had a son named Aioth, who was *chwith*'. The meaning of *chwith* here is certainly neither 'left-handed' nor 'clumsy'. The adjective rather refers to the mental defectiveness of the child, its funda-mental 'wrongness'. The epithet *chwith* in MW personal names such as *Dauid Chuyth, Howel Whith, Llywelyn Chwith* can be translated as 'simple' or 'crooked', and not necessarily as 'left handed' (*pace* Gw. Peredur Jones BBCS iii. 33).

In a poem in praise of Owain Glyndŵr, Gruffudd Llwyd says of King Arthur *chwith fu neb wrthaw* (IGE[2] 126 l. 6) 'anyone was *chwith* compared to him'. Appropriate translations would seem to range from 'foolish' to 'awkward, unfitting, wrong'.

---

2   On Gereint mab Erbin, see TYP[2] 356–60.

The theme of wrongness, this time with grave consequences, seems to be present in the title given to a triad in the Red Book of Hergest (TYP² 144-5): *teir gvith baluavt ynys prydein* 'the three *chwith* hand-slaps of Britain', two of which resulted in war (the slaps given to Branwen and Gwenhwyfar), while the story behind the third is unclear. Bromwich freely translates 'harmful', where an approximate translation 'wrongful', perhaps 'overturning', would seem to do better justice to the context of the triad. *Gwith* instead of expected *chwith* may be compared with other examples of *gw-* for *chw-* (e.g. *guero* beside *chwerw* 'bitter', Bromwich TYP² 53).

All this is not to say that the meaning 'left' is not attested. For one thing, *chwith* is the normal word for 'left' in many varieties of Modern Welsh as well as in the northern-based modern standard language (GA s.v. left; Fynes-Clinton, *The Welsh Vocabulary*, 333). Note that the South Welsh dialect dictionary of Meredith Morris (*Glossary of the Demetian Dialect*) has *ase* = Mod.W *aswy, aseu* for 'left', which is missing from the North Welsh dictionary of Fynes-Clinton, while *whith* exclusively means 'amiss, askance'. The first clear instance of the meaning 'left' dates from the 15th c.: *ar with hen ssyr Rys* (ID 57) 'to the left of old Sir Rhys'. From the early 17th c. may be quoted *o'r ddeheu i'r ysgwydd chwith* (Salisbury, EH 11, 1618) 'from the right to the left shoulder'; *chwith, sinister, laevus. Insolitus, insuetus*' (D, 1632) and various instances of the derivative *chwithig* 'left-handed' (also 'wrong').

The evidence discussed so far would seem to suggest that the meaning 'left' is a later development out of a primary meaning 'amiss, wrong, out of order'.

2. BRETON *c'hwitañ*

The idea that 'wrong, not right' can lead to 'amiss' and hence 'missing' is borne out by the Modern Welsh expression *bod yn chwith ar ôl rhywun* 'to miss someone', lit. 'to be *chwith* after someone'. The development to 'missing, being without' bridges the semantic gap between *chwith* and its only likely cognate in Breton, *c'hwitañ* (Ernault, *Glossaire*, 329).

Mod.B *c'hwitañ* means 'to fail, be unsuccessful, miss; (of plan) to miscarry, to prove abortive' (Delaporte, *Geiriadur*, s.v.) and is always intransitive. Its earliest occurrence is in Grégoire de Rostrenen's dictionary of 1732 as *huytout*, Vannetais *dihuyteiñ, dihuytout*. Vannetais has *ne huit quet* 'rather well, passable' and *ne huitan* 'I'm not too bad'. The obvious formal problem is that the expected counterpart of W *chwith* would be Mod.B *c'hwizhañ*. Now formally *c'hwitañ* is very similar to EMod.W *chwitio*, an alternative form of Mod.W *cwitio* 'to quit, renounce, acquit, absolve'. This is clearly a borrowing of English *to quit*, which itself derives from

French *quitter*, whose Breton descendants are *kuit* 'gone, away' and its derivative *kuitaat* 'leave'. I suggest that Mod.B *c'hwitañ* replaces an earlier **c'hwiðañ* by analogy with *kuit*, and that **c'hwiðañ* is a derivative of **c'hwið*, the counterpart of W *chwith*. The reason for the replacement would be the superficial formal resemblance and the semantic similarity of 'fail, miss' and 'leave, quit'. Similarly, *chw-* in Mod.W *chwitio* may well have been supported by the semantic similarity to *chwith*.

3. IRISH *citt-*

W *chwith* is usually connected with EMod.Ir. *cittach* 'lefthanded, awkward', Mod.Ir., Sc.G *ciotach* 'id.', Mod.Ir. *ciotóg*, Sc.G *ciotag* 'left hand', Mod.Ir. *ciotrainneach* 'clumsy, unfortunate', Sc.G *ciotachd*, *ciotaireachd* 'left-handedness, clumsiness'.[3] These forms presuppose an OIr. **citt* or, conceivably, **cicht* (cf. O'Brien, *Celtica* ii, on the sporadic change of Ir. *cht* to *t*, e.g. *littiu* < *lichtiu* 'porridge').

On the basis of **cicht*, a common Insular Celtic form can only be reconstructed with great difficulty. As to Goidelic, the underlying form would be **kext-i-s* > Pr.Ir. **kixtih* (raising) > **cicht* > *citt-* (with sporadic change *cht* > *t*). In British, however, one would need to posit **skext-i-s*, with mobile *s-*. This would then develop into PBr. **xwextih* (PCelt. **sk-* > **xw-* probably only before **e*; Schrijver BBCS xxxix.1-15) > **xwixtih* (final *i*-affection of **e*, Schrijver SBCHP 265-68) > W *chwith* (**ixt* > **īð* > *ith*). Two untrivial assumptions are required. The first is that the allomorphs with and without mobile *s-* were retained until the split-up of Insular Celtic.[4] Secondly, Ir. *t* must reflect **cht* by a sporadically attested development. Both assumptions do little to inspire confidence; were one nevertheless to accept these reconstructions, this only leads to an etymological dead end.

The reconstruction that is usually endorsed departs from Ir. *citt-* < **kitt-*. In order to uphold this, one must again assume mobile *s-* in order to arrive at British **hw-*. Worse, short *-i-* of Goidelic **kitt-* cannot be regularly connected with long *-ī-* of British **skītt-* unless one is prepared to accept that Goidelic **kitt-* goes back to **kēttu-* and British **xwið-* to **skītt-* < pre-PCelt. ** skētt-*, with a morphologically highly problematic lengthened grade. Even if one were to ignore this problem, the traditionally proposed etymology of this Celtic complex itself faces insur-

---

3   Stokes, *Wortschatz*, 308, Foy IF vi.317, Pedersen KZ xxxviii.389, Pedersen VKG i.77, Walde–Pokorny, *Vergleichende Wörterbuch*, 2.537, Pedersen-Lewis CCCG 19, Vendryes, LEIA C–108.

4   A possible parallel is OIr. *fet* 'whistling or hissing sound', MW *chwythu* 'blow' < **(s)wisd-*; alternatively, however, *fet* may simply reflect the generalized lenited form.

mountable problems: Celtic *-tt-5 and *-ĭ- or *-ĕ- cannot be reconciled with
*skaiwos (or *skeh₂iwos) 'left' in Lat. scaevus, Gr. σκαιός 'left'.

It therefore appears not only that a satisfactory IE etymology is lacking but
also that the inner-Celtic connection between chwith and citt- is highly problematic. Once chwith is divorced from its would-be Irish cognate, however, an
alternative etymology presents itself.

4. OLD DUTCH swifter-

A remarkable and hitherto unrecognized cognate of chwith can be found in Old
Dutch *swifter 'left, north', which is attested in the place-name Swifterbant
(Suifterbant 793, copy 10th c.), lit. 'Left or Northern Settlement', which was
situated in the province of Gelderland.6 It contrasts with Teisterbant (Testeruenti
709, copy 1191, Testarbanto 815–16, copy 1170–75), lit. 'Right or Southern
Settlement', whose first member reflects PGm. *tehs(i)-ϑera- < *deksi-tero- 'right'.
Old Dutch *swifter- survives as the rare Middle Dutch suchter, as Pijnenburg has
argued (Bijdragen, 89). *swifter > suchter reflects PGm. *swif-tera- and may be
directly compared with MW chwith < *swix-to- < *swiφ-to-. The root common to
both forms is *swip-, *swib- or *swibʰ-.

5. PROTO-GERMANIC *sweib-

The next etymological step becomes acceptable once we remember that the oldest
attested meaning of chwith is approximately 'wrong, amiss' and that 'left' probably
developed from this. Under these circumstances a connection with the Germanic
strong present stem *sweib- is both formally and semantically attractive.

OIc. svífa ordinarily means 'rove, ramble' and 'turn', as in sumir svífu at nautum
(Sturl. iii 241)7 'some went roving after cattle', and sveinn sýsliga sveif til skógar
(Hým.) 'the lad turned briskly to the wood'. The common feature is a curved,
wave-like motion. If only a single curve is envisaged, a meaning 'turn' arises, and if
a number of waves are called to mind, this leads to 'turn left and right, move to
and fro'. A specialized application of the second type is 'drift', as in Sigfús sveif at

---

5   Walde-Pokorny, Vergleichende Wörterbuch, 2.537 suggest that Celtic -tt- reflects *-tn- before
    a following stressed vowel. Even if this rule is correct for Celtic (Lühr, Sprachwissenschaft
    x, 274–346), the difference in formation between *(s)kĭtnV- and *skaiwos remains
    formidable.

6   In this section dates are those of Künzel et al., Lexicon.

7   In this section abbreviations of texts are those of Cleasby, et al., Icelandic-English Dictionary.

landi (*Bs.* i.139) 'S. drifted ashore'. In order to express the lack of control by the subject, the latter often appears in the dative case, while the verb is in the 3rd person sg., as in *sveif þá skipinu frá landi* (*Fms.* vi.108) 'then the ship drifted off-shore'. Another specialized meaning, this time deriving from 'turn', is found in *láta samþykki sitt svífa til* 'to let one's consent swerve towards', i.e. 'to agree to'. The reflexive *svífask um* 'to be active, bustle about' can easily be connected through 'to move to and fro'. In the sentence *segir þórðr at svífi yfir hann* (*Sturl.* iii 286) 'þ. says that he was suddenly taken ill', the specific use of *svífi* no doubt primarily involves the notion of dizziness.

OIc. *svífask einskis*, lit. 'turn oneself away from nothing', means 'stop at nothing'. This provides a semantic bridge for connecting Goth. **sweiban* 'cease'.[8] This occurs only twice, both times in combination with the negation. Like the OIc. verb, it is a class I strong verb:

> Luke VII. 45: *iþ si, fram þammei innatiddja, ni swaif bikukjan fotuns meinans* 'but she, from the time I entered, has not stopped (οὐ διέλειπεν) kissing my feet';

> Ephes. I.16: *unsweibands awiliudo in izwara* 'without ceasing (οὐ παύομαι) I thank you'.

Further formal equivalents are OE *swifan* 'to move around, turn, sweep, interfere in a matter' (intrans.) and OFris. *swiva* 'waver, be uncertain'.

In the German and Dutch areas of West Germanic we find two derivatives, **swib-ē-* and **swaib-ō-*. **swib-ē-* is a weak class 3 verb. The IE stative suffix **-eh₁-* provides it with an approximate meaning 'to be in a state of turning, of moving to and fro'. This fits in well with OHG *swebēn* gl. *no, cohortor, fretus* 'to drift, move to and fro, go in and out (of the tide)', *bi-swebēn* gl. *emico* 'to stick out' (< 'curve, swell'?), MHG *sweben* 'move to and fro' (floating or flying), MDutch *swēven* 'float to and fro'.[9]

*swaib-ō-, a weak class 2 verb, is attested in OHG *sweibōn* 'to turn, roll (a wheel), float (through the air)'. This looks like a denominative verb derived from **swaibaz* in e.g. OHG *sueib* 'movement, rolling', or, alternatively, from **swaibō*, which survives in OIc. *sveif* (f.) 'tiller, handle fixed to the top of a rudderpost to

---

8   This is the standard etymology (e.g. Lehmann, *Gothic Etymological Dictionary*, S179); Seebold's hesitation (*Vergleichendes und etymologisches Wörterbuch*, 484–85) seems unjustified.

9   Under OHG *ir-swebben* gl. *restagno* 'to be inundated' may be hidden the Old Saxon equivalent (in view of -*bb*-) of OHG *swebēn*. This is supported by the stative semantics. The alternative, viz. -*swebben* < **-swibjan*, does not account for the -*e*-, and it requires positing a first class weak verb for which there is no other evidence.

serve as a lever in steering it', in other words, the instrument that controls the sideways movements of a ship. It is not clear whether OHG *swebōn* (in glosses) 'pendeo, sedeo, pervolito' reflects a separate derivative *swib-ō-*, is a cross between *sweibōn* and *swebēn*, or represents *sweibōn* with northern monophtongization.

Germanic *sweib-* probably reflects PGm. *sweibʰ-*: the voiced reflex of Gothic *unsweibands* cannot be explained as a Verner variant of *sweif-* < *sweip-*, as strong verbs with a root ending in PIE voiceless stop always generalize a voiceless fricative in Gothic (*galeiþan, urreisan, gateihan, þeihan, þreihan, weihan* are examples from the first class of strong verbs).

Beside PGm. *sweib-* there exists a similar root, PGm. *sweip-*, with highly similar meaning. The strong verb *swaip-a-* (originally VIIth class) occurs in OIc. *sveipa* 'to cast; to wrap (trans.)', OE *swāpan* 'to sweep, move by sweeping (trans.), swing (e.g. a sword); to sweep, have a sweeping motion (intrans.)', *ymb-, be-swāpan* 'to wrap (a mantle)'; OHG *sweifan* gl. *certo* 'to fight' (8th c., Pfeiffer, *Etymologisches Wörterbuch*, 1258), OHG *bi-sweifan* gl. *palliatus* 'to cloak', *umbi-sweifan* gl. *amicire* 'to wrap around', MHG *sweifen* 'to cause sth. to roll, swing; to wrap (one's arms around someone)', also intrans. 'to move in curves, curve', OSax. (pret.) *forsuuēp* 'expelled'.

While all instances of *sweib-a-* are connected by a common bundle of features that can be approximated by the gloss 'the subject moves along a curving path', in the case of *swaip-a-* the appropriate translation is 'the subject moves the object (a sword, broom, mantle, arms, the enemy etc.) along a curving path, in a curve'.

To this same root belong a number of weak verbs and nouns. OIc. *svipa* < *swip-ō-* 'move swiftly (of a sudden but noiseless motion, e.g. flying bird, intrans.), refl.: to look after (*at*), around (*um*)' seems to be derived from the noun *svipr* < *swip-a-* 'sweeping movement; sudden loss; brief glimpse; look, countenance'. Similarly, OIc. *sveipa* < *swaip-ō-* 'to sweep (e.g. a hair (Dsg.) from one's forehead), strike (e.g. with an axe or sword (Dsg.)), to swathe, wrap (transitive)' may be derived from the noun underlying OIc. *sveipr* < *swaipa-* 'fold, folding, curl in the hair; sudden stir; kind of headdress'. OIc. *sveipa* < *swaip-ja-* 'sweep (e.g. a hair (Dsg.)), wrap, swaddle', OHG *sweifen* gl. *eversio* 'overthrow', MHG *sweifen* 'to swing, roam' could be denominative, too, or it reflects a causative-iterative *swaip-ija-* < *swoib-eie-*. MHG *sich swīfen* (refl.) 'to move, swing' < *swīp-* no doubt is a cross between *swīban* and *swaipan*.

The semantics of Goth. *midja-sweipains* 'deluge' (lit. 'middle [= world] sweep'), which occurs only in Luke 17.27, is highly reminiscent of OHG *swebēn* 'float, move in and out (of the tide)', *ir-swebben* 'be inundated'.

For the semantics of OE *swipor*, OHG *swepfar* 'clever, handy' < **swip-ra-* we may compare Engl. *versed*, German *gewandt*. OE *swift* 'quick' (of a horse, wind, bird etc.) < **swifta-* may belong to either **sweip-* or **sweib-*.[10]

The alternation between a PGm. voiceless (in this case **p*) and voiced obstruent (in this case **b*) in one and the same root has been the subject of an extensive study by Rosemarie Lühr (*Expressivität*). She argues that in such cases, which are very frequent throughout Germanic, **b* is primary and **p* resulted from the operation of Kluge's Law, which turned **-bn-* into **-pp-*. This development occurred mainly in *n*-stems or **no-* derivatives, all of which are nominal. Once **-pp-* had arisen in this way, analogy would have given rise to a root ending in ungeminated **p*, which patterned up more regularly with **pp* than **b* did. In Germanic, the geminate could obtain a sound symbolic function, especially in verbs.

Lühr discusses our etymon in connection with two forms with geminate **-pp-*, viz. OHG *swipfen* 'to move quickly' < **swippija-* (p. 360) and **swipp-an/ōn* 'whip' attested in MLG *sweppe, swoppe* (f.), MHG *swippe* (m. f. *n*-stem), OHG oblique *sukphxn* gl. *aben* [=*suiphun* gl. *habena*] (*Expressivität*, 247-48).[11] The latter also occurs without gemination in *svipa* (f. *n*-stem), OE *swipa* (m. *n*-stem), *swipe, swipu* (f. ō-stem), MDutch MLG *swēpe*. As *n*-stem forms are widespread, it is possible to explain the forms with geminate **-pp-* from **-bn-* according to Kluge's Law. This would indeed solve the problem of the double root: for reconstructive purposes, PGm. **sweib-*, from IE **sweibh-*, would suffice to account for all Germanic forms. Yet there is room for some doubt. The geminate in OHG *swipfen* may just as well be due to the West Germanic gemination before **j*. Once it had arisen in the verb, it could be transferred by analogy to the word for 'whip'. Another problem is that it is hard to see how *p(p)*, arising as it does in nominal forms, could be plausibly made to spread to the primary seventh class strong verb **swaipan* (but not, arbitrarily, to the primary first class strong verb **sweiban*).

A preliminary conclusion can now be drawn. Germanic **sweib-* and **swaip-* are semantically and formally so closely connected with one another that it would be unjustified to reconstruct two completely different roots just on the basis of the difference in phonation of the labial obstruent. In fact, the formal problem is not insurmountable in light of Rosemarie Lühr's treatment of these and similar etyma,

---

10   OHD *swift* 'silent, quiet' and its derivatives MHG *swiften*, MDutch *swichten* 'to make quiet' would seem to be semantically closest to Goth. *sweiban* 'cease' (Heidermanns, *Etymologisches Wörterbuch*, 581, with references). Alternatively, these forms belong to **swigan* 'be silent', *swift(en)* being a hypercorrect High German form based on such models as MLG *nichte*, MHG *niftel(e)* 'niece'.

11   For the semantic connection of 'whip', see section 8 on Avestan.

although the particular solution involving Kluge's Law is far from self-evident. Matters are complicated by the fact that *b, not *bʰ, must be reconstructed for Slavic too (see section 11 below).

One issue will become especially relevant at a later stage: in Germanic, IE *sweibʰ- has become mixed up with reflexes of PIE *weip- 'to swing, move to and fro, quiver' to such an extent that the origin of individual meanings and forms can hardly be ascribed to the one root to the exclusion of the other:[12]

> OIc. *sweipa* 'to wrap', OE *ymb-, be-swāpan* 'to wrap around (a mantle)', OHG *bi-sweifan* gl. *palliatus* ('to cloak'), *umbi-sweifan* gl. *amicire* ('to wrap around') :: Goth. *bi-waibjan*, OIc. *veifa* 'to wrap', OE *wǣfan* 'to clothe', *be-wǣfan* 'to wrap'.

> OIc. *sveipr* < *swaipa- 'kind of headdress' :: *veipr* 'headdress', Goth. *waips* 'wreath', *weipan* 'to crown', *wipja* 'wreath', OHG *weif* '(head)band'.

> OIc. *svīfa* etc. 'to rove, ramble', OHG *swipfen* 'move quickly' :: OHG *wipphōn* 'to ramble', MHG *wippfen*, MDutch *wippen* 'move up and down'.

> OIc. *svipa* (f. *n*-stem), OE *swipa* (m. *n*-stem), *swipe, swipu* (f. *ō*-stem), MDutch MLG *swēpe* 'whip' :: ME *(h)wip* 'whip', with unetymological *h*.

> OHG *sweibōn* 'to turn, roll (a wheel), float (through the air)' :: OHG *weibōn* 'to swing, roam'.

In Germanic the mesh has in some cases become impossible to disentangle. While it is clear that Engl. *whip*, being isolated and attested later than OE *swip-a/e/u*, is an innovation, it is not possible to decide whether for instance OHG *sweibōn* and *weibōn* are both original or whether the one was based on the other. The crossing of *sweibʰ- and *weip- does little to ease the problem of the forms with PGm. *p, however, for which a scenario like the one presented by Lühr must still be invoked.

6. WELSH *chwyfu*

The formal and semantic possibilities opened up by Germanic *sweib- enable us to take a fresh look at the Welsh verb *chwyf-*, whose meaning is closely comparable to the Germanic type 'move to and fro'.

---

12   Lat. *vibrāre* 'tremble', which belongs to the root *weip-, probably took its *b* < *b, *bʰ from *sweib(ʰ)-.

A typical MW instance is WM 455.36-8 (CO) *Ny chwyuei ulaen blewyn arnaw rac yscawnhet tuth y gorwyd y danaw yn kyrchu porth llys Arthur* 'not a tip of a single hair on his head stirred (moved up and down?), for so light was the canter of the horse under him as he made for Arthur's court'. The stem *chwyf-* is used particularly in order to describe a stirring of the body, as in HMSS i.40 *y marchawc racko yssyd yn kyscu heb chwyfu ohonaw* 'yonder knight who is asleep without stirring', and HMSS i.93 *heb allel chwyfu na throet na llaw* 'without being able to move foot or hand'. Early Mod.W instances indicate a meaning 'move up and down, to and fro', as in the gloss in Llst 189 '*chwifio*, to be never at a stay, to wander up and down', which is also found in the compound *chwyfiwr*, *chwifiwr* 'wanderer, vagabond'. The compound *cyhwfan* < **cy-chwyfan* means 'to move like a wave, shake, fly (of a flag), hover'. Compare finally EMod.W *fel ac ŷ gallent. . .chwyfan eu Hadenydd* (TS 150) 'as if they could flap their wings', and *y Saethau yn chwifio o'r naill Lû at y llall* (T. Evans, DPO 122) 'the arrows moving to and fro from one host to the other'.

In view of the closely matching semantics of *chwyfu*, *chwifio* and Germanic **sweib-*, we may confidently claim that both reflect one and the same root, which may be reconstructed as Western IE **sweibʰ*. W *chwyf-* reflects the zero grade, **swibʰ*. The MW assimilation observed in **chwyfio* > *chwifio* is regular.

7. BRETON *fiñval, koc'hu(i)*

W *chwyfu* has long since been connected with MB *fifual* (Barbe 275.4), Mod.B *fiñval*, root *fiñv-*.[13] Semantically there is no obstacle, as *fiñval* means 'to stir', especially of bodies or body parts, a use it has in common with *chwyfu*. The comparison faces three formal difficulties, however.

The first is that *fiñval* has *-ñv-*, which points to lenited **-m-* rather than lenited **-b-*. While *chwyfu* may have either, Gm. **sweib-* and W *chwith* certainly exclude **-m-*. While it is true that in most instances B *-ñv-* does indeed reflect lenited **-m-*, there are well-known instances of confusion. There is no doubt, for instance, that B *a-dreñv* 'back' is to be compared with W *adref* 'homewards', *tref* 'village', OIr. *treb* 'house, farm' < **trebā*. Another instance is MB *cleze(u)ff*, Vann. *klean* 'sword' < **kladibos*, cf. OIr. *claideb*.[14] A particularly early example is OW *uiidimm* (Ox. 2), OB *guedom* beside *guodob* (both OrlCC) 'billhook' < **widu-byo-* 'wood-cutter', cf.

---

13 Stokes, *Wortschatz* 323; Ernault, *Glossaire*, 290; Henry, *Lexique*, 122; Vendryes, EC iv.
14 These instances are missing from the relevant section on secondary nasalization in Jackson, HPB 643.

OIr. *fidbae*, Gallo-Lat. *uidubium*. It is possible therefore that *-ñv -*in *fiñval* is not to be taken at face value but rather reflects **-β-* < lenited **-b-*.

The second problem concerns the vocalism of *fiñval*. On the basis of a comparison with *chwyfu*, the expected vocalism in Breton is *-e-* < PCelt. short **i*. It is easy, however, to generate OMB *-i-* from **-e-* by the Old Southwest British secondary *i*-affection, which raises any PBr. short vowel to *i* before a preserved *i*, whether syllabic or non-syllabic (type *bran* 'raven', pl. *brini*; *mab* 'son', pl. *mibien*, see Jackson HPB 299ff.). This of course presupposes that the Old South-West British paradigm of *fiñval* must have contained forms with *-i-* in the inflectional suffix. I shall return to this consequence in section 12.

The final problem is the initial *f-*. To W *chw-* normally corresponds B *c'hw-* (with orthographical variants *c'hou-*, *c'ho-*), as in W *chwech*, B *c'hwec'h* 'six', W *chwil*, B *c'hwil* 'beetle'. Yet there is evidence for a development *c'hw* > *f*, which in the case of some words spread through wide parts of Brittany. Accordingly, B *c'hwibu* 'gnats' has yielded *fibu*, *fubu* (MB already *fubuenn*, Cath.), and *melc'houed* 'slugs' has become *melfed*. What is exceptional is therefore not the development of **c'hwiñv-* to *fiñv-* but the fact that the latter seems to have completely ousted the former throughout Brittany.[15]

There is, however, one derivative that has retained original *c'hw* but is in all other respects identical to *fiñval*.[16] MB *cochuy* (Cath., late 15th c.), *cochy* (Dictionary of Quicquer, 1632) 'market hall', whose Mod.B descendants *koc'hu*, (Vannetais) *covu*, etc. and the French loanword *cochu* also mean 'bustle, crowd', derives from **kochwiµ* (Ernault, *Glossaire* 249). The loss of final **-µ* after an unstressed syllable is also found in e.g. *ene* 'soul' < MB *ene*, *eneff*, *kleze* 'sword' < MB *clezeff*, *cleze* (Jackson, HPB 624 ff.). It reflects the same compound as W *cyhwfan* discussed in section 6. Semantically, the connection may probably be envisaged as starting from 'wavelike movement, movement to and fro', whence 'activity, bustle' and finally 'place of activity and bustle, market hall'.

As none of the formal problems confronting the connection between *fiñval* and *chwyfu* is decisive and the semantics clearly favour the connection, we may adopt a Proto-British reconstruction **hwιβ-* < **swib-* for both.

---

15 Falc'hun, *l'Histoire de la langue bretonne*, 131 ff., Jackson, HPB 389–90. On alleged OB *fimre*, see Fleuriot-Evans, *Dictionary*, 455.

16 I have not been able to trace the form *gwiñval* mentioned by Henry, *Lexique* 155, and Favereau, *Geriadur* 316.

8. AVESTAN *xšuuaēβa-, xšuuiβi-, xšuuiβra-*

Germanic **sweib-* is usually connected with a group of Avestan forms, whose meaning is given as 'quick, speeding, swinging quickly'. As the Western IE forms have the semantic features 'movement' and 'curved' (leading to 'to and fro' or 'crooked, amiss') in common, it is interesting to note that these features appear also to be present in Avestan.

xšuuaēβa- occurs three times. As it yields important semantic information, Yašt 8,6 may be quoted in full:

tištrim stārəm raēuuaṇtəm / xʷarənaŋuhaṇtəm yazamaide / yō auuauuat xšuuaēβo vazāite / auui zraiiō vouru.kašəm / yaϑa tiγriš mainiiauuaså / yim aŋhat ərəxšō xšuuiβi.išuš / xšuuiβi.išuuatəmō airiianąm / airiiō xšuϑaŋ haca garōiat / xʷanuuaṇtəm auui gairīm

'We worship the shining radiant star Sirius, who moves as *xšuuaēβa-*in the direction of the sea of wide bays as an arrow through the realm of spirits, which (i.e. arrow) *ərəxša-* the bowman, the best bowman of the Aryans, shot from Mount A. to Mount Xᵘ.'

Hübschmann (KZ xxvii.107) translates 'schnell', Bartholomae (*Altiranisches Wörterbuch*, 560-1) 'rasch', which hardly applies to the movement of a star. As Kellens pointed out (JIES v/3.198), the compound *āsu.xšuuaēβa-* 'quick-xš.' (Yašt 8,37), also an epithet of Sirius, suggests that *xšuuaēβa* must have denoted something else than just speed. Kellens himself proposes that the root *xšuuiβ-* 'only applies to things with a brief, quick, repeated movement—the vibration of a flexible rod, arrow or whip, the wriggling of the snake or of the tongue, the quivering of nervous horses'. He translates the adjective in Yašt 8,6 with 'sparkling, scintillating, twinkling'. Although this is quite conceivable, it is not the only possible interpretation. As the adjective describes Sirius' path rather than Sirius itself, 'sparkling' would not seem to be particularly apt.[17] As Sirius' orbit is compared with the path of an arrow shot across fabulous distances, the context would rather suggest a translation 'moving along a curved path, curving'. Not only does this translation fit better in this particular passage but it also ties in with the semantics of the Western IE cognates.

The second occurrence of *xšuuaēβa* is Vidēvdāt 18.65 *ažaiiō xšuuaēβåŋhō* which Bartholomae (*loc. cit.*) translates as 'sich rasch (im Bogen) schnellende Schlangen',

---

17   The argument is only valid, of course, if one is prepared to accept that the poet did not mix his metaphors.

while Hübschmann (KZ xxvii.107) opts for 'losschießend'. Although the vague context allows various shades of meaning, a translation 'with curving movement' would suit the context as well as fit in with Yašt 8,6 and with the meaning of the Western IE cognates. Kellens' translation 'wriggling' (JIES v/3.198) comes very close to this, but it should be noted that this differs considerably from the meaning 'quiver, flicker' he proposes for the other instances, which diminishes the overall likelihood of his proposal.

Curving movement is clearly present too in *xšuuaēβaiiaṱ.aštrā-* (Yašt 5.130) 'swinging the whip'. The first member is a present participle of a causative verb **xšuuaēβaiia-* 'cause to curve, swing' ('kreisen lassen', Bartholomae *loc. cit.*, 'schwingen', Hübschmann, KZ xxvii.107). Kellens has 'making the whip vibrate' (JIES v/3.199), which is a less than ideal description of what a whip does.

To these forms also belongs *xšuuiβi-* in *xšuuiβ-išu-* (Yašt 8.6 above, 10,102, 17.12) 'archer', probably from 'one who makes his arrows curve', and *xšuuiβi-vāza-* in Yašt 8.37 *tištrim stārəm. . . xšuuiβi-vāzəm* 'the star Sirius, moving ahead curvingly' (but Bartholomae, *Altiranisches Wörterbuch*, 563 has 'schnell dahinfahrend, fliegend'). Kellens (JIES v/3.199) proposes 'with vibrating arrow' and 'with sparkling, twinkling movement', which are close to one another but clearly diverge from 'wriggling' in Vidēvdāt 18.65. Once again, describing a movement as twinkling seems inappropriate.

Finally, there is the adjective *xšuuiβra-* in Yasna 62.4 *dāiiå mē xšuuiβrəm hizuuąm* 'give me a *xšuuiβra-* tongue' (Kellens: 'vibrating'). It is also found in the personal name *xšuuiβrāspa-* (Yašt 13.111, 13.112, 13.140), which is interpreted as 'having swift horses' (Bartholomae, *Altiranisches Wörterbuch*, 563 'mit schnellen Rossen', Mayrhofer, *Die iranische Namen*, 101 'mit flinken Rossen', Kellens, JIES v/3.198-99 'with quivering horses', out of nervousness). I shall return to these forms below in connection with Skt. *kṣiprá-*.

We may conclude that there can be no reasonable doubt that the Avestan forms are cognate with the Western Indo-European set discussed earlier. What this means, of course, is that the etymon cannot be considered a West IE innovation but must go back to PIE.

9. VEDIC *kṣip-*

Av. *xšuuiβ-* has of old been connected with Ved. *kṣip-* (Mayrhofer, EWAia 437). On the morphological side, the identification is supported by the fact that both languages have a *ra-* adjective and (near-) identical compounds: Av. *xšuuiβrāspa-* corresponds to Skt. *kṣiprāśva-* (JB). In composition, instead of the adjectival suffix

-*ra*-, -*i*- appears in the most archaic layer of IE forms. The compound therefore replaces an older formation, **xšuuiβi-aspa-*, **kṣipi-aśva-*. The archaic type survives in Av. *xšuuiβi-išu-*, which corresponds to innovated Ved. *kṣipréṣu-* (RV 7,46,1). The alternation of -*ra*- and -*i*- after the root suggests a Caland system, which in turn suggests the original presence of a root noun. This is indeed attested in Ved. *kṣip-*. Here a semantic problem needs to be overcome, as *kṣip-* means approximately 'finger' (see below).

In West IE and Avestan (causative *xšuuaēβaiia-*), there are primary, i.e. non-denominative verbal forms. The same is true of Vedic, which has a *tudáti*-type present, *kṣipáti*, approximately meaning 'shoot, hurl' (see below). The morphological similarity contrasts with phonological dissimilarity, however. To begin with, **-w-* is missing in Skt. This problem can be overcome. Skt. *kṣ-* and Av. *xšuu-* require the reconstruction of I-Ir. **ksw-* or **kʷsw-*. An almost exact parallel for the loss of *w* in Vedic and its preservation in Avestan is to be found in the word for 'six', Ved. *ṣaṣ-*, Av. *xšuuaš* < **k'swek's*.[18] The corollary is of course that since Vedic requires an initial velar stop, this must be reconstructed for the Germanic and Celtic cognates too.

The other phonological problem is rather more difficult to account for, viz. the root-final -*p*,[19] which matches neither Avestan -*β*-, Celtic **-b-*, Germanic **-b-* < IE **p*, **bʰ*, nor Germanic **p*. There is evidence for **p* in Western Iranian, too (Szemerényi KZ lxxv.190, n. 3; Kellens JIES v/3.200, with references). For the moment I take the position that this mismatch of Vedic and Avestan is irritating but does not provide sufficient grounds to abandon the etymology. The Indo-Iranian situation is no more (nor less) problematic than the situation in Germanic. We have seen that in Germanic, **sweib-* was intensively crossed with IE **weip-* 'shake to and fro, quiver', which is semantically and formally close. A similar suggestion may be made for Indo-Iranian: Ved. *vip-* 'tremble, be excited' (< 'move to and fro') is semantically related to **k(w)sweibʰ-* 'move curvingly'. There is a partial morphological match, too: Ved. *vépate* 'trembles' occurs beside the root noun *víp-* 'excited speech' and the adjective *vípra-* 'trembling, excited', which approximately match *kṣipáti*, *kṣíp-*, *kṣiprá-*. It would therefore seem possible that **ksweibʰ-* replaced its **bʰ* by **p* on the model of **weip-* in Indic and Western Iranian.[20]

---

18   Thus Hübschmann (KZ xxvii.105–7). The fact that **s* became *ṣ* in Vedic, **x* > *š* by palatalization in Slavic and *š-* in Lithuanian as a result of the *ruki*-rule in my opinion suffices to demonstrate the original initial **k-* or **K-* in the word for 'six'.

19   A well-known problem, see Mayrhofer, EWAia 437, with references.

20   Av. *xšaēpā-* 'back, bottom, tail', if from 'swinger', may represent influence by **k(w)sweibʰ-* on the root **weip-* 'move to and fro, shake'; cf. OCSl. *ošibĭ* 'tail' and see section 11.

In view of this problem, however, more than normal weight is carried by the semantic side of the comparison: if on top of the phonological divergence there exists a semantic mismatch between Avestan and Vedic, as has been suggested notably by Kellens (JIES v/3), there would certainly be a good reason to be suspicious of the etymological connection.

As it turns out, however, the semantic feature 'having a curved path, curving' fits in with Vedic too. More specifically, as Av. *xšuuiβ-* was associated with the curved path of an arrow and the plying of a whip, so too is the Rigvedic present *kṣipáti* 'to make something curve':

> RV 5.83.3a *rathíva káśayáśvāṁ abhikṣipánn* lit. 'as a charioteer, plying with a whip in the direction of (*abhi*) the horses';

> RV 4.27.3c-d *sṛjád yád asmā áva ha kṣipáj jyā́m / kṛśánur ástā* 'when the bowman *Kṛśnu-* shot at him (i.e. the eagle) (and) let the bowstring curve off'.

A remarkable feature of this example is that the object is 'bowstring' rather than the missile that is being launched, as is the case in all other Rigvedic instances:

> RV 2.30.5a *áva kṣipa divó áśmānam uccā́* 'cast down (make curve) the stone from high up in heaven';

> RV 10.68.4b *avakṣipánn arká ulkā́m iva dyóḥ* 'as lightning cast off from heaven the fire glow (torch)';

> RV 10.182.1c *kṣipád áśastim ápa durmatiṃ hann* 'he (BRhaspati) cast the curse (or curser) off';

> RV 1.129.8g *kṣiptā́ jūrnír* 'the cast torch'.

In view of Av. *xšuuiβi-išu-*, Skt. *kṣipréṣu-* 'who has curving arrows, who makes his arrows curve, arrow-archer' it is likely that the object of the verb originally denoted the arrow rather than the bowstring, although it is easy to see that the two may be closely connected in the mind of the speaker. A similar ambiguity seems to be present in *kṣiprá-*. As a non-verbal form, this adjective is naturally ambiguous as to verbal voice and valency distinctions: it can mean 'curving' in the sense of moving like an arrow through the sky or like a wriggling snake (Germanic *sweib-*), and it can mean 'curving' in the sense of making something curve, like a bowstring or an arrow (RV *kṣipáti*). The latter is clearly present in one of the two Rigvedic instances:

RV 2.24.8a-b *ṛtájyena kṣipréṇa bráhmaṇas pátir / yátra vásṭi prá tád aśnoti dhánvanā* 'with his *kṣiprá*-bow with truthful string, Brahmanaspati hits wherever he wants'

kṣiprá- is translated 'schnellend' by Grassmann (*Wörterbuch* 369), 'schnellschießend' by Geldner (*Der Rig-Veda*), and 'springing, flying back with a spring, elastic' by Monier-Williams (*Sanskrit-English Dictionary*). Similarly, *kṣiprá-dhanvan-* (RV 9.90.3) has been interpreted as 'mit schnellendem Bogen' or 'with flexible bow'. It seems, however, that the one remaining instance of *kṣiprá-* in the Rigveda swings the evidence in favour of a translation 'setting or being on a (quick) curving course' rather than 'flexible':

RV 4.8.8a-c *sá vípras carṣaṇīnā́m / śávasā mā́nuṣāṇām / áti kṣipréva vidhyati* 'this eloquent one with his force outdoes (lit. hits further, through and through) (the speech) of peoples and men, like a (quick) curving one'

The archer terminology (*áti vyadh-*, *kṣiprá-*) makes clear that the words of the eloquent one hit their target, not because they are flexible like a bow but because they fly like a well-shot arrow. This passage elucidates Yasna 62.4 *dāiiā̊ mē xšuuiβrəm hizuuąm* which can now be interpreted as 'give me a tongue that speeds (and hits target) like an arrow'.

The military connotation of the root *kṣip-* in the Rigveda is further borne out by *kṣipaṇí-* (RV 4.40.4a) 'whiplash' and *kṣipaṇú-* (RV 4.54.6d) 'missile'. As the use of *kṣip-* and Av. *xšuuiβ-* with missiles and arrows contains a special reference to the quick arching motion of these projectiles, one wonders whether Skt. *kṣiprā́śva-* and Av. *Xšuuiβrāspa* 'having quick (?) horses' originally referred to horses running on a race circuit. As much has been argued for by Létoublon and de Lamberterie (*Revue de Philologie* liv) in order to account for the semantics of Gr. τρέχω 'turn → run', and it may apply to OE *swift*, too.

There is one Vedic cognate which is semantically remote from all other Indo-Iranian forms and whose appurtenance has therefore been called into question (Mayrhofer, EWAia I 432). This is the Vedic root noun *kṣip-* (f.). In the Rigveda, it appears almost exclusively in hymns dealing with the preparation of soma. It refers to the fingers that 'work' the soma plant in order to purify it (5.43.4a, 9.8.4a, 9.14.7a, 9.15.8a, 9.46.6b, 9.80.4b-5b, 9.85.7a, 9.86.27c, 9.97.12d and 57c). In one example the 'fingers' rub fire from sticks (3.23.3a), and in another the word seems to refer to the shoots of the soma plant (9.79.4b). In view of the last example, it seems likely that the core semantic feature is not 'active' but rather 'curved, crooked', whence perhaps 'flexible'. This would fit in with the basic sememe of the verbal forms found in Germanic and Celtic. A direct association of the root *kṣip-* with manual activity can be found in Vedic *kṣipra-hasta-* (AVP) 'with dexterous, flexible hands'.

In conclusion, Av. *xšuuiβ-* and Vedic *kṣip-* etymologically belong together, not only because of the formal resemblance, but also semantically. This confirms the earlier impression that the different phonation type of the root-final stop does not constitute enough reason to abandon the etymology. It may be suggested that the *-p-* of Vedic and Western Iranian is due to the influence of the semantically and formally close root **wip-* 'move to and fro, shake'.

10. OSSETIC *æxsirf* AND GREEK ξίφος

A remarkable semantic development is found in Ossetic (Digor) *æxsirf*, (Iron) *æxsyrf* 'sickle', which reflect Iranian **xšifr-* (Benveniste, *Études*, 38). This is an exact match of Ved. *kṣiprā-* and Av. *xšuuiβra-* (Ossetic *f* can reflect either β < **bʰ* or *f* < **p*). The development of **xšw-* to **(x)š-* by dissimilation to the following labial is common in Iranian forms of this root, cf. Middle Persian *šeb-* 'move quickly' (Szemerényi KZ lxxv.190). Ved. *kṣiprá-* and Av. *xšuuiβra-* mean 'with (quick) curved motion (like an arrow)', as we have seen. The etymological connection of these adjectives with *æxsirf* is most attractive if it were not for the semantic difference. Needless to say, a meaning 'sickle' can hardly be explained on the basis of the translations 'schnell'[21] and 'werfen, schleudern, mit einer Waffe treffen'[22] of *kṣiprá-* and *kṣip-* respectively (Čop KZ lviv.232, Frisk, *Nominalbildung*, 19). Once it is recalled that the core semantic feature of the root **k(ʷ)sweibʰ-* is 'curved motion', however, the meaning 'sickle' immediately comes within reach, as this is exactly what describes the action of a sickle. Therefore there is no obstacle to regarding Ossetic *æxsirf* as a substantivization of the PIE adjective **k(ʷ)swibʰ-ro-* 'having curved motion'.

Once this connection is accepted, it is only a small step towards including Gr. ξίφος 'sword'. Čop (KZ lviv.232) was the first to propose the connection of Greek

---

21   This translation leads Abaev, *Jazyka*, to reject the etymology on semantic grounds and prefer the formally problematic connection with Russ. *serp* 'sickle', Lat. *sarpō* 'cut, harvest', which leaves Ossetic *xs-* unexplained (Benveniste, *Études*, 40).

22   Benveniste's 'lancer d'un détente brusque' (*Études*, 40) lacks the essential sememe 'curved motion'.

and Ossetic, but he separated these from the older Indo-Iranian cognates for semantic reasons that cannot be endorsed. Heubeck (*Minos* vi/1.60) accepts Čop's etymology but includes the Vedic and Avestan forms, assuming that the basic meaning of the root *k(ʷ)sweibʰ-/-p-* was 'heftige, schnelle, schwingende Bewegung', which agrees well with what I have argued for in detail.

Formal arguments are in favour of a connection. Mycenaean has a dual *qi-si-pe-e* (Pylos, Ta 716; Heubeck, *Minos* vi/1). The latter is generally interpreted as evidence that ξίφος reflects *ksibʰ-os*, but this leads to the well-known problem of why later Greek does not have *φίφος (cf. Myc. *Mo-qo-so* > Μόφος and Vedic *kṣáp-* 'night', Gr. *φέφας 'darkness'; Heubeck, *Minos* vi/1.57; Szemerényi, *Studi micenei*, i.36, with references). On the basis of the proposed root *kswibʰ-[23] rather than *kʷsibʰ- this problem may well vanish, however, once we are prepared to accept that phonological /kswi/ was spelt *qi-si-* rather than a laborious *ki-si-wi-*. In later Greek, *kswíphos regularly lost *-w- and yielded ξίφος.

As to morphology, a Caland system consisting of root noun, compound form in *-i- and adjective *-ro- has been reconstructed for Indo-Iranian. The Greek s-stem perfectly ties in with this system. Its zero grade root was no doubt taken from the *ro-*, *i-* or (unattested) *u-*stem Caland counterparts, as is the case in Ionic θάρσος, θράσος 'courage', which replace θέρσος (still found in Aeolic) on the model of the adjective θρασύς 'bold'.[24] Neuter s-stems usually represent *nomina rei actae* of the type *kʹléwos 'that which one hears' → 'fame' (Risch, *Wortbildung*, 77). Accordingly, ξίφος originally denoted 'that which one curves, swings in a curve'. Given the known associations of the root with weaponry in Indo-Iranian and Germanic (OE *swāpan* 'swing, e.g. a sword', OHG *sweifan* 'fight') and the parallel of Ossetic 'sickle',[25] the semantic transition to a more specific 'weapon that one swings' and thence highly specific 'sword' is not unexpected.

II. SLAVIC[26]

Slavic has a verbal root *šīb-* with a semantic profile that is by now familiar: Russ. *šibát'*, *šibít'* 'to hit', *sušibát'* 'to wipe off (e.g. sth. off the table)', *ošibát's'a* 'to be in error', ORuss. *šibati* 'to hit (repeatedly)', *šibiti* 'to hit (thunder, lightning), beat',

---

23   As *kwu > *ku is regular in Greek, *kwswibʰ- > *kswibʰ- is a possible reconstruction, too.

24   For these and other examples, see Risch, *Wortbildung*, 78

25   Cf. ξίφαι· τὰ ἐν ταῖς ῥυκάναις δρέπανα ἢ σιδήρια (H) 'the *sickles* or irons in planes'.

26   I am indebted to Dr Willem Vermeer and Dr Rick Derksen for sharing their thoughts on the Slavic material.

OCSl. *šibati* 'to whip', SCr. *šïbati* 'to whip', *šibíti* 'to bend, weaken', Slovene *šíbati* 'to whip, flog', *šibíti* 'to bend', Pol. *szyb* 'projectile, missile', SCr. *šïba*, Slovene *šíba* 'rod', Russ. *šíbkij* 'quick'. The initial *š-* is the result of palatalization of **x-* by the following front vowel. Initial **x-* arose from **s* that was preceded by **k*: cf. Russ. *šest'* 'six' < **k'swek's*. As in the word for 'six', the **w* was lost. We may therefore reconstruct the initial consonant cluster as **k(w)sw-*, which agrees with the evidence of its cognates.

While the derived ā-verb, PSl. *šïbati*, belongs to accentual paradigm (a) in view of Slovene and Serbo-Croat, *šibíti* has mobile accentuation (class (c) in Russian and Slovene). In Russian, the latter uniquely has a thematic present, *šibú*, *šibёš* (class c),[27] which may be directly compared with Germanic **sweiban* < PIE **sweibʰ-oH* or Ved. *kṣipáti*. To this thematic present belongs a preterite feminine *šíbla*, with retracted accent, and a participle ORuss. *šibenŭ* 'hit' (whence ORuss. *šibenije* 'thunder').

Although the semantics, morphology and segmental phonology leave no doubt as to the etymology of the Slavic forms,[28] the accentuation presents a difficulty. The combined evidence of the SCr. short *ï*, the Slovene rising *í* and the Russian preterite *šíbla*, with its retracted accent, point to a PSl. acute root vowel. This can go back to a PIE laryngealized root, hence **ksweHibʰ*, in which case the Russian retracted accent is a reflex of Hirt's law (**ksweHibʰ-láH > *kswéHibʰ-laH*). Such a reconstruction faces the insurmountable problem that non-Slavic cognates with a short root vowel, such as Skt. *kṣipáti* and Germanic **swib-*, **swip-*, disallow the reconstruction of a laryngeal. Alternatively, the acute root vowel is a reflex of Winter's Law, which leads to a reconstruction **ksweib-* (not **ksweibʰ*).[29] In that case the retracted accent of the Russian preterite is analogical after laryngeal roots (as in *jéla* 'ate' < **ēd-láH* < PIE **ed-*). As there seems to be no way around this conclusion, Slavic **ksweib-* offers a direct comparandum to PGm. **sweip-*, which forces us to recognize the existence of **ksweib-* beside *ksweibʰ* (Germanic, Greek) and **ksweip-* (I-Ir.). The Celtic and Avestan forms are ambiguous, allowing as they do both **ksweib-* and ** ksweibʰ*.

---

27 Dr. Willem Vermeer suggests to me that the expected infinitive to the thematic present would be **šïbti > šïti*, which would have been identical with *šïti* 'to sow' and was therefore bound to be replaced. *šibíti* which had probably arisen as a denominative verb derived from **šïba* (attested in SCr. and Slovene), was pushed into service. The infinitive *ošíti* 'make a mistake' was made up by Miklosich (*Lexicon*, s.v.).

28 The connection with Skt. and Gm. is at least as old as Zupitza, *Beiträge*, 93.

29 The third logical alternative, viz. the reconstruction of a PIE lengthened grade ***kswēibʰ*, is highly unlikely on morphological grounds (there is no evidence for a Narten present).

What remains is the problem why the thematic present does not show columnal initial stress on the acute root, which one would certainly expect on the basis of **kswéibeti* (cf. Germanic *sweiban*). The probable answer is that Slavic has the equivalent of Skt. *kṣipáti*, i.e. a zero grade root and originally columnal stress on the thematic vowel. Early in Balto-Slavic, the stress regularly shifted from internal syllables in non-mobile paradigms to the end of the word (the so-called 'Oxytonesis' as discovered by Ebeling, see Derksen, *Metatony in Baltic*, 25). This turned forms like 3sg. **kswibéti*, 2pl. **kswibéte*, 3pl. **kswibónti* into **kswibetí*, **kswibeté*, **kswibontí*. At a much later date in Proto-Slavic, the stress retracted from final **ĭ* and **ŭ*, so that **šibetŭ*, **šibeté*, ** šibóntŭ* arose (with typically Slavic remodelling of the endings) and subsequently, by generalization of the stress on the first syllable of the ending, the attested Russian paradigm. Therefore, the Slavic present reflects PIE **kswibé-* (Skt. *kṣipáti*) rather than **kswéibe-* (Gm. *sweiban*). This seems to be confirmed by the semantics: Slavic *šibe-*, like *kṣipáti*, means 'to make sth. curve', not 'to move oneself in a curve'.

In view of Ossetic *æxsirf* 'sickle', Gr. ξίφος 'sword' and the Indo-Iranian connection of the root with archery, it may be possible to include **ksweip-* in Slavic **šipŭ-* > Russ. *šip* 'thorn, goad, spike', SCr. *šip* '(iron) nail', Czech *šíp* 'arrow', Upper Sorbian *šip*, Lower Sorbian *šypa* 'arrow'. If this is correct, **šipŭ-* constitutes the only evidence for **p* outside Indo-Iranian.

12. IRISH *scibid*

The Indo-Iranian, Greek and Slavic evidence points to the reconstruction of a PIE initial consonant cluster **k(ʷ)sw-* rather than **sw-*, as might have been supposed on the evidence of British and Germanic.[30] This legitimises a reconsideration of the old inner-Celtic connection of W *chwyf-* 'move, stir' with MIr. *scibid* 'move' (Vendryes, LEIA S-44).

There would seem to be two ways in which **k(ʷ)sw-* could have yielded W *chw-* and Ir. *sc-*:

(1) **k(ʷ)sw-* became **sk(ʷ)-* at a stage common to Irish and British, and this developed regularly into OIr. *sc-* and W *chw-*. The development of **sk-* to

---

30   The parallellism in the treatment of the initial cluster in **k(w)sweibh-* and **k'swek's* 'six' breaks down in the centum languages (Gm. *sw-*, Ir. *sc-* in the former, but Gm. *s-*, Ir. **sw-* > *s-* (lenited *f-*) in the latter). Whether this should be ascribed to the different velar (Germanic?), to the dissimilatory loss of the initial velar in the word for 'six' (Celtic?), or to both factors, is unclear.

chw- was a conditioned development, which probably depended on the quality of the following vowel. The only reliably ascertainable context in which **sk-* became *chw-* is before **e* (W *chwynnu*, MIr. *scendid* < PIE **skend-* 'rise'; W *chwedl*, OIr. *scél* < **sketlom*, PIE root **sekʷ-*), while the evidence for **sk-* before **i* is ambiguous (W *chwyd* 'vomit' < **ski-tV-*, OIr. *scëid* 'vomit' < **skei-eti-* < PIE **sk(e)i-*; but B *skejañ* 'cut' < **skid-y-*, PIE root **skid-*; perhaps *chwyd* is analogical after *e*-grade forms while *skejañ* represents the regular development before **i*; see Schrijver BBCS xxxix). This means that **k(ʷ)sw-* > **sk(ʷ)-* > W *chw-* is possible if **sk-* > *chw-* is not only the regular development before **e* but also before **i*; or, if **sk-* > *chw-* was indeed limited to the position before **e*, *chwyf-* was analogical after the *e*-grade form **k(ʷ)sweibh-* > **skeib-* > **skēβ-*. This full-grade happens not to be attested in Celtic but, as we have seen, it must be reconstructed for Germanic.

(2) Alternatively, **k(ʷ)s-* through no common intermediate stage developed into British **sw-* > *chw-* and Irish **sk(ʷ)-* > *sc-*. In this case there are no phonological parallels to either support or incriminate the development.

As there is no compelling formal reason to think that *chwyf-* cannot be connected with MIr. *scibid*, it is time to turn to the semantic side of the comparison. *Scibid* is semantically closest to W *chwyf-* where it refers to body movements and can be translated as 'stir':

> *ni buí scibudh anma na betha[d]* (CCath. 2091)[31] 'there was no stirring of breath or life';

> *in fheoil 7 na cnama do impodh in crocund immorro dianechtair cen scibhiudh* (RC ix.470.9: *Voyage of Mael Duin*) (of a magical animal) 'flesh and bones turned round, but the skin did not stir on the outside';

> *ind eóin . . . can scibud ette náa cosse* (LU 1361: *Dá Brón Flatha Nime*) 'the birds . . . without stirring wing or leg'.

In the following instance the subject is lifeless:

> *scibis in n-id co ranic remur in chorthe* (TBC 566) 'the withe slipped (down) and reached the thick part of the pillar'.

---

31 Abbreviations of texts in this section are those of the DIL.

The second semantic type has no parallel in Welsh, but it has in Germanic (OIc. *swífa*, OHG *swebēn*): *scibid* refers to the movement of a flood, of waves:

> *corscib dím in díliu* (*Ériu* iv.130.15: *Suidigud Tellaich Temra*) 'the Deluge flowed away from me';
> *o ro scib . . . tuile srotha dona muighibh* (CCath 2375) 'when the rising of the flood flowed from the plains';
> *forscibset na tonda for culo* (RC x.88.4: *Voyage of Mael Duin*) 'the waves flowed back'.

Closely related to this is the use of *scibid* to describe the movement of a vessel:

> *céin co scibtis na rathanna o tir* (CCath. 2646) 'so that the rafts would move away from the land';

> *co scibdis na longa(ib) seacu* (BB 7a18) 'so that the ships moved past them'.

Metaphorically, *scibid* refers to the movement of a mass of people:

> *do sgib cach d'indsoigid araile dib re bordbiledhaib* (*Ériu* viii.32.22: *First Battle of Moytura*) 'each man pressed forward against his neighbour with the edge of his shield';

> *ró sgiobsad na buidhne . . . do fhriothólamh na hiomghona sin* (CRR² 29 (84.5)) 'the troops moved in order to prepare for that slaughter'.

The semantic profile of *scibid* is such that it fits in perfectly with other attestations of the root $*k(^w)sweibh$-. It may therefore be concluded that the etymology is correct. *Scibid* is attested too late to be certain about its OIr. inflectional type. In MIr., it has an *s*-preterite and an *a*-subjunctive, which would fit in with an original AII present. As the form has zero grade of the root and shows no lowering of the root vowel, we can be reasonably sure that *scibid* reflects an old stative present $*skib-\bar{\imath}$- < $*k(^w)swibh-\bar{e}-ye/o$- 'to be in curved motion' *vel sim.*, which is also attested in Germanic (OHG *swebēn*). This reconstruction is confirmed by British. As we have seen in section 7, the -*i*- in Breton *fiñval* can only be explained if the following syllable contained a Proto-British $*-\bar{\imath}$- < PCelt. $*-\bar{\imath}$-.

13. SUMMARY

In spite of the necessity to reconstruct $*bh$, $*b$ and perhaps also $*p$ (if this was not taken from $*weip$-), the phonological and semantic correspondences between the forms dicussed above are such that the reconstruction of a single PIE etymon, $*k(w)sweib^h-$ ($*k(w)sweib-$, $*k(w)sweip-?$), cannot be doubted.[32] The basic semantic connection can be represented as a 'curving movement'. Morphologically, a Caland system based on a root noun is reflected in Indo-Iranian ($*\bar{k}(w)swib^h-i-$, $-ro-$) and Greek ($*k(w)swib^h-es-$). The following primary verbal forms can be reconstructed:

$*k(w)sweib^h-e-$ (intrans.) 'move to and fro, along a curved path' (Germanic);

$*k(w)sweib^h-eh_1-$ (intrans.) 'be in a to and fro motion' (Germanic, Celtic);

$*k(w)swib-e-$ (trans.) 'make curve, make something move along a curved path' (Slavic, Vedic ($*-p-$));

$*k(w)swoib-e-$ (trans.) 'make curve, make something move along a curved path' (Germanic);

$*k(w)swoib(^h)-eie-$ (iterative-causative) 'make curve, make something move along a curved path' (Avestan).

The correlation 'intransitive – $*b^h$: transitive – $*b$', which may well be accidental, calls for further investigation. As to the starting point of this article, W *chwith*, this can now be reconstructed as a verbal adjective in $*-to-$ derived from the intransitive present stem $*k(w)swéib^h-e-$ or the transitive present $*k(w)swib(^h)-é-$. Its basic meaning was 'curving, curved, bent', which developed into 'wrong' and thence 'left'.

---

32 *Pace* Walde-Pokorny, *Vergleichendes Wörterbuch*, I 241, 501, 520; Pokorny, IEW 625 1041–42.

Rowynniauc, Rhufoniog:
the orthography and phonology of /μ/ in Early Welsh

Paul Russell

W ORKING with early Welsh phonology can sometimes resemble the life of an Eskimo out on the ice-floes jumping from one section of solid ice to another across murky channels of freezing water. There is much which is secure, or seems secure, and recent work by Peter Schrijver in particular has done much to make these areas more secure and to bridge some of those channels.[1] Even so, it is frequently the case that these apparently secure areas are more slippery than expected or, like any self-respecting iceberg, nine-tenths of it is under water and unknown. My aim in this paper is, like our Eskimo, to perch on the edge of one of these ice flows and delve into the murky channels and see what emerges, and it may be useful to explore an issue where it seems to me that the orthographical aspects have largely been ignored and that by exploring them the problems may be, if not solved, at least more clearly understood.

I

The starting point is the range of spellings of what in its standard form is usually spelt *Rhufoniog* /rʰuvoni̯og/, the territorial unit in Denbighshire.[2] It shows a wide range of orthographical variants: in the *Brutiau*, we find *Roweynauc* (AC 816); *Ryuonyawc* (BT (Pen. 20)), *Rywonyauc* (ByS 816), *Rywynnyavc* (ByS

---

1   Schrijver, SBCHP. Jackson, LHEB, remains indispensable. Research for this paper was supported by the British Academy with a grant from the Neil Ker Memorial Fund.
2   For the historical background, see Lloyd, *History of Wales*, I.240; Owen, *The Description of Penbrokeshire*, III.195n, 199n, 200n, IV.506.

1118); *Rywynyawc* (BT (RB) 816); *Rywynnyawc* (BT (RB) 1118); in genealogies (EWGT), *Rywynnyawc, Rhyfonyog, Rryvonioc*; in verse, *Rowynniauc* (BBC (LlDC 22.14)), *Rywonyaбc* (Prydydd y Moch (CBT V, 24.63)), *Ryvonioc* (Gutun Owein); it is also frequent in documentary sources:[3] *Rowennyok* (1247 (*Litt. Wall.*, p. 7)), *Rowenyok* (1253 (Roderick, BBCS x.255)), *Reweniauk* (1254 (*Valuation of Norwich*, 160)), *Rowennak* (1277 (*Cal of Ch Roll Var*, 160)), *Roewynnok* (1282 (ibid., 241), *Rowaynok* (1334 (SHD 1), *Rewaynok* (1334 (ibid., 50, 154)).[4] It is assumed that this form is a derivative of the personal name *Rhufon* (< **Rōmānus*), presumably going back to **Rōmāni̯āko-*.[5]

For our purposes the striking orthographical feature is the consistency of the spelling -w- where one might usually in Middle Welsh literary orthography have expected -u- or -v-, and ultimately -f-.[6] There are other curious aspects of the orthography of these forms, such as the -y- or -o- spelling in the first syllable and the apparent vowel affection in the second syllable. All of these features would perhaps in other instances encourage us to wonder whether all these forms were really attempts to spell /rʰᵤvoni̯og/ vel sim. But given that it is a local name and that in most cases the location and circumstantial detail all point to present-day Rhufoniog makes such speculation less fruitful in this instance. Part of the confusion can be clarified fairly straightforwardly. While there may have been some scribal confusion (in *Bonedd y Seint*, for example, there seems to have been occasional confusion with *Rheinwg*[7]) it seems quite likely that in some instances the base was re-analysed as containing *Rhufein* (from the plural *Rōmāni*) rather than the singular *Rhufawn* (< *Rōmānus*); in other words the derivative was analysed as 'belonging to the Romans' rather than as 'belonging to Rhufon' (derivatives based on plurals being relatively widespread in Welsh[8]). Furthermore, the influence of Latin *Roma, Romani*, etc. may have encouraged the -o- spelling of the first syllable. Even so, none of this helps to explain the -w- spelling. Essentially, the issue is this: is this a spelling for /v/, as it can be in certain manuscript orthographies? Does it reflect a sound change of /v/ to

---

3   On documentary sources, see Russell, ÉC xxix.

4   I am grateful to Maredudd ap Huw for supplying some of these references.

5   See Russell, *Celtic Word-Formation*, 54–6; Melville Richards, JRSAI xcv.208; id., *Enwau Tir a Gwlad*, 13, 26; Williams, *Y Llenor* ix.229;

6   See, e.g., Russell, *Introduction to the Celtic Languages*, 213–9; id., NLWJ xxix.146 (Hand B), 149 (hand C), 153 (Hand F).

7   See EWGT, 56 (§ 13).

8   See Russell, *Celtic Word-Formation*, 45–6, 118–19; Zimmer, *Studies in Welsh Word-formation*, 558–60.

/u̯/? Or is it an attempt to spell some intermediate sound such as /μ/ or a nasalised /u̯/? Given that there is good evidence for -w- representing /v/, it might be thought otiose to pursue the question further.9 However, there is also a phonological issue here in that there is a widespread but ill-defined set of circumstances in early Welsh where /u̯/ developed to /v/, e.g. *Difiau* < *dyw iau*, and in other cases alternated with /u̯/, e.g. *cawod/cafod*. Since the more usual usage of -w- is to represent /u̯/, it seems worth exploring the situation further. But before moving on to the phonology, it will be useful to establish more clearly what we know about the orthography of an original /m/ and its lenited variant. The rest of this paper, therefore, falls into two sections, orthography and phonology. There are clearly points of overlap at most stages but it is probably simpler to discuss the two aspects consecutively than to run the risk of confusing them.

II

We may begin by outlining what is the traditional view of the orthography of lenited /m/ and lenited /b/ in early Welsh. In doing so, however, we immediately run up against the problem of potentially confusing notation. Jackson uses /ƀ/ for the bilabial fricative arising from lenited /b/, and /μ/ for its nasal counterpart.10 He then used /ṽ/ for the weakened form of /μ/ and /v/ for the labio-dental fricative which was the outcome of the merging of original /ƀ/ and /μ/. As recent work by Hajek and others has shown, a nasal fricative is an extremely unstable element, and in universal terms is a very rare segment indeed.11 Mayerthaler has observed that the passage of air through the nasal cavity affects the level of airflow through the oral cavity, thereby reducing the amount of friction normally associated with fricatives.12 We should perhaps, therefore, be wary of reconstructing a fully nasalised fricative rather than a nasalised vowel followed by a non-nasal fricative. For such reasons I should be inclined to treat /μ/ as representing [˜β] in most cases. As regards notation, in the present discussion the following will be used: /β/ bilabial voiced fricative; /μ/ bilabial nasal fricative; /u̯/ bilabial continuant; /v/ labio-dental voiced fricative; /˜/ preceding vowel nasalised.

---

9   For details, see below, p. 00.
10 Jackson, LHEB 413–4, 480–95.
11 Hajek, *Universals of Sound Change in Nasalization*, 156–8; cf. Maddieson, *Patterns of Sound*, 84.
12 Mayerthaler, 'Markiertheit in der Phonologie', 225; cf. also Hajek, *Universals of Sound Change in Nasalization*, 157.

In Old Welsh it seems that in certain environments the nasal and non-nasal bilabial fricatives were still distinct and, it is thought, *b* was used for /β/ and *m* for /μ/. In Middle Welsh, by which time the phonemes had fallen together, the resulting /v/ could be spelt as *v*, *u*, the developed ʊ-form of *v*, in some manuscripts as *w*, and in final position in the first instance as *f*.[13] It is the last of these which has emerged into the modern spelling system as the spelling of /v/ in all positions. The use of *v* and *u* is already attested in the *Liber Landavensis*, and in Meinir Lewis' formulation (who distinguishes two phases of Old Welsh orthography and places the *Liber Landavensis* wholly in Phase B) the *Liber Landavensis* would then illustrate the orthographical bridge between Old and Middle Welsh.[14] However, more recent work on the *Liber Landavensis* has demonstrated that it contains a chronologically wide range of material and so has to be evaluated charter by charter.[15]

We may begin with a number of observations the relevance of which will emerge in due course. First, the inventory of sounds and signs in early Welsh. It has long been observed that, because of the rise of fricatives and spirants within the history of British, early Welsh was seriously understocked in signs to represent the full consonantal inventory.[16] The situation may be summarised as follows:[17]

	Phonemes			Signs
Dentals	/t d ð δ n/	5	: 4	t d th n
Gutturals	/k g χ (γ) ŋ/	3 [4]:	3	c g ch[18]
Labials[19]	/p b f m v (μ)/	5 [6]:	9 [10]	p b f(f) m v u ʊ w f (ph)

---

13 See, for example, Russell, *Introduction to the Celtic Languages*, 214–17; Charles-Edwards and Russell, NLWJ xxviii.422–3.

14 Lewis, 'Disgrifiad o Orgraff Hen Gymraeg', Phase A, v–viii, 22–189; Phase B, viii–ix, 190–644.

15 See W. Davies, BBCS xxviii; Koch, SC xx–xxi; Sims-Williams, BBCS xxxviii, and below for further discussion.

16 Charles-Edwards and Russell, NLWJ xxviii.421–5; Russell, *Introduction to the Celtic Languages*, 214. The same is also true of front and central vowels but is not relevant here.

17 The numbers indicate the numbers of phonemes matched to the number of signs in the late Old Welsh period; numbers in square brackets indicate the early Old Welsh situation. N.B. not all variants for /ð/ and /χ/ are indicated; see Jenkins and Owen, CMCS vii.119. For a discussion of the range of spellings for /ð/, see Russell, NLWJ xxix.141–3.

18 On /ŋ/, see T. A. Watkins, BBCS xxi; id. BBCS xxiii.

19 Including labio-dentals.

The dentals are particularly problematic and continued to be so until the rise of the *dd*-spelling for /ð/.[20] Life became easier among the gutturals after a reduction in the phonemic inventory with the loss of /γ/.[21] In contrast, it is striking that there is no problem among the labials and labio-dentals which seem to be comparatively well-stocked, if not indeed over-stocked, with signs. Partly it is because this was the one area where Latin had a fricative to be spelt and had used *v* for it, and also because this *v* had been split into two letter forms, *v* and *u*; still later within early Welsh the *v*-form also split into two, the out-curling form of *v* and the inward curling ꝟ.[22] But that is not the whole story. For within the labial group we may also note that it is /v/ in particular which is surprisingly over-stocked with signs, *u, v, w, f* (and in some manuscripts *uu* and *vv*), some of which also do duty as signs for rounded vowels.

The second observation concerns *w*. Issues of form are not directly relevant here but, in passing, it is worth remarking that it is not always clear whether we are dealing with *w, vv* or *uu* (and editorial transcriptions are not always helpful in this regard[23]). The form of *w* can vary: the usual type has four points which can be formed either by two overlapping *vs* (with outcurling first strokes) or by two overlapping ꝟs. However, there are instances (notably in the Black Book of Carmarthen (BBC)) of a three point *w* formed by adding a central stroke to a ꝟ.[24] Another form characteristic of the some of the scribes of the Red Book of Hergest has the form of a tall, elongated *u* followed by a *ʒ*-like form.[25] Whichever form the *w* takes, it is used for /v/ by some scribes in some manuscripts but it is by no means widespread. It is used by the scribe of NLW MS, Peniarth 44, NLW, Llanstephan 1, BL, Cotton Caligula A.iii, scribes D and F of the Black Book of Chirk (they also use *uu*), the scribe of the Dingestow manuscript, and the scribe of BBC.[26] On the other hand, it is not

---

20 Apart from the one OW example of *meddimnich* (see Russell, NLWJ xxix.174, n. 34), the earliest example of the *dd*-spelling for /ð/ seems to be in the Black Book of Chirk (Russell, NLWJ xxix.150–1); see also Charles-Edwards and Russell, NLWJ xxviii.432–3.

21 The loss of /γ/ occurred within the OW period; cf. Jackson, LHEB 433–70.

22 See Charles-Edwards and Russell, NLWJ xxviii.423.

23 E.g. Latin Redaction C of the Welsh Laws where *uu* was transcribed as *w*, etc. (see Russell, NLWJ xxix.168, 175, n. 69) Note also the tendency to print ꝟ as *w* in edited texts; see Charles-Edwards and Russell, NLWJ xxviii.423 (and 461, n. 21). It is on occasions admittedly difficult to be sure whether to treat a pair of *us* or *vs* as a *w* or not.

24 Cf. *welugan, meinwi* (1v4) with a four-point *w* beside *awyrlaꝟ* (5r8), *kywystraud* (5v1) with a three-point *w*. There seems to be no detectable difference in value.

25 See Gifford Charles-Edwards, NLWJ xxi.248–9 (Diagrams 2 and 3).

26 On Llanstephan 1, see *Brut y Brenhinedd*, xxviii–xxix; on the scribe of Peniarth 44, etc., see Huws, 'The Manuscripts', 119–36 (and Plates 1 and 2 facing pp. 122–3) (= MWM

found among the scribes of the Hendregadredd manuscript.[27] In most of these manuscripts use of *w* for /v/ is sporadic (and in a minority usage in comparison with other uses of *w* for /u/ and /u̯/), and it is difficult to tell in each case whether it is a deliberate spelling by the scribe or traces of the orthography of the exemplar.[28] However, in BBC this spelling for /v/ is more common than any other and deserves careful examination.[29]

The Black Book of Carmarthen (BBC) has occupied an important position in the study of early Welsh orthography ever since Ifor Williams' comments about its orthography.[30] He claimed, partly on the grounds of its date (12th century, according to him, subsequently re-dated by E. D. Jones to the mid-13th [31]), that the orthography of the Black Book of Carmarthen formed the bridge between between Old and Middle Welsh orthographical practices. Although the re-dating of the manuscript together with recent advances in the study of the orthography of other 13th century manuscripts have reduced the validity of his arguments, the manuscript still remains an extrememly important document for the study of early Welsh orthography. Apart from a few minor additions in a later hand, the whole text (as we have it, and it is missing at least three quires) was written by the same scribe probably over a long period. According to Daniel Huws, it is the product of fourteen phases of writing and rubrication.[32]

While the spelling of *t* for /ð/ has always been regard as characteristic of this manuscript, the use of *w* for /v/ is far more common than in any other manuscript.[33] It is at least as frequent, if not more so, that *u* and *v*. Of the 846

177–92 (and Plates 25 and 26 on pp. 180–1)); Russell, CMCS xxv; on hands D and F in the Black Book of Chirk, see Russell, NLWJ xxix.148–51 (hand D), 152–4 (hand F); on the Dingestow MS, see Russell, CMCS xxxvii; for the Black Book of Carmarthen, see below.

27   Only one doubtful example can be found: *kywrenhin* (75v18 (= p. 189.3) (second stratum, hand G) where the *w* may stand for /vv/, i.e. /kəvvrenin/; see Charles-Edwards and Russell, NLWJ xxviii.

28   For this approach, cf. Charles-Edwards and Russell, NLWJ xxviii.420–1; Russell, NLWJ xxix.134–5; Russell, CMCS xxxvii.91–2.

29   What follows is part of a fuller forthcoming study of the orthography of the Black Book of Carmarthen; fuller discussion and complete statistics will be presented there.

30   For Williams' comments, see PKM xii–xx. For a facsimile, see J. Gwenogvryn Evans, *The Black Book of Carmarthen Reproduced and Edited* (Pwllheli, 1906); for an edition, see LlDC; and discussion, see Huws, *Five Ancient Books*, 7–11 (= MWM 70–72).

31   See LlDC, xiii–xxiv.

32   Huws, *Five Ancient Books*, 8 (= MWM 71).

33   Note that *t* for /ð/ is not universal; cf. *arderchauc* (22.14), and also *t* for /d/, e.g. *bit* 'world' (35.4).

cases of a spelling of /v/ by the main hand in this manuscript w is used in 47.75% of them (408 instances). Furthermore, when that figure is broken down into position in the word, it is clear that w was the preferred spelling in final position (73.9% of cases). Internally, w is the single most common spelling for /v/ (39.5% of cases), a quarter of which are in compounds containing the prefix cyf- /kəv/, spelt cyw-. Initially, however, w only occurs in 16.2% of cases, v- being the predominant spelling (61.9% of cases).[34] In addition to its use for /v/, w also occurs as a spelling of both /u̯/ and /u/. Spellings of /v/ take up just over half (51.5%) of the occurrences of w; some 40% represent /u̯/ and the remainder are for /u/ and in diphthongs. There are also occasional examples of m for /v/, relics of what has been conventionally regarded as an Old Welsh-style spelling, e.g. amtimeid (3.6) /amðivaid/. The very frequent use of w in final position is particularly striking, both in polysyllables, e.g. chaffaw (2.22), drossow (3.36), modridaw (7.3), gobuyllaw (7.17), archaw (3.30, etc.), uchaw (17.25), and in monosyllables, e.g. new (5.78, etc.), gniw (26.26), etc., though in some poems it seems to be being replaced by -f, notably in poems 16 (Afallennau) and 17 (Oianau). In these two poems final -/v/ is spelt -f in 61.2% of occasions (w in 24.5%), and internal -/v/- is spelt -f- in 33.3% of cases (-w- in 25.5%).

One point to note about -/v/ in final syllables is that historically it is in most cases to be derived from an original /μ/ rather than an original /β/, especially given the frequency of superlatives, 1st singular verbs and 1st singular conjugated prepositions, and the dearth of words ending in -/β/.[35] We may also note that the frequent use of -w- in the prefix kyw-, etymologically derive from *kom-. Statistically, when we take the the forms in BBC with a sound etymological base, 79% of the forms where w represents /v/ derive from an original /μ/, 21% from an original /β/. It is difficult to gauge the significance of this: overall within Welsh forms containing an original /β/ (< */b/) are far less common than forms deriving from /μ/ (< */m/); as a crude indicator (based on initial consonants) GPC devotes 126 pages to the letter B but 251

---

34 For the purposes of the present discussion, no further breakdown will be attempted here, though there is significant variation between poems and groups of poems which will be discussed in the fuller study.

35 Probably the most common example in BBC is, in modern spelling, twrf (< Latin turba), variously spelt turuw and in compounds goduryw, etc. (cf. especially poem 37 Goduryw a glyuaw). A minimal pair or two would be helpful, but the only possible example seems to be W. rhwyf 'oar' < Lat. rēmus (cf. Br. roeñv) beside W. rhwyf 'lord' (M. Br. roue). However, the etymology of the latter is uncertain and the Middle Breton form makes it possible that the -f in Welsh is secondary; see Ernault, Glossaire moyen-breton, 579–82.

pages to *M*. Nevertheless, one possibility, admittedly unprovable, but worth considering, is that the use of *w* for forms containing an original /µ/ in BBC represents a relic of an older, or perhaps different, spelling system which was developed at a period when /µ/ was still at least partially distinct from /β/. If so, then it would also help to explain the overstocking of signs available for labials and fricatives in early Welsh since presumably it was taken over and used for /v/. However, given the compilatory nature of BBC, poems could easily be of widely different dates of composition and we might expect some orthographical variation anyway, but the question is whether we can rescue some of the original orthographical patterns. Daniel Huws, however, has commented on the orthographical consistency of BBC which might imply the imposition of an orthographical template on material collected from different sources.[36]

Another spelling feature which may be relevant here is the sporadic use of *w* to represent /vu/-, usually initially but occasionally internally, e.g. the scribe of Peniarth 44, Llanstephan 1, and Cotton Caligula A.iii: *wy* 'more' for /vui/ Dingestow scribe: *wy, wyhaf, gowyaf*, etc.[37] In almost all the examples the /v/ is to be derived from an original /µ/. It is of course possible that the *w* represents a merging of *vu-* or *uu-* in initial position, but in the light of the present discussion it may be relevant. There are occasional examples in BBC, e.g. *gawi* (17.133) for Mn.W *gafwy*.[38]

At this stage it may be useful to move backwards in time from BBC to consider the orthographical habits attested in the remains of Old Welsh. As far as we can tell, /µ/ merged with /β/ during the Old Welsh period. There are no examples of *w* in the extant Old Welsh sources though there are two examples of *uu* in *dauu* (Ox. 1), *Frauu* (Asser, 49.6). It is, however, now possible to move the discussion a little further forward. It is well known that in the *Liber Landavensis u*, *v*, and *f* spellings for /µ/ and /β/ can be found alongside *b* and *m*; this has usually been put down to modernising on the part of the scribes. However, in a detailed discussion of orthography and related matters in the *Liber Landavensis*, which builds on the work of Wendy Davies and John Koch, Patrick Sims-Williams has provided a new way into the rich linguistic material to be found in that collection.[39] The effect of his work has been to provide a

---

36   Huws, *Five Ancient Books*, 10 (= MWM 72). Detailed statistical analyses, however, suggest that it is not as consistent as it might at first appear; full consideration must await a fuller study of BBC.

37   See Russell, CMCS xxv.79, and CMCS xxxvii.90–1 for details and further examples.

38   Cf. *(g)afwy* (18.126 (the later addition to *Englynion y Beddau*)).

39   Sims-Williams, BBCS xxxviii; see also W. Davies, BBCS xxix and Koch, SC xx/xxi.

valuable new source for the phonology and orthography of early Welsh stretching back to the early eighth century at least or even earlier. Sims-Williams has discussed a range of features and, schematising his material in graphs, has shown that it is possible that the orthography of names in the *Liber Landavensis* do reflect the orthographic patterns of the periods when these charters were written.

Figure 1: the incidence of *m, u/v, f* for /μ/ in the personal names in the charters of *Lib. Land*

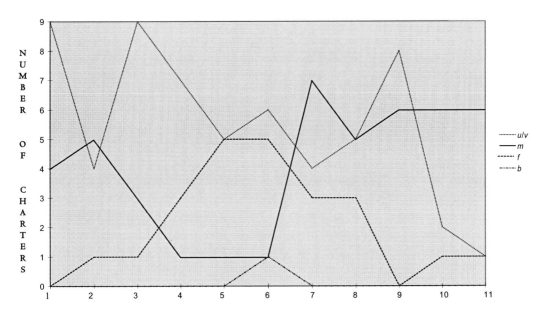

Groups of Charters (in chronological order)

Figure 2: the incidence of *u/v, b, f* for /β/ in the personal names in the charters of *Lib. Land.*

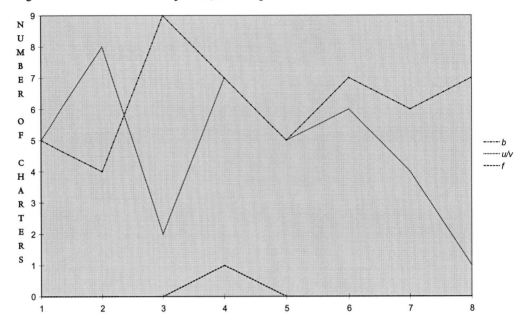

Groups of charters (in chronological order)

A similar approach can be used on the orthography of /μ/ and /β/. The material in the charters is presented in date order rather than textual order;[40] this obviates the issue of a copying scribe tidying up the spelling as he goes. Personal names listed in the charters containing /μ/ and /β/ were collected. Three signs are used for each: *m, u* and *f* for /μ/ (and one example of *b*) and *b, u* and *f* for /β/. The data are presented in Figures 1 and 2. Charters containing relevant forms were divided into groups; in Figure 1 they were divided into eleven groups, in Figure 2 into eight groups. The graphs show how many charters in each group contain the features in question. To avoid the distorting effects of the multiple repetition of one name, in any given section if a charter contained one or more examples of, for example, *m* for /μ/ it was counted only once. If a charter contained, for example, two examples of *m* and three of *u* for /μ/, it was counted once for *m* and once for *u*.[41] For /μ/ 98 charters con-

---

40   The date order used here is that suggested in Davies, *The Llandaff Charters,* 31–82, and used (with minor modifications) by Sims-Williams.

41   For details, see Sims-Williams BBCS xxxviii.42–4.

tained relevant material, for /β/ 71 charters. For /μ/ 60 charters contained examples of the *u/v*-spelling, 45 of the *m*-spelling, and 23 of the *f*-spelling. For /β/ 38 charters contained examples of the *u/v*-spelling, 50 of the *b*-spelling, and 1 of the *f*-spelling.

In both sets of data there is clear evidence that the *b/m* type of spelling only seems to emerge as the dominant pattern at a relatively late stage and that in the earlier stages each was in competition with *u*. For /β/, the *f*-spelling is of no significance (one example: *Gafran* (180); usually *Gabran* (158, etc.)) but it was a significant way of spelling /μ/ from an early period in final position, e.g. *Heinif* (198), *Condaf* (140, etc.) and especially at the beginning of the second element of a compound, e.g. *Confur* (148, etc.), *Cinfic* (207), etc.[42] This is probably the source of *f* for /v/ in Middle and later Welsh. Rather than the standard Old Welsh spelling being superseded by a *u-*, *v-* or *f*-style of spelling in late Old Welsh and on into Middle Welsh, the latter spelling patterns seem to have been in use from the earliest evidence onwards.

In view of the fact that *f* became the regular spelling of /v/ in later Welsh, it may be worth considering whether there is any force in the claim that the *f*-spellings in the *Liber Landavensis* are later modernisations, as had always been claimed under earlier views of this collection of charters.[43] Two features would militate against this. First, apart from *Gafran*, all instances show *f* for /μ/;[44] if this was a later modernisation (after the merging of /μ/ and /β/) we would expect a more even spread of use of *f* across forms with original /μ/ and /β/. Secondly, according to Wendy Davies' analysis of the charters, the names containing *f*-spellings occur in her groups C, E and F which have in common the possibility that they were 'copied at Llancarfan, in or after the late 9th century, after the demise of the principal houses which had collected them'.[45] In other words, if some modification did occur it is likely to have happened at Llancarfan 'in or after the 9th century'. Is it possible then that the *f*-spelling was

---

42   It is assumed here that *Confur* contains /μ/ rather than /β/, whether from *-/moːros/ or *-/muːros/ (see Sims-Williams, BBCS xxxviii.63 (and n. 4); for /β/, see Jackson, LHEB 485 (< *-/burros/). On the first element, see Sims-Williams, BBCS xxxviii.40. One possibility for the use of *f* was as a means to break up a row of minims.

43   The relevant forms are *Condaf* (140), *Confur* (*148, 180b, 188b, 187, 189, 184, 188a, 178, 198a, 199a), *Heinif* (190a, 198b, 199bi, 216a), *Conficc* (199bi), *Cinfic* (207), *Cinfall* (171b), *Gurcinnif* (168). Notation follows that of Wendy Davies, *The Llandaf Charters*; note in particular that * is used to mark a suspect charter (of which there is only one in this group).

44   As will be observed below, it is clear that /μ/ and /β/ seem to have merged earliest before /r/; see p. 39.

45   W. Davies, *The Llandaff Charters*, 91.

being experimented with at Llancarfan at this period?

Remains of the Llancarfan cartulary do survive, preserved in *Vita S. Catoci*, §§55–70, and it is possible to check our speculation about *f*-spellings. The material from Llancarfan presents a different picture.[46] Consisting of only 43 items, it is sparse but some observations can be made. Overall, there are 34 examples of a *b/m*-spelling and only 9 of a *u/v*-spelling; among the former there are 20 cases of *m* for /μ/ and 14 of *b* for /β/, while of the latter four clearly contain *u* for /μ/, one has *u* for /β/, and the others are uncertain. The date span of the surviving elements of the Llancarfan charters is thought to be from 650–765;[47] if so, it approximately matches sections 2-7 of Figure 1 and to sections 2–6 of Figure 2. In comparison with the *Liber Landavensis* there is a far greater proportion of *m* and *b* spellings. It is possible, therefore, that the Llancarfan charters derive from a different scribal milieu than some of the charters in the Llandaf collection, one where *b* and *m* spellings were in more frequent use earlier. In the surviving material, however, there is no sign of *f*-spellings. It still remains possible that *f*-spellings were produced at Llancarfan at a relatively late stage but, if so, there is no surviving evidence.

This is not the place for a full exploration of the implications of these findings, but two points are worth making: first, recent work on Middle Welsh orthography has begun to reveal a range of different orthographical systems in use, often restricted to particular scriptoria or more often to different individual scribes.[48] Presumably what we are seeing here in the *Liber Landavensis* is the varying orthographical habits of the scribes writing the original charters which have been copied into the collection; there is certainly no evidence of tidying up by a later master hand. Secondly, it has been standard to assume that Old Welsh orthography did not mark lenition and that this was one of the main orthographical changes which marked the shift into Middle Welsh. Such an stance was based on the evidence of the Old Welsh gloss and commentary

---

46   See VSB 125–41. For discussion of these charters, see Koch, SC xx/xxi.45, Sims-Williams, BBCS xxxviii.29–30. The evidence for forms containing /μ/ or /β/is as follows (by charter): 55 *Guornemet, Heilbiu, Colbiu*; 56, *Iunemet, Guobrir?*; 57, *Catman, Beduan*; 58, *Nantcarban, Boduan*; 59, *Hierbrith*; 60, *Herbic, Nantcaruan*; 61, *Temit, Rimogeat*; 62, *Conmogoy, Nedauan, Boduan*; 63, *Boduan*; 64, *Conmogoi, Conmil*; 65, *Guorcinnim, Carbani, Conmoe, Conmil, Guallimir?* (cf. *Guallunir*), *Cornouan*; 66, *Conbelin*; 67, *Conmil, Nant Carban*; 68, *Gorbrith, Brocmaili, Rumceneu, Conmogoe, Conmil, Guorcinnim*; 70, *Cinmur, Chumurth.*

47   Sims-Williams, BBCS xxxviii.29–30.

48   For a summary, see Russell, *Introduction to the Celtic Languages*, 213–9; see also Charles-Edwards and Russell, NLWJ xxviii; Russell, NLWJ xxix, CMCS xxv, CMCS xxxvii.

material which shows few examples of anything other than *b* and *m*. However, these recent approaches to the charter material of the *Liber Landavensis* have opened up new avenues into Old Welsh. If the analysis of this material is correct, it would appear that with the labials and labio-dentals at least (where the orthographical resources were available in the form of Latin *u* and *v*) lenition was marked at least by some scribes.[49] In contrast with this material it is striking that generally the monumental inscriptions do not show lenition nor do the Latinised forms of Welsh names.[50] Is it from that style of writing that the *b*/*m* spelling pattern arose? A consequence anyway of this analysis is that, while we have been happy to accept *b*/*m* spellings as Old Welsh, we cannot now say that *u*/*v* spellings are not Old Welsh.

With regard to the distinction between /μ/ and /β/ it looks as if some scribes might have been trying to use *f* to maintain the distinction. If so, they were using it to mark /μ/ not /β/. Moreover, it would seem that *b* for /β/ was slightly more common that *m* for /μ/ and that *u* was correspondingly less common for /β/ than for /μ/. So perhaps at each stage a distinction was maintained but differently by different scribes. What is clear is that unsurprisingly *w*, or even the double letters, seem not to have been part of the repertoire.[51] The use of *w*, then, as we see it fully fledged in BBC, looks like a development which either occurred later or in a milieu which is not otherwise represented in the surviving remains of Old Welsh. For a scribe who was using the *u*-type of spelling for these fricatives it would be the case that without *f* he would not be able to make all the required distinctions. Did he start doubling his *u*s or *v*s to make the distinction clearer?[52] Put another way, the BBC pattern of orthography may have arisen in an environment where *f* was not an option and so a scribe needed other strategies to make the necessary distinctions. By contrast with the bulk of BBC, in the *Afallennau* and *Oianau f* is far more common. The use of *f* in these poems does not does not necessarily imply a later orthography, merely a different one; they could be seen as deriving from a

---

49 There is, of course, no evidence for initial mutation since the names are embedded in a Latin context.

50 See Jackson, LHEB 549–50. On the other hand, there is evidence for attempts to spell spirants, e.g. VAILATHI FILII VROCHANI (CIIC 460), BROHOMAGLI (CIIC 401); see Sims-Williams, *The Celtic Inscriptions of Britain*, 134–9.

51 A striking example of a double letter, which also shows evidence of confusion between /μ/ and /β/, is *uiidimm* (Ox. 2) where -*mm* represents /β/ (cf. Gallo-Latin *vidubium*); see the comments of Peter Schrijver elsewhere in this volume (pp. 10–11).

52 In discussion Pierre-Yves Lambert reminded me that this is what Middle Breton scribes did who used *ff* for /μ/ beside *f* for /v/.

milieu where use of *f* was already a preferred strategy.

If we accept the general trend of the argument, it means we can become more relaxed about *u*-spellings of fricatives in Old Welsh. For example, Jackson was positively dismissive about the possibility that O.W. *dauu* and *Frauu* could represent /dauμ/ and /frauμ/ respectively, but under the present scheme such forms present no problems at all.[53]

III

With these orthographical aspects in mind, it may be helpful to rehearse what we think we know about the phonological development of /μ/ and /β/. As ever in such situations, we may start with Jackson's formulation.[54] The general development is clear: lenited /b/ and lenited /m/, i.e. /β/ and /μ/ respectively, remained distinct in the Common Brittonic period (and continued to be so in Breton) but gradually fell together in Welsh. The presumed developments may be summarised as follows:

/m/ > /μ/ (? = [˜β]) > W /v/, e.g. *haf* 'summer' < **sam-* (but cf. B *hañv*)

/b/ > /β/ > W /v/, e.g. *afon*, B *-aven* 'river' < **abon-*

There is already evidence in the *Liber Landavensis* of confusion, e.g. *treb/trem* (cf. *Treim-* (V S. Catoci, §49)), *Rubon* : **Rumaun* (cf. *Rhufawn* above).[55] Jackson dates the loss of nasalisation in Welsh to the 12th century, but there seems to be evidence for confusion long before that.[56]

Matters are more complicated when it comes to the clusters, not least because there seems to have been long-standing instability in clusters involving /m/ and /μ/: compare, for example, the simplification of /mw/ to /u̯/, e.g. OIr. *coir*, MW *cyweir* < **kom-u̯ar-*, MW *kywir*, Gaul *Couiro-* < **kom-u̯ir-*; the assimilation of /u̯n/ to /μn/, e.g. OIr. *amnair* < **awn-*, OIr. *omun*, W *ofn* < **ownos*;[57] the development of /mn/ to /u̯n/, e.g. *Vellauno-* < **u̯ellamno-*, *alauno-*

53 Jackson, LHEB 416–7; for an earlier discussion, see Förster, *Der Flussname Themse*, 616–85 (though criticised by Jackson, it remains an excellent collection of evidence).

54 Jackson, LHEB 413–24.

55 Cf. also O.W. (Ox. 2) *uiidimm* 'hand-axe' , Mn.W. *gwddf* usually thought to go back to **u̯idubi̯o-* (cf. Gallo-Latin *vidubium*).

56 Jackson, LHEB 699

57 McCone, *Towards a Relative Chronology*, 48–9; cf. also McCone, MSS liii. He assumes

< *alamno-;[58] and the apparently Gallo-Brittonic change of /nm/ to /nw/, e.g. Gaulish *anuana* < *anm- (cf. OW *anu*, etc.), W *menw(yd)*, B *meno* < *menm-.[59] Most of these instances pre-date Common Brittonic and do not figure in Jackson's discussion. He nevertheless presents a number of scenarios where the outcome of /m/ and /β/ is less than straightforward:

(i)   /μ/ or /β/ adjacent to R (= /l r n/) > /ṃ/ or /β/ (the vocalic variant is usual in Cornish and Breton but there is variation in W), e.g. after R: W *twrw*, *twrwf* < Latin *turba*, *cwrw*, *cwryf* < *curmi-, ? *mynwent* < Latin *mon(i)ment-*; before R: *diawl* (cf. pl. *diefyl*) < Latin *diab'lus*, *dŵr*, *dwfr* < *dubr-, *dwfn*, Pembr. /down/ < *dumn-, *cein/cefn* < *cebn-, cemn-.

(ii) /μ/ or /β/ adjacent to /u/ > /ṃ/, e.g. after /u/: *lugubelino- > *Llywelyn*, *lugumarko- > *Llywarch* (*Loumarch*, *Leumarch*, *Lugua(r)ch*, *Luuarch* (*Lib. Land.*)); cf. also *luguualiion > *Lliwelydd*; before /u/: (especially before /ui/), *afwyn*, *awyn* < Latin *(h)abēna*, *Sawyl* < *Samuēl*, *Tawe* < *Tamouia- (cf. BBC *Tawue* (LlDC 34.25, 26)), *Breguoin* (HB) /breṵṵin/ < *Bremēn-.

(iii) loss of final /μ/ (and perhaps /β/): e.g. monosyllables: OW *dauu*, MW *daw/dawf* < *dām-, *Frauu* < *frōm-, *llaw* (but *llof-*) < *lām-, MW *prawf* (cf. also *praw* (1632))< *prōb-; polysyllables: OW *igridu*, *didu* < *-bis, OW *erchim* (Chad 2), *diterni* (Comp.), OW *-cum/cu*, *Adda/Addaf*, etc.

(iv) early loss of distinction between /μ/ and /β/: OW *abruid*, *amcibret* (cf. OB *gucobret*), [co]*bracma*, *Cobreidau* (*Lib. Land.* 202) (= W *cyfraith*).

The above summarises the evidence presented by Jackson in various parts of LHEB. Most of his discussion is descriptive rather than analytic, and he is rarely concerned with orthographical matters except for instances such as *dauu* and *Frauu*.

   A number of further observations can be made. The one possible instance of a development affecting /μ/ and not /β/ seems to be the monosyllables in (iii), namely the loss of the fricative after /au/. The case of *prawf* might indicate that the same change did not affect /β/.[60] Precisely what the Old

---

that /ṵn/ gave /bn/ with a subsequent assimilation to /mn/ and thence to /μ/. As will emerge from the following discussion, a change from /ṵn/ directly to /μ/ would be unexceptional; his assumption of a stage /bn/ may have been prompted by forms such as Gaulish *Exobnus* beside *Exomnus*, where the -*b*- may be orthographic.

58   Lambert, 'Welsh *Caswallawn*', 213–4.
59   See Schrijver, SBCHP 463; see below, p. 47.
60   See below, p. 40.

Welsh orthography indicates here is not clear. Jackson firmly states that *dauu* cannot represent /dauμ/ but perhaps rather /dauu̯/ or /dāuu̯/ since '-auṽ . . . would cerainly be spelt -*aum*'.[61] Following the above discussion, we would not necessarily share his confidence about the certainties of OW orthography, though in view of the evidence in (i) to (iv) above the environment of a rounded vowel is where one might expect a relatively early loss of /μ/, or at least its development to /u̯/. It seems to me that the final -*u* in these OW forms could represent any one of the stages between -/μ/ and -/u̯/ and even a spelling of the diphthong -/au/. Matters are complicated further by the fact that in MW we also find *dawf* and the compound form of *llaw*, namely *llof-*, e.g. *llofrud*, etc. The latter is less surprising since the end of the first element of a compound seems to be a protected position where the consonant is treated as if it were internal. The former is more difficult to account for in a systematic way. There are also doubts about whether this development is unique in being restricted to /μ/ or whether it applied to /β/ as well.

   An important word seems to be *prawf* which is attested in most early sources, but *praw* is attested in Dafydd ap Gwilym and Iolo Goch (Dr John Davies' *Dictionarium* (1632) quotes both forms). This form is problematic in that its etymology is not as clear as it might be. The usual view is that it is derived from Lat. *probāre* with a short first vowel.[62] If so, the noun *prawf* (deriving ostensibly from */proːb/-*) would have to be regarded as a back formation based on the verb *profi* on the analogy of, for example, *llawn* 'full' : *lloni* 'fill'. But it is as likely that it is derived from Lat. *prōmere* 'bring forward, bring into the open', in which case *prawf* would show a reflex of /m/, not /b/. The same verb may have had some influence on OIr. *promaid* 'prove' which has the short first vowel of *probāre* but the -*m*- of *prōmere*.[63] It may well be that the -*f*- was restored in *prawf* on the pattern of the verb and other derivatives, e.g. *profiad*, etc. In contrast, *llaw* does not have a corresponding verb and the surviving plural does not contain -*f*- so that there were fewer forms, apart from the compound form *llof-*, to exert any analogical pressure.[64] In short, it is possible that final -/β/ was also lost phonologically in monosyllables, but by no means certain, since the only possible example is etymologically uncertain.

---

61   Jackson, LHEB 416.
62   Lewis, *Yr Elfen Ladin*, 45–6.
63   Cf. LEIA, *P* 15–16, where confusion between /β/ and /μ/ is assumed. It is not impossible that W *profi*, etc. also arose through a crossing between these two Latin verbs.
64   W. *llaw* may not have had a fully functioning plural in early Welsh, as the dual form *dwylaw* would have been far more common (cf. Zimmer, *Studies in Welsh Word-formation*, 32).

It is also the case that the merging of /μ/ and /β/ happened earlier in some environments than others. In Old Welsh forms such as *abruid,* (iv) above, the *b-*spelling suggests that nasalisation was lost in this environment, i.e. before /r/, earliest. The developments towards /u̯/ in (i) and (ii) above involve both /μ/ and /β/ and indicates that in these environments too the distinction was at least partially neutralised. Adjacency of /u/ seems to be crucial and, if this condition is broadened to include the /au/ diphthong, the important condition may well be rounding; the fricative, whether /β/ or /μ/, appears to assimilate to the preceding or following rounded vowel and thus lose its fricative feature giving /u̯/ which then merges with original /u̯/. In both cases the nasal segment, which phonetically may belong to the preceding vowel, is lost or at least unrecorded in the orthography. The other environment is adjacent to a continuant /R/ (= /l r n/). In this instance the cluster seems to resolve itself either as /Ru̯/ or /u̯R/ or as /Rβ/ or /βR/ (in this last case epenthesis seems inevitable). However, variation between /u̯/ and /β/ is not restricted to this environment.

It has been frequently observed that in addition to the material discussed above there are other doublets in Welsh, one of which contains /u̯/, the other /β/, e.g. *cawod* (also *cawad*) : *cafod* 'shower', *tywod* : *tyfod, briwo* : *brifo, gwywo* : *gwyfo, cywoeth* : *cyfoeth,* etc.[65] Similarly, there are forms where etymologically we would expect /u̯/ but find /v/, e.g. *deifio, edryfant* : *edrywiant, Difiau* < *dyw iau, dwyfol* < *dwywiol,* etc. The most discussed of these is perhaps W *tafod* 'tongue' which, if it represents an earlier */taŋu̯a:t/~* requires an explanation for why it contains /v/, especially as for *ewin* 'nail' (< */aŋu̯i:na/~) no variant in /v/ is attested in Welsh. The alternation between /u̯/ and /v/ has long been recognised and acknowledged but always left unexplained; McCone, for example, characterises it as 'an undeniable but as yet ill-understood tendency'.[66] Likewise, if we widen the perspective to consider the Brittonic languages as a whole, there are cases where the *w*-form is found in one language and the *v-*variant in another, e.g. W *diwedd* : MB *divez,* W *llewenydd* : B *levenez,* W *glawog* : B *glavek,* etc.[67] There is no doubt that the evidence is less than straightforward, and it may well be that more than one thing is going on here (and perhaps at different periods).

The material seems to be divisible into a number of categories, and part of the confusion may lie in a failure to separate out these categories. Three groups

---

65   For a collection of these forms, see Parry-Williams, RC xxxv.342–4; see also Koch, 'Indo-European *g^{wh} in Celtic', 84. For *tywod,* see WDS 372.

66   McCone, *Towards a Relative Chronology,* 40.

67   Parry-Williams, RC xxxv.343; see also Jackson, HPB 239–40.

seem to be distinguishable:

(i) It has been observed by John Koch that there is a tendency for a cluster of /ṷi/ to give /v/ in, for example, *edryfant* < *edrywiant*, *Difiau* < *dyw iau*, *dwyfol* < *dwywiol* (but also MW *duwiau*, *duwiol*, etc.).[68] This development may also account for the dialectal variation found in verbal noun formations: southern Welsh *briwo*, *gwywo* beside northern *brifo*, *gwyfo*.[69] It is well known that verbal noun suffixes had northern and southern reflexes with and without -/i̯/-; thus, a northern **briw-i̯o* would give *brifo* beside a southern *briwo* containing the version of the suffix without /i̯/.[70] Phonetically, this may involve the retraction of the articulation of the bilabial continuant towards a labio-dental position in anticipation of the /i̯/; this would inevitably give rise to a fricative pronunciation.

(ii) That the alternation between /v/ and /ṷ/ seems to be a tendency rather than a thorough-going sound-change is suggested by the fact that it is detectable in relatively late loanwords into Welsh from English, e.g. *pwfer* < *power*, *lwfans* < *allowance*, *lwfio* < *allow* (15th c, onwards), etc.[71] Sims-Williams also mentions the alternation in the loanwords from Latin *cavella* which seems to give both *cawell* and *cafell*.[72] However, this need not be quite the same kind of alternation. In Welsh *cawell* and *cafell* are not simply formal variants; they mean different things: *cawell* 'basket' preserves the general sense of the Latin, while *cafell* 'chancel, sanctuary' seems to have a specialised ecclesiastical meaning. It is possible that the alternation arose in Latin with *cawell* deriving from a more conservative pronunciation with /ṷ/ rather than a more 'vulgar' /v/ pronunciation, or from different chronological layers of Latin. In this instance, the former explanation is perhaps less likely in one respect: we would perhaps have expected the ecclesiastical term to retain the more conservative pronunciation.

(iii) Another environment where /ṷ/ tends to give /v/ is in the environment of a rounded vowel (often /u/ and /au/ but also /o/). This was noted for *tafod* by Pedersen, and a similar approach might account for *cafod* and

---

68   Koch, 'Indo-European **gʷʰ* in Celtic', 84.
69   See GPC svv.
70   See Russell, *Celtic Word-Formation*, 39–60; Thomas, BBCS xl.26–8.
71   Parry-Williams, RC xxxv.343; id., *The English Element*, 234; cf. also W *berfa* < OE **barwe* implied by Middle English *barewe*.
72   Sims-Williams, 'Indo-European **gʷʰ* in Celtic', 212

tyfod.[73] Matters are not helped by these words having opaque etymologies. *Cafod/cawod* 'shower' (with a variant *cawad* perhaps showing vowel assimilation[74]) seems not to have troubled the etymologists; one possibility is that it is a compound of the **pot-* root seen in *odi* 'fall', perhaps **kom-pot-* though the devlopment of */mp/ is unclear (possibly /mp/ > /mu̯/ > /u̯/ or /v/). *Tyfod/tywod* 'sand-dune, seashore' may be related to *tywyn* 'sand-dune', *tywynnu* 'shine'; possibly *tywod : tywyn* is related as collective : singulative (cf. *tywodyn* 'grain of sand'), and the verb *tywynnu* is a metaphorical extension from the sand, i.e. 'gleam, shine (like the sand on the beach)'.[75] None of this, however, helps without the etymology. A doublet where the etymology is clear is *cyfoeth/cywoeth* < **kom-okt-* (cf. OIr. *cumachtae*); in this case, /μ/ is flanked by rounded vowels. In such cases we may be dealing with a dissimilatory tendency to unround the continuant before (and/or after) the rounded vowel. What is striking is that it does not in most cases seem to be a simple sound change whereby the form in /v/ replaces an earlier form in /u̯/ or *vice versa*; in many cases the forms seem to co-exist in the language. Hence presumably the tendency to call it a 'tendency'.

A similar co-existence of variants involves the clusters of /μ/ or /β/ adjacent to R (= /l r n/) giving /u̯/ or /β/, e.g. W *twrw : twrwf* < Latin *turba*, *cwrw: cwryf* < **curmi-*, *diawl* (cf. pl. *diefyl*) < Latin *diab'lus*, *dŵr : dwfr* < **dubr-*, *dwfn* : Pembr. /down/ < **dumn-*, *cein : cefn* < **cebn-/cemn-*.[76] Such double treatments may be accounted for in a number of ways: they could be historically differentiated; one form could be a secondary analogical development of the other based on a different stem pattern or accentual pattern. For these particular forms, there is some evidence that there may be a regional or dialectal explanation. The indications are that, where in Welsh there is a /u̯/ : /v/ alternation (excluding the /u̯i/ to /v/ change), the /v/ reflex is northern and the /u̯/ reflex is southern (the latter may in many instances simply the preservation of the inherited form): thus southern *cawod* : northern *cafod*. Similarly

---

73 Pedersen, VKG, I.107.

74 The variant *cawad* may show the unrounding of vowel or assimilation of vowel to preceding /a/.

75 See WDS 372: the dialectal distribution is unclear; the word obtained a nil response or an active refusal at many points. The most common form is *tywod* but there is a small cluster of *tyfod* in Flintshire.

76 For *dwfn*, see Awbery, *Pembrokeshire Welsh*, 95–7; /down/ is not recorded in WDS 308.

with clusters, those containing vocalisation of the fricative seem to be southern: the form *cein* 'ridge, back' is attested in the *Liber Landavensis*; OW *ceintiru* (Ox. 1) beside northern *cefnder(w)* again is likely to be a southern reflex and comparable with southern Welsh [kendɛr] and to be constrasted with Bangor [kevndar].[77] Pembrokeshire Welsh is particularly rich in vocalised consonants in such clusters, e.g. *sofl* (Pembr. [sowl], northern [sovol]), *cefn* (Pembr. [kewn], northern [keven]), *ysgafn* (Pembr. [əsgawn], northern [əsgafan]).[78] Another such form is *ysgafn* 'couch, bed' (< Lat. *scamnum*): there are 18th century examples of *ysgawn* and *ysgon* is reported as 'ar lafar yng ngogledd Cered(igion)'.[79] The alternation is also found in a group of forms in Welsh conventionally regarded as containing the stem *tafl-*, e.g. W *tafol*, *tafl* (< Latin *tab(u)la*), *taflod* 'hayloft' (< Latin *tāblātum*), and W *taflu* 'throw' (of uncertain origin). For *taf(o)l* there is no evidence for a vocalised form in Welsh, though in Breton it seems to have been vocalised from an early period, e.g. MB *taul*, Mn.B *taol* (but OB *tablor* gl. *tabellarius*).[80] Vocalised forms of *taflod*, however, are well documented in the south.[81] Likewise, for *taflu*, *tawlu*, etc. is well attested in modern southern dialects, and in Breton and Cornish, e.g. MCo. *teulel*, MB *teuleur*, *teurell* (showing dissimilation of /l/).[82]

---

77   See Charles-Edwards, BBCS xxiv.108. I would be inclined to take Cyfeiliog [kemdɛr] (recorded by Sommerfelt, *Cyfeiliog Welsh*, 66, 104) as an assimilation of a basically northern type in which the nasal assimilated to the labial (labio-dental?) fricative, as opposed to the Pembrokeshire type where the fricative assimilates to the nasal. On [kendɛr], see WDS 415, where it is recorded for the whole of south Wales.

78   See Awbery, *Pembrokeshire Welsh*, 95–7; see also WDS 304 (*sofl*); 367 (*ysgafn*), 294 (*cefn*; where [kewn] is not recorded). It is worth noting, however, that this feature is not universal in Pembrokeshire Welsh and the evidence of WDS suggests that the vocalised variants are disappearing or have disappeared. There are also forms like [oːvon] and [treven] where a matching epenthetic vowel has developed instead. Awbery (*Pembrokeshire Welsh*, 97) may well be right to characterise it as 'gradual spread of an innovation through the vocabulary'; she is not clear on what she thinks is the innovation, but the evidence would point to the epenthesised forms as be the innovation.

79   I am grateful to Andrew Hawke for supplying this information from the GPC slips before the publication of the relevant fascicule of GPC.

80   See Jackson HPB 239–40, 252; the Old Breton spelling suggested to Jackson that the change had occurred after the Old Breton period; but the -*b*- spelling could simply be influenced by the Latin form it glosses, *tabellarius*.

81   GPC 3416; WDS 413.

82   For the Welsh forms, see GPC 3414; WDS 370. For the dissimilation of /l/ in the Breton forms, see Jackson, HPB 806.

The evidence of Breton suggests that the vocalisation was largely a phenomenon of late Middle Breton and early Modern Breton in that spelling representing the fricative are well attested in Middle Breton sources, e.g. MB *guefl*, Early Mn.B *gueaul*, Mn.B *géol* 'throat' (cf. W *gwefl*).[83] On the other hand, in MB *taul*, etc. the change seems to be earlier. Jackson seems to want to distinguish between cases where loss of the fricative produces dipthongisation, and instances where the fricative is simply lost with no apparent change in the vocalisation. As an example of the latter, he offers Mn.B *kenderv*, V *kenderù* 'cousin', attested as *quenderu* in Middle Breton (Catholicon). But we may also compare MB *queyn*, Mn.B *kein* 'back', and it is at least possible that forms such as *kenderv* represent a weakened **kein-* in unaccented position. The general impression is of a tendency to vocalisation in both Welsh and Breton (and presumably Cornish as well, though the evidence there is less clear), but it seems to be differentiated both regionally and chronologically. We find vocalised forms in southern Welsh mostly after /a/, /o/ and /u/ but less often after /e/; compare, for example, the singular *diawl* 'devil' and its plural *diefyl*. Jackson interprets the Breton evidence similarly;[84] the vocalisation after back vowels had already happened in Middle Breton, but after front vowels vocalisation is only complete by the 17th or 18th century.

Where then there are forms like *tafod* and *ewin*, both containing an original -/ŋu̯/-, with single but different reflexes, it is possible that the variant has dropped out. Alternatively one might wish to see phonological reasons why, for example, the -/u̯/- of *ewin* was preserved; for example, could we make something of the fact that the /u̯/ is followed by a front vowel? With these forms it may be an error to concentrate so completely on Welsh. Taking a wider dialectal perspective, it emerges that the variant occurs in other Brittonic dialects: compare, for example, W *ewin* : MB *ivin*, W *tafod* : MB *teaut*, B *teod*, W *tafol* 'dock-leaf' : B *teaul(enn)*.[85] The development of **-/ŋu̯/-* to either /u̯/ or /v/ is unclear. Hamp suggested a shift -/ŋgu̯/- > -/gu̯/- > /u̯/ which then gave /β/ after a back vowel but remained as /u̯/ before a front vowel (as in *ewin, priod* < Lat. *privatus* (which shows a subsequent loss of /u̯/ before the rounded vowel)).[86] Sims-Williams, however, regarded a development of -/ngʷ/- > British -/ŋu̯/- > /u̯/ s 'quite attractive *prima facie*' but perhaps as an instance of a special treatment of Celtic **gʷ(h)* before nasals, and so not offering

---

83 See Jackson, HPB 240, 630–7 (esp. 635).
84 Jackson, HPB 635–7.
85 See Hamp, EC xiv.462. For *ivin*, see Jackson, HPB 458.
86 Hamp, EC xiv.462

counter-evidence to the view that */gʷh/ gave internal /gʷ/ in British as well as in Irish.[87] The Breton forms show the same alternation of forms with /v/ and /w/ as is found in reflexes of /μ̞/, and one possibility raised by the present discussion is that -/ŋμ̞/-, did not simply develop to /μ̞/, since it is not clear that simple /μ̞/ alternated with /v/; as we have seen, usually some other element has to be involved, e.g. /μ̞/ + /i̞/, etc. It is possible that -/ŋμ̞/- was perceived phonetically as very close to /μ/, perhaps as a nasal bilabial continuant or with a preceding nasalised vowel [˜u̞]. If so, it would be reasonable to suppose that it fell together with /μ/ and followed the same relatively complex development within which two possible environmentally determined reflexes were /μ̞/ and /v/: the latter where there was a preceding back vowel and a following rounded vowel, the former where an adjacent front vowel encouraged retention of the rounding. The example of *priod* with a preceding front vowel and following rounded vowel suggests that the preceding vowel was the important factor. In Breton there seems to have been a complex set of circumstances in which /β/ and /μ/, were resolved as /v/, /ṽ/ or /ũ/ with or without loss of nasalisation.[88]

One form which has been left to one side so far is *enw* (O.W. *anu*). The development in British would fit prefectly well with the developments noted above for a cluster of -/nm/- with subsequent dissimilation of the /m/ to /μ̞/ in contact with /n/. The example of W *mynwent* (where the same change occurs) is used by Schrijver to show that the change is relatively late since it must post-date the syncope of Latin *mon(i)menta*.[89] But that is to assume that *monimenta* had not already lost its /i/ in Vulgar Latin; if it had, then it would simply have gone the way of **anm-* and the dating would be less clear. If, however, we accept that the cluster in *mynwent* is a relatively late outcome of syncope in British, then the cluster arising must have been -/nμ̞/- (developing to -/nμ̞/-), since before syncope the -/m/- would have been in leniting position. Morover, in Gaulish both *anman-* and *anuan-* are now attested, and that raises the question of the significance of the change; the variation may suggest attempts to spell a poorly perceived phonetic variation.[90] It has been assumed that these developments in both Welsh and Gaulish are related and

---

87　Sims-Williams, *Hispano-Gallo-Brittonica*, 213.

88　See HPB 601–3 for a summary of the details.

89　Schrijver, SBCHP 463; see also Schrijver, ÉC xxxiv.135–6.

90　The latter is found in the Larzac inscription in the form *anuana*; the former has now appeared in the recently discovered tile from Châteaubleau in an instrumental plural, *anmanbe*; see P-Y. Lambert, ÉC xxxiv.89.

thus it forms a significant plank in the argument for Gallo-Brittonic unity. Even Peter Schrijver, who is sceptical about Gallo-Brittonic, acknowledges the specific nature of the change.[91] However, as we have seen, clusters involving /m/, and especially clusters of /m/ and another continuant, seem to have been very unstable; in the cluster /nm/ there seems to have been a fairly straightforward dissimilation going on. If so, it is no more specific than any other dissimilation of a cluster. The fact that it involves the same word may simply be coincidental; after all, there are not that many words containing this cluster anyway. Beside *enw*, etc., only W *menw(yd)*, B *meno* (cf. OIr. *menmae*) seems to contain the same cluster and there it develops in the same way.

Phonologically, if we start from the fricative bilabial nasal -/μ/-, which seems to be inherently unstable, the close relationship between /u̯/ and /v/ in these forms should not be surprising. In Welsh and Cornish terms, the nasal feature is unstable and prone to loss (though it remains more fixed in Breton); if so, we are then faced with an unstable scenario in which a distinction has to be maintained on the one hand between a bilabial fricative (i.e. denasalised /μ/) /β/ and the bilabial continuant /u̯/, and on the other between a bilabial fricative /β/ and a labio-dental fricative /v/. It would then crucially depend on which feature was perceived to predominate: if the bilabial feature, it would have fallen together with /u̯/; if the fricative, then it would have gone with /v/. A further complication would have arisen with the cluster /ŋu̯/, which developed in the preforms of *tafod* and *ewin*. One way of explaining why it seems to have behaved in a similar way to some of the forms discussed above is to assume that it was perceived phonetically as close, if not identical, to /μ/, and thus underwent the same chequered development.

To return briefly to *Rhufoniog* and the question with which we began about the phonological status of the *w*-spellings in BBC: in view of the dialectal variation between /v/ and /u̯/ discussed above, we may simply observe that it is not impossible that in some areas this form would have been pronounced /rʰu̯'u̯oni̯og/. The widespread *w*-spelling would, as suggested above, reflect one of the possible inherited spellings for the range of sounds from /μ/ to /v/. A further possibility is that some of the *w*-spellings in BBC which have been assumed to stand for /v/ may indeed have been understood to represent /v/ at the time of copying but at an earlier period of composition may have represented /u̯/.

---

91   Schrijver, SBCHP 463–5.

Old English literacy and the provenance of Welsh *y*

Peter Kitson

To people in neighbouring scholarly disciplines it can often seem that ones on the other side of the fence are not asking the interesting questions, or not formulating the questions they ask in quite the right way.[1] This is especially liable to happen with a relatively self-enclosed field like Celtic studies. For reasons both of modern cultural history and the difficulty of the subject-matter, activity in general linguistics overlaps a good deal less with Celtic studies than it does with historical English studies, for example. This may mean the observer from outside the specialism is not up to date with what those inside it are saying to one another. Whether that is so in ways significant for this paper, readers must be the judge. But just as liable to apply is Gödel's theorem, pointing out that for any intellectual system there are questions formulable from within the system but only answerable from outside it. That has to be true of the main question to be asked here: where does the letter *y* in Welsh spelling come from? Data to establish a probability on it must of necessity come from outside Welsh.

Welsh *y*, as most readers will know, denotes two sounds, called by Welsh grammarians since the fourteenth century clear and obscure *y*, respectively a rather broad retracted *i*-sound and a reduced vowel with values approximating to schwa, but spreading as far as standard English *u* especially before nasals, where mediaeval spellings often show it alternating with *a*.[2] The clear sound occurs in syllables which were stressed, and obscure *y* in syllables which were

---

1   A version of this paper was given at the International Congress of Celtic Studies in Cork on 29.vii.1999. I thank Paul Russell for suggestions improving its completeness on the Celtic side.
2   Evans (GMW §3) gives many examples including *amherawdyr*/*ymerawdyr* 'emperor'.

unstressed, before the shift of the accent from final to penultimate syllables in the transition from Old to Middle Welsh around 1100.[3] Historical grammarians such as Morris Jones (*Grammar* §§65–66) and Jackson (LHEB §§6–7) have detailed where the sounds come from. Clear *y* is the main reflex of older British *i* outside diphthongs, though *i* can survive as such and *y* can derive from *e* in particular phonetic environments. Obscure *y* results from reduced vowels, oftenest *o* because of the many prefixes containing it, but in principle any vowel irrespective of quality.

That is reasonable enough; but Welsh grammarians, at least those whose works I have ever seen, do not seem to have asked where the Welsh *spelling* comes from. They tend to approach *y* from the direction of modern Welsh, where it is a datum. Thus Morris-Jones (*Grammar* 10) just records its presence in 'the earliest Welsh alphabet given as such', the Red Book Grammar in the fourteenth century,[4] Evans (GMW §13) variation 'at an early period' tending to more uniform *y* from the mid-thirteenth century on. And they tend to project back the connection between the two sounds spelt *y* in modern Welsh onto earlier periods of the language as if it were a datum.[5] I don't suppose there are any minimal pairs involving clear and obscure *y*. But the same would go for obscure *y* and just about any other vowel. It must still in reason be considered a separate phoneme.[6] Mediaeval grammarians whose intellectual framework was phonetic not phonemic would anyway have been likely to think of it as an entity distinct from any front vowel. On the other hand there are plenty of pairs of related words where clear and obscure *y* alternate, singular *mynydd* /mənɨð/ plural *mynyddoedd* /mənəðoɨð/ and so on, and that might have been enough to keep them yoked in early as in modern perceptions. A fourteenth-

---

3   The date of the accent-shift will matter for the argument below. A classic treatment, with fair reference to opposing views, is that by Jackson, SC x. Russell (*Introduction*, 119–121) reviews more recent scholarship.

4   Current scholarship, e.g. Huws, MWM 60, would place the Red Book at the very end of the fourteenth century. The alphabet is not a separate item but the beginning of the grammar traditionally attributed to Einion Offeiriad, which Gruffydd, PBA xc.4–5, thinks he wrote 'fairly early in the 1320s', and of which the Red Book is the earliest surviving copy. It is edited by Williams and Jones as Grammar A (*Gramadegau'r Penceirddiaid* 1–18).

5   Thus Morris Jones (WG §16) proceeds from '[Mod.W.] y has two sounds, the clear and the obscure' to 'In O.W. the sounds of *y* are denoted by *i*, and are therefore not distinguished in writing from the sound *i*.' Evans (GMW §4) phrases 'The vowels *y* (both [ɨ] and [ə]) and *i*' as two terms with subdivision of one, not as three terms.

6   As it is by phonemically minded modern Welsh grammarians, e.g. Thorne, *A Comprehensive Welsh Grammar* 4.

century grammarian who comments on them[7] does so in terms of the written letter *y* having *deu ryw datkanyat* 'two kinds of pronunciation', which does not suggest he felt any organic connection between the two; his examples, *ystyr* and *llythyr*, could be argued either way.[8]

Old Welsh used the symbols *i* and *e* for these sounds. The grammars treat *i* as norm for both and *e* as an occasional variant.[9] This is potentially dangerous, and the assumption that spellings for the two developed together is doubly dangerous. They did not do so in the other P-Celtic languages; nor in these matters did the three languages develop together. The normal reflex of British *i* in Middle Cornish and Breton was *e*; the early development according to Jackson was through a lowered *i* not a retracted one.[10] The shift to *e* is nearing completion in the eleventh-century Old Cornish of the translation of Ælfric's Glossary; *i* always predominates in Old Breton spellings, though there is some increase in *e* in late Old Breton. For the reduced vowel Middle Cornish has no standard symbol; Lewis presents *e* as primary but lists beside it *o* and *u* and a set of digraphs mainly involving *u*.[11] Breton, as the textbooks present it, does not seem to have had a schwa phoneme; accentual reductions and fallings together are part of the history of individual vowels, and spellings preserve their etymological value much longer than in Welsh and Cornish.[12] So the question of *y* in Welsh has essentially to be considered in isolation from Cornish and Breton.

The tenth-century Old Cornish of the Bodmin manumissions[13] does in fact show *y* beside *i* for the stressed vowel. That is pretty clearly a temporary stage in the development from *i* to *e*, not directly related to the Welsh usage, though with some implications for it which we shall consider. It is substantially earlier than *y* appears regularly for either value in Welsh, though Paul Russell has

---

7   Dafydd Ddu of Hiraddug (Gruffydd, PBA xc.14–15, etc.), near the start of his revision of Einion's grammar, Williams and Jones's C (*Gramadegau'r Penceirddiaid* 39–58), extant in Peniarth 20, a manuscript of *c*.1330 (Huws, MWM 59 etc.). Matonis, *Modern Philology*, lxxix.130, quotes and translates the relevant passage.

8   My own view is that his non-mention of the change of pronunciation of the second syllable in the plural of these words is far more significant than the pedagogic neatness of instancing both sounds in a single word.

9   Thus Morris Jones as quoted in the previous note.

10   LHEB 284 (where he spells it *i̯*), HPB 91–93 (spelling *ɪ*).

11   '*e* (gall fod fel Cym. *e*... ac i y dywyll Gymraeg a ddynodir yma gan yr arwydd *ə*, a chynrychiolir y sain hon hefyd gan *eu, ue, u, uy, o, ey*)', with typically four or five variant spellings for a single word (Lewis, LlCC 6).

12   Compare the silence of Lewis (LlCC 7) with the vowel by vowel treatment of Jackson (HPB 145–54).

13   Freilassungsurkunden.

pointed out to me that it is present in two texts that are otherwise in Old Welsh orthography. One is the Computus fragment, dated by its editor Williams ('Computus' 245), apparently on grounds of palaeography not content, also to the tenth century, and satisfyingly different in its usage from the Bodmin documents. The other is the *englyn* to St. Padarn's staff, in the margin of a manuscript written in the late 1080s.[14] These two outliers are of radically different kinds, as will be shown below.

What principles governed the distribution of *i* and *e* for these sounds in Old Welsh is something about which we can now only speculate. People with databases of mediaeval Welsh might try to look for chronological, geographical, or phonetic patterning, but so little Old Welsh writing survives that it is very unlikely that any such findings would be statistically reliable. Since in items such as stop consonants Old Welsh, Cornish and Breton spelling was famously conservative, *i* might be expected to be kept for stressed *y* out of historical inertia. There might have been comparable conditioning for the unstressed vowel, with *i* preferred for what historically was reduced *i*, *e* for reduced *o* as *e* represents the *i*-mutation of *o*. On the other hand people who heard stressed *y* as closer to *e* than to *i*, and so spelt it, would have little historical use left for *i* outside diphthongs, so might use it for the reduced vowel as being the nearest thing available in their existing inventory to a distinct symbol. That may be what is going on in the inscription from Tywyn (Towyn), Merionethshire, which Sir Ifor Williams (BWP 36–37) called 'in all probability . . . the earliest example[s] on stone of the Welsh language', and where he found two instances of OW *e* corresponding to modern Welsh stressed *y*, beside *i* for unstressed *y*.[15]

If Welsh, or some Welsh, shared at first the Cornish and Breton lowering, a possibility Morris Jones favoured (*Grammar* 16) but Jackson seems to discount, that, where it applied, would be a factor favouring *e*. Then again, there may very well have been different preferences at different scribal centres, as there certainly are in different Middle Welsh manuscripts.[16] The paucity of extant Old Welsh, combined with a strongly neogrammarian and non-variationist approach in most of the standard scholarship, means that non-uniformities in it, especially dialectal ones, are likely to be overlooked or ignored. If the quantity of surviving Old English were as little as there is of Old Welsh, it is very

---

14　Williams, BWP 181; Haycock, *Blodeugerdd* 241.

15　Stressed, *celen* for *Celyn*, and less certainly *tricet* for *trigyd*; unstressed, *cimalted* for **cyfalltedd*. For a different interpretation, see Koch, *Grammar of Old Welsh* (forthcoming) §§64, 251; see also Sims-Williams, *Celtic Inscriptions of Britain* 50, 128.

16　Morris Jones (WG 15) gives examples.

unlikely that our picture of the dialects would be accurate even at the broadest level. I am not concerned to take up a position on this; the principles governing the variation need not have been the same throughout the Old Welsh period, and as already stated I think it unlikely that enough data survive for them to be recoverable at all accurately. But the basic starting-point for the discussion of *y* must be that *e* and *i* were both current as symbols it supplanted.

So now, whence and how did the *y* come in? Obviously from somewhere where it was current as a written letter, and presumably in a value, or values, either identical or felt to be analogous to those in which it was current there. There is only one first-millennium European language where *y* was current, and that is Old English. It was not widely current in scribal Latin; *y* in Greek-derived words had for centuries routinely been spelt *i*.[17] Old Welsh scribes' vacillation between *e* and *i*, but never *y*, for sounds they clearly felt not identical with either *e* or *i*, is in itself a strong indication that *y* was alien to the Latin alphabet they operated with. So in a left-handed sort of way is what is otherwise a large red herring, the ninth-century *alphabetum Nemnivi*.[18] It is an alphabet by a Welshman which does contain a *y*, yet it is not a Welsh alphabet, but invented on the basis of English runes, those letter-names with intelligible meanings being translated from English rune-names.[19] By contrast with all the names of such vowels as are known from Old Welsh texts and even with the factitious diphthong-names, the name given to *y* does not begin with that letter itself. It is *oyr*, probably adapted from the Old English rune-name *ȳr*. It shows some relation too to the names given to *u*, *uir*, and to *au*, *aur*. The whole set may well be a calque on a group of rune-names which includes diphthongs.[20]

Since the only land in whose orthography *y* was current is also the neighbour of Wales, the overwhelming general likelihood is that Welsh *y* was borrowed from there. But in what value? The difficulty with an English derivation always has been that the basic value of OE *y*, the only one that is common Old English, was not either of those for which the letter is used in Welsh, but a rounded front vowel, modern French *u* or German *ü*, whose pronunciation was identical or all but identical to that of Welsh *u* at this period. That is the

---

17   Though some scribes, including some Welsh ones, did still use *y* in such words: Paul Russell points out repeated *syllaba* by hand B on fol. 16 of CCCC 153 (the Corpus Martianus Capella), a Cambro-Latin manuscript of 850x930 with Old Welsh glosses.

18   Zeuss, *Grammatica Celtica* 189–190; for a facs. see I. Williams, 'Notes on Nennius' facing p. 381.

19   Expounded by Derolez (*Runica Manuscripta* 157–9). For Old English rune-names cf. Dickins, *Runic and heroic poems* 12–23, Page, *Introduction* 69–89, and Elliott, *Runes* 45–61.

20   Beside *ȳr* *y* there are *ūr* *u*, *īor* *io*, and *ēar* *ea*.

reason no doubt why Welsh scholars have not pursued the question further.[21] The occasional modern Celticist with whom I have raised it has indeed been satisfied with the idea of *y* as a variant of *i* as in modern English. For reasons which will emerge I think that is anachronistic by a couple of centuries, given that *y* is fully present in some Welsh manuscripts already around 1200, even if *y* does alternate with *i* in some of these manuscripts. That a new letter should be picked up by scribal accident from a foreign language and then just happen to be found just the thing that phonetic economy in the scribes' native language needed is also enormously improbable on general grounds. Adoption of *y* as a standard spelling must represent deliberate choice; adoption of *y* as a letter is much likelier to have been also deliberate, to express one or other of the distinctions not previously expressible in Welsh spelling which standard *y* was afterwards to express. Notice, however, that I have said 'choice' not 'a choice'. Adoption of *y* in either use may well have had more than one point of Welsh origin, and it is likely that the clear and obscure uses were imported separately and that the coordination apparent in pairs like *mynydd–mynyddoedd* is a secondary effect of standardization.

This sounds very well in the abstract, but is not much practical use unless it is possible to show what the English points of origin are likely to be. For the clear *y* this is actually rather easy, and it is surprising no-one has done it before. In southern Old English from the late ninth century on there is a secondary source of *y*-spellings, as the reflex of 'early West Saxon' front vowel diphthongs before *r* and *l*, and of simplex *i* in some words before *r* and in labial contexts. Some reputable scholars have expressed doubts whether secondary *y* had rounding.[22] If it did not, it can only have been a retracted and/or lowered *i* more or less identical with Welsh clear *y*. Subsequent history of the relevant words shows in my opinion that secondary *y* did have rounding,[23] but it can have been no more than could be caused by accommodation to neighbouring consonants, less than in primary *y* which is the *i*-mutation of underlying *u*. So give or take the exact degree of rounding, this is a plausible phonetic source for Welsh clear *y*. It was current throughout 'late West Saxon', that is in most of

---

21 Thus Charles-Edwards and Russell, NLWJ xxviii.422, are content to speak of the 'extra symbol, *y*, introduced into Welsh orthography, probably from English, in the tenth century and more widely used in the eleventh'.

22 The kind of argument involved is illustrated by Hogg (*Grammar* §5.163 n. 3).

23 E.g. OE **risc** > 'rush' (with *u* sporadically from the 970s on), or the phonetic conditioning in Campbell, *Old English Grammar* §§318, 325. There is more detail on this in my *New foundation*, ch. V.

southern England and the south midlands, including Gloucestershire, and (beside alternatives) in Worcestershire; and of course especially at West Saxon kings' courts. The earliest literary text to show significant amounts of it is the Old English translation of Orosius made in the 890s, whose dialect must be placed in Bristol or somewhere very close.[24] The first Welshman who we can be sure knew of it probably is Asser at king Alfred's court. With the participation of Hywel Dda and his underlings in English kings' grants of charters from the 920s on, appreciable handfuls of literate Welshmen will have been acquainted with West Saxon vernacular literacy. More than one of them may have found the advantage in it of an unambiguous symbol for their clear *y*.

This is likely to be the origin of the earlier of the pair of Old Welsh outliers Paul Russell noted. The Computus fragment uses *oy* consistently (five attestations) in *loyr* 'moon',[25] = Mod.W *lloer*, with *y* followed by *r*, the commonest phonetic context for secondary *y* in Old English (LWS *byrht* for LWS *beorht* 'bright' etc.), but only sporadically beside *oi* in *oes* 'is',[26] a phonetic context where *y* could not occur except by *i/y* levelling in Old English, and not at all for simplex vowels whether obscure or clear, both of which are normally spelt *i*. Thus *did* (x 4) = *dydd* 'day',[27] *ir* consistently = both *yr* 'the' (x 16)[28] and *er* 'for' (x 4),[29] *is(s)i(d)* = *y sydd* 'that is' is unstable consonantally but has both vowels consistently *i*.[30] There are only isolated exceptions; for the obscure vowel *cen nit* beside *cinnit* = *cyny* 'though not',[31] for the clear vowel *tritid, triti, trited* all = *trydydd* 'third'.[32] The governing principles seem to be much as canvassed for the Towyn stone above. The function of *y* in *oy* is to disambiguate the Mod.W diphthong *oe* from *wy*, for which the spelling *oi* is also used in *blwyddyn* 'year' (twice),[33] and *wyth* 'eight' (once, as part of a compound *oithaur* ≈ *oeth awr* 'eight hours'),[34] but *ui* in *abruid* = *abrwydd*

---

24 The arguments and pertinent evidence are set forth at length in Kitson, *Studia Linguistica Posnaniensia* xxx; 'main dialect' if you think patches of forms incompatible with a Bristol origin make it more seriously composite than I do (*Studia Linguistica Posnaniensia* xxx.25–27).

25 I. Williams, BBCS iii.256, lines 2, 4, 9, 11, 21.

26 Once *hoys* (line 14), once *hois* (line 6). With these belongs *oit* = *oedd* 'time' (line 20).

27 Lines 1, 3, 14, 18.

28 Lines 1, 2, 4, 6, 7, 8, 9 (x 3), 14, 16, 17, 18, 20 (x 2), 21.

29 Lines 2, 9, 20, 21.

30 Line 5 *issi*, 12 *isid*, 15 *issid*.

31 Lines 11 and 14 respectively.

32 Respectively lines 1, 5, 2.

33 Lines 20, 22 (both *bloidin*).

34 Line 4.

'difficult' and in *hinnuith* = *hwnnw* (x 4)[35] and *hunnuith* = *honno* (x 1)[36] 'that (m./f.)'.

The obvious explanation for this last divergence is that it is accentual, with *ui* retained in the syllable stressed in Old Welsh, *oi* reflecting some kind of pretonic reduction.[37] To judge by absence of diphthongal spellings for *hwnnw*, *honno* in even the earliest Middle Welsh (MSS from *c*.1200 on),[38] the second element of their *oi* was already by the time of the Computus fragment probably reduced to vanishing-point. It seems then that the scribe felt the need to use *oy* for a diphthong of *o* and a low front vowel second element that was not reduced. Variability in *oes* may thus have to do essentially with its variable sentence-stress, and correlation between consistency of *oy* and quasi-Old English consonantal contexts be no more than felicitous coincidence. Either way, though, there is a very strong likelihood that updating of ±diphthongal spellings in the formulation of late West Saxon orthography furnished the impetus for this particular device in Welsh. Granted overlap at all with what became regular in the later language, it is as remote from it as it can be, the kind of exception that proves the rule that *y* does not come in until Middle Welsh.

Development of primary *y* in Middle English varied dialectally. It was retracted to a darker *u*-like sound in a broad west midland-centred area (including the parts of Wessex mainly relevant to court West Saxon), lowered to *e* in a broad south-eastern area, and unrounded to *i* in northern and eastern England and the far south-west.[39] Developments of secondary *y* are geographically less tidy and only partly identical. Levelling of *y* and *e* is well known as a feature of 'Kentish' Old English. So is *i* for *y* in the Middle English of Devon.[40] The Old English start of that tendency must be where *i*/*y* alternation in the Bodmin

---

35   Lines 9, 11, 14, 15, and scribal error *hinnith* line 6 (believing Morris Jones, WG 295, against I. Williams, BBCS iii.261, for the gender of *loc* < Latin *locus* m. in lines 6 and 14).

36   Line 20.

37   If there is anything in Henry Lewis's etymology for *oes*, quoted by Charles-Edwards, *Astudiaethau ar yr Hengerdd* 50, by which *wys* would be regular, then low sentence-stress would have to be invoked for the word as well as for its spelling *ois*. But it seems more satisfactory to keep Morris Jones's etymology (WG 350), by which *oes* is regular, and consider the Computus fragment's diphthongal spellings as a whole group. Charles-Edwards's explanation of the contrast *oy* and *oi* as one of openness/closeness accounts for less of the data than that adopted here.

38   GPC 1931–2.

39   A standard account is that of Jordan, *Handbuch* §§39–43.

40   Bohman, *ME Dialects* 53–85

manumissions comes from. Not so well known[41] is that the west midland *u*-development is already present in favourable phonetic contexts in late Old English.[42]

This dialect geography is why I called *i/y* alternation as a possible origin for clear *y* an anachronism. If *y* came in by scribal accident, it should be from the part of England with which Welsh scribes were most in contact. Not until the fourteenth century did *i/y* alternation become normal in Middle English of the west midlands, and then not by organic development but by spread of forms from neighbouring dialects, and those not the ones that had cultural prestige in Anglo-Saxon times. If this origin for clear *y* is accepted, then discounting the north-east as unlikely to be relevant to Wales, we are more or less forced to accept the corollary of a model in *Devonian* Old English, and the lack of match of chronology with the Cornish *y* tells against that. Indiscriminate *y* for *i* in the Black Book of Chirk may show, as Morris Jones thought,[43] a scribe *c*.1200 treating *y* and *i* as identical, or may just show one in whose speech the sounds were nearly enough identical that though acquainted with the idea of spelling clear *y* as a third vowel-phoneme and deferent to authorities propounding it, he was hopelessly confused trying to put it into practice.

Less well known still than the pre-Conquest origin of the west midland *u*-region for primary *y* is that these levellings in stressed syllables, where alone it occurs etymologically, have knock-on effects in unstressed syllables, which show sporadic instances of *y* for *e* far outside the Kentish dialect area.[44] Not known at all in currently published scholarship is that some Old English scribal centres made systematic use of the symbol *y* in other than its standard Old English value, and that these two phenomena come together to produce a

---

41 Because barely hinted at in standard grammars, e.g. Campbell, *Old English Grammar* §§315–8.

42 The processes are examined at some length in my *New foundation*, chapter V, and data presented in detail in my *Guide* §§8.3.17.1–10, 8.3.18.1–2. The prime example is the word **pyll** 'tidal creek or similarly flat inland tributary of a major river', which occurs in more than fifty features in the Severn estuary region (mapped 'OE dialect distributions' map 20), more than 60 spelt *pull*. The northern half of the distribution, Worcestershire, Gwent, NW Wiltshire, and most of Gloucestershire, spells it *pull* without exception. For these parts it is clear that the formulation usual in histories of English, of OE [y(:)] being retained in pronunciation with ME *u* for it merely a spelling-change, will not do. For the mid-south country the question remains open, but since either way usage there tells against an equation *y = i*, it is rather unimportant for our argument.

43 He cited (WG 15) *yx* for the Roman numeral nine.

44 A random example is *æt Uptuny* beside several correct *-e* in a Herefs./Worcs. charter *c*.1020 (S1460).

possible model for the Welsh use of *y* systematically as symbol for an obscure vowel sound, *ipso facto* as symbol simultaneously for a clear and an obscure vowel, at one centre supposed to be in the region of England geographically most promising as a source for cultural influence on Welsh, the west midlands. To make these phenomena and this possibility known to Celticists is my main reason for producing this paper.

We must not of course beg the question of whether, when Welsh scribal authorities adopted *y* as a standard symbol, they did so first for the clear vowel then extended its use to the obscure vowel, or *vice versa*, or propounded both together. All three relations are in principle possible. But however exactly it happened, the causes ought to be at least in a general way recoverable from the general history of the language. In the unlikely event that Welsh scholars could come up with convincing statistical data on the question I would defer to them. Pending that, the adoption looks from the Anglo-Saxon side of the fence, where we are used to the large effects stress position has on sound-change in Germanic languages, intrinsically likely to have been motivated primarily for the obscure vowel. It must have happened within at most a generation of the accent-shift around 1100. That shift left reduced vowels no longer naturally correlated with low stress but, what in general phonology is highly anomalous, largely the reverse. That, I suggest, is when and why a need was felt for a special symbol for a reduced vowel. It was adopted either on a particular model to be suggested below, or just possibly by creative adaptation of wider changes in late Old English; and the Old English distinction of three front vowel phonemes was copied with it.

The *englyn* on St. Padarn's staff tends to corroborate both that the adoption was of this kind, and the approximate dating. For it has *y* consistently for the reduced vowel (4 x),[45] and *uy* for its single instance of *wy*.[46] It is not decisive evidence because it does not contain any vowel that should be clear *y*, but does at least positively fit first regular use for obscure *y*. Its mixture of mainly Old Welsh orthography with Middle Welsh usage in this particular is just what is to be expected at the start of a transition from a fossilized orthography to one reflecting current language relatively closely. Logically the first things to be addressed would be distinctions the older system did not make at all; only later would attention be turned to ones where all it needed was updating.

---

45   The words are *trynit*, *trylenn*, *trybann*, and *cyrruenn*, which I. Williams (BWP 189) translates 'much accomplishing, much loved, [triple] limits, Cyrwen'.

46   *Amdifuys*, which Williams translates 'wonderful'.

To turn then to the possible models in Old English. The wider changes mentioned above are a conceivable model but not at all a plausible one. They are developments widespread in so-called 'late West Saxon' manuscripts, of *weorC* to *wyrC*[47] and *sel* to *syl*.[48] Both these can be said to show loss of distinction in front vowels resulting in a spelling *y*; both occur in an environment, before liquids, where reduction of vowel quality as such is likely. But this is not close to the generality of the Welsh usage, and its pertinence is undercut still further by another of the unknown[49] local Old English scribal conventions, where creative use of *y* before *r* clearly does not involve a reduced vowel. A late tenth-century memorandum from a York manuscript, S1453,[50] sometimes mistakenly cited as evidence for a 'West Saxon standard', really exhibits a literary dialect that mixes 'Anglian' features with specifically those 'West Saxon' ones current at Worcester, and an item not found anywehere else in literary texts, *yrcebiscop* twice so written in full beside twice *arceƀ* as abbreviation of standard *arcebisc(e)op* (including both side by side in one sentence).

What makes this look like an available local convention rather than an individual idiosyncracy is that a West Riding charter boundary, 959 S681(ii), twice writes *Yr* for the river Aire. Reading that as normal Old English *y* led Smith[51] to a vanishingly improbable etymology from ON *eyjar* 'islands' for an English river-name. Reading it as in S1453 as what would be written *æ* (probably = *ǣ*) in southern Old English removes what he thought were insuperable phonetic difficulties in Ekwall's otherwise much likelier etymology from *Isara* well attested for other rivers in the stratum of names we now call 'Old European'.[52] Ekwall himself ('Etymological notes' 9–10), returning late in life to the difficulty of *Yr* understood in a standard Old English way for his etymology, stated that the Old English pronunciation of Aire 'will have been something like *Æger*'. With the contraction to a monophthong which S681(ii)'s spelling shows had already happened, that would be *ǣr* just as I have suggested for S1453. Ekwall's explanation was quite different. He compared the personal name OScand *Eirikr*, found in Old English mainly as *Yric*, and suggested 'that in

---

47 Campbell, *Old English Grammar* §§320–4 represents this as a change of *weor* and *wyr* to *wur*, but that is erroneous; *wur* where it occurs is secondary, due to the west midland-centred development of *y*, as I have shown (*English Studies* lxxiv.19–21 etc.).

48 Campbell, *Old English Grammar* §325.

49 Except to those who heard my 'Natural and literary dialects'.

50 Most conveniently edited, with translation, by Robertson (*Anglo-Saxon charters*, no. LIV).

51 *PN WRYorks* VII 118–120.

52 Ekwall, ERN 1–3. Ekwall's book is brought in in relation to '*alteuropäisch* hydronymy' in Kitson, TPS xciv.

some dialects OE ȳ before *r* had a pronunciation that rendered it liable to be substituted for OScand *ei*, or that OScand. (ODan.) *ei* in this position had a pronunciation similar to OE ȳ'. But both the individuals Old English sources record with this name, the mid tenth-century king at York Eric Bloodaxe and Cnut's earl Eric in the first half of the eleventh century, were Norwegians; and in Norway the normal form of the name-element was (and still is) *øy*.[53] As a front rounded vowel ONorw. *ø* could only be rendered in standard Old English as *y*. So Ekwall's parallel vanishes, unless the tenth-century pronunciation was Scandinavianized as he posited, but to **Ør* not to his posited *Eir*. Anyway it is likely enough that contact with the wider variety of Scandinavian (±long) front vowels somehow underlies these York-based Old English writers' strange use of *y*.

That is interesting for the things that could be done with *y* in Old English, but geography renders it unlikely as a source for the Welsh. The usage I do think important for the Welsh is that of a gloss conventionally known as the Cambridge Psalter. Unmentioned in voluminous published scholarship on Old English psalter-glosses but actually the most conspicuous phonological feature of this psalter is a near-complete use of *y* for unstressed *e* when followed by a consonant, thus *wætyr(-)* 24, regular *wæter(-)* only 3. As *e* is much the commonest Old English unstressed vowel, both as a real front vowel in inflections and to show syllabified consonants as here, examples are extremely frequent. As can be seen either from Wildhagen's edition or the *Microfiche Concordance*, the proportions are much the same throughout. The Cambridge Psalter is famous as a rare instance of a copied gloss whose original, or almost its original, survives: it was copied from one very nearly identical to the extant Vespasian Psalter, which of course has regular unstressed *e*.[54] So the small proportion of *e* in this usage in the Cambridge Psalter can be confidently put down as relict forms. The high degree of regularity of the *y* should, at least by the reasoning of most scholarship on dialect copying, imply a norm cultivated at a scriptorium not just by an individual scribe; though since this gloss was written by just a single scribe that is open to argument. Ker dates him to the mid-eleventh century,[55] so if we grant this comes from somewhere where Welsh savants might also come, it shows the model in existence some half a century before the accent-shift would make it urgent for them.

---

53   Noreen §§63.14, 68.8; cf. §55 and de Vries, *Altnordisches etym. Wörterbuch* 106.

54   Pulsiano, *Anglo-Saxon England* xxv.60–62, contains some discussion of this. Cf. Kitson, *English Studies* lxxxiii–iv, where the Cambridge Psalter's special use of *y* is visible *passim.*, perhaps most strikingly at lxxxiii.478, 485–6.

55   Ker, *Catalogue*, no.13.

Where does it come from? The conventional answer to that is Winchcombe in the north of Gloucestershire. But the conventional reason is no more than prominence its litany gives to St. Kenelm, whose cult was centred at Winchcombe. Cultic localizations of literary texts can be spectacularly wrong; for instance the Life of St. Machutus whose cult-minded editor wanted it to be from Winchester but whose dialect belongs in the Cotswolds.[56] Michael Lapidge has made and withdrawn ('Germanus' 128) a suggestion that the Cambridge like the Vespasian Psalter was copied at Canterbury; his current theory is Winchcombe monks at Ramsey. The consistency of this maximally un-Kentish usage of *y* makes copying at Canterbury anyway incredible; and for our purposes if the scribe was trained at Winchcombe it does not much matter where he did his copying. The south-west midlands, especially Gloucestershire, were to judge by Middle English spellings the heartland of retracted reflexes of Old English secondary *y*.

Properly dialectal features in the Cambridge Psalter are not consistently cultivated as in Vespasian, nor has it been as systematically studied, but visible indications do seem to point to the south-west midlands. Of items extant in large enough samples mapping tidily enough in charter boundaries to be a reliable framework for placing literary texts,[57] vocabulary and phonetics of words for 'between' mix strongly 'Anglian' more or less relict forms with choices that fit at the west midland Severn Valley end of 'West Saxon'.[58] The Hwiccean masculine gender of **hyll** is not usually corrected to 'West Saxon' feminine as it usually is in the other psalter derived from the Vespasian-like model, the Junius Psalter[59] supposed to come from a West Saxon scriptorium.[60]

---

56 Contrast Yerkes, *OE Machutus* xlii, with Kitson, *English Studies* lxxiv.35–41. Yerkes, *Manuscripta* xxx, presented palaeographic data fitting a west midland origin as against the Winchester one he had favoured as editor. Actually even his cultic data are at best double-edged: Lapidge, 'Germanus' 78, 86, 90, points to commemoration of Machutus in the Cambridge Psalter, essentially a Winchcombe manuscript, and in Harley 2904, from Ramsey, explaining it from the activities of Germanus, first prior of Ramsey and first abbot of Winchcombe.

57 As shown in my *English Studies* lxxiv. My *New foundation* (esp. ch. IX) carries this a good deal further. Complications of relict forms are treated at length in Kitson, *English Studies* lxxxiii–iv.

58 *Betwih* 6, *betwuh* 5, *betwyh* 3, *betwux* 6, *betux* 2, *betweonan* 1; case governed usually accusative. Cf. Vespasian *betwih* 20, *bitwih* 2 (consistently acc.), *betwinum* 1; Junius *betwih* 12, *betwuh* 6, *betweoh* 3, *betweonum* 1.

59 **Hyll**: psalter-glosses DEFGHIJK only fem.; A (Vespasian) only masc.; C (Cambridge) 4 m., 1 f., 1 sub–f.; B (Junius) 3 f., 1 m. The Sisams (*Salisbury Psalter* ix–x) conveniently expound sigla and standard editions; Kitson, *English Studies* lxxxiii.474 is somewhat fuller.

Items of more restricted distribution in topographic vocabulary point the same way. The general Old English word for a valley is **denu** 'dene', used by all the prose psalter-glosses, including C, that translate 64_{14} *valles*, and 83_7 *in valle*.[61] All but this one use it too for 103_{10} *in convallibus*. C is from far enough north to prefer here **dæl** 'dale', which was not current any further south than Gloucestershire.[62] On the other hand it participates in what charter boundaries show to have been a broadly southern late simplification of the *wō-* declension, and does so with a consistency that more thoroughly 'West Saxon' glosses do not.[63]

---

60 Cf. Kitson, *English Studies* lxxiv.44, 46; *English Studies* lxxiv.219; *New foundation* ch. IX.

61 64_{14} ACDEFGHK; 83_7 ABCDEFHIJK. The verse gloss P has *dene* for the latter but *wangas* conditioned by alliteration for the former. See the tabulation in Kitson, *English Studies* lxxxiii.486.

62 It is in complementary distribution with cognates **dell** 'dell' (south-eastern) and **crundel** (mid–southern): (Kitson, *English Studies* lxxiv, map 1; *Medieval dialectology*, map 4). None of the three is found in charter boundaries of Somerset, Devon, and Cornwall. The general sample size is such that that very probably constitutes evidence of absence not just absence of evidence (cf. Kitson, *Medieval dialectology*, 50, 72). Any doubt about this is irrelevant for our purposes because the word for 'valley' which becomes general there, supplanting **denu**, is **cumb** (Kitson, *Medieval dialectology*, 93–94 and map 20).

63 Kitson, *Medieval dialectology*, map 2, maps it from the word **mǣd** 'mead(ow)'. A transitional zone in the Hwiccean counties, where oblique case-forms with and without *-w-* both occur, was drawn on the evidence then available as comprising most of Gloucestershire and small parts of N. Somerset and S. Worcestershire. It really stretched appreciably into Warwickshire (perhaps therefore also Oxfordshire); this is shown by southern *w*-less forms in a recently discovered charter of Coundon, Warwickshire (under the **m** of **mǣdw-** on the map). The *wō-*declension word usable for comparison in psalters is **sc(e)adu** 'shade, shadow'. The sample is much smaller than for charter **mǣd** but still enough to be suggestive. Oblique case-forms of this word should in principle occur at 16_8, 22_4, 56_1, 87_7, 106_{10}, 106_{14}, and Canticle 9_{12}. Exact numbers in a text vary according to whether it uses instead the word **scua** (as do A always, B and the verse portion of P usually, and E occasionally), or substitutes as it were a dictionary nominative, or conversely turns some of the nominative singulars at 43_{20}, 79_{10}, 101_{11}, 108_{23}, and 143_4 into plurals. I give therefore the number of instances without *-(u)w-* as a fraction of the total number of non-nom.-sg. case forms for each text: K 7/7, C 6/6, G 5/5, J 2/2, P (prose) 2/2, (verse) 1/1, L 1/1, D 5/7, H 4/6, E 3/5, B 1/2, F 1/3, I 1/8. D is widely regarded as the archetypal 'West Saxon' psalter-gloss. What is significant here is that it is the earliest (extant copy mid-tenth-century). Its derivatives FGJH (of which in variants that seem dialectally as opposed to stylistically important G and J are a closely related pair drawing on some independent tradition, H stays fairly close to D, F has some things tantalizingly in common with I) are all extant in mid eleventh-century manuscripts, as is P. I and probably C are earlier eleventh-century, K c.1100, E c.1150. C's outscoring H as well as D on this variable is part of the careful attention to detail which produced the

In one gloss, 67$_{27}$ *de fontibus: of springum ꝇ æwylmum*, it actually combines a strongly non-West Saxon word adapted from the A tradition with a strongly West Saxon word, not used in any of the D-type psalters so presumably native to the dialect of its composition. The overwhelmingly common word for 'spring' in charters, with over three hundred instances as substantive element and many more as qualifier, is **wylle** 'well'. The compound **ǣwylm** 'river-spring' is found thirty times, the northernmost in north Gloucestershire, at Cutsdean four miles ENE of Winchcombe. **Spryng** only occurs twice as substantive, once in Staffs (in the compound **wylspryng**), the more southerly in N. Gloucs, at Hawling four miles SSE of Winchcombe. It is also used once as a qualifier, at Grittleton in NW Wilts three miles from the Gloucs border. The natural inference, bearing in mind that charter samples are much smaller for 'Anglian' than for 'West Saxon' counties, is that **spryng** in this sense was dialectally 'Anglian'. Perusal of the *Microfiche Concordance* confirms this, and shows that the compound **wylspryng** was the normal form: it occurs in literature more than thirty times, **spryng** just in one gloss (to a corrupt lemma, so even this may be doubtful). The only 'West Saxon' prose author to use **wylspryng** is Ælfric, whose dialect is for other reasons to be placed at the north-west edge of Wiltshire; Grittleton is in the west lobe of the small area shaded for him in my 'Ælfric's dialect' map 8. Literary **ǣwylm** is almost confined to works of king Alfred (plus the Orosius); a parallel compound **ēspryng** occurs in strongly 'Anglian' texts, including psalter-glosses AB for this verse. So what C is doing here is partly toning down the 'Anglian' word of its received tradition, partly adding a West Saxon synonym. This is just the kind of behaviour to be expected of linguistically serious scribes in the mixed 'Anglian'/'West Saxon', predominantly 'West Saxon', county of Gloucester-shire. Though we should not place too much weight on single items with small samples, the charter evidence does seem to point quite strongly to north Gloucestershire as the only area where the particular combination of 67$_{27}$ would be likely; and to the extent that they can be pressed, the charter instances of the two words bracket Winchcombe very nicely indeed. The traditional hypothesis is distinctly strengthened by this evidence; Winchcombe is not guaranteed to be right, but it is guaranteed not to be far wrong.

The use of *y* to represent reduced vowels, and its use simultaneously for

---

unstressed *y* spellings, turning an A-type gloss into something acceptable in a particular part of the 'late West Saxons' cultural realm. Distribution of relevant forms in F and H matches that in D. I's very low score is one of many signs of an origin in north-west Gloucestershire or adjacent parts, where ~w~ forms continued to be preferred.

reduced vowels and retracted high front vowels, can thus be seen to have arisen by organic processes within a language where *y* was current in writing, and been cultivated systematically a good generation before *y* for the reduced vowel is found in Wales, in at least one scribal centre close enough to Wales for it not to be absurd for us to posit adaption of its usage by Welsh scribes when they felt an urgent need to reform their own spelling. Urgent need was first felt, I suggest, at some scribal centres as a result of the accent-shift around 1100. The first Welsh use of *y* as a standard symbol was thus for the obscure sound, and it began as an orthographic variant of *e* not *i*. Origin in that value is intrinsically likely because, outside Wales, *i* was not ever a symbol for a reduced vowel in any language in which *y* was current, and in Old English the only use of *y* in unstressed syllables is as a variant of *e*.

The point should perhaps be stressed that there is a very strong presumption that a spelling-reform in a medieval language *should* have arisen organically, as a result of sound-changes varying the practical phonetic value of letters. It is theoretically conceivable (as the editor of this volume has suggested to me) that a Welsh scribe acquainted with the vaguely West Saxon idea of *y* as a (lowered?) variant of *i* in purely diphthongal contexts as in the Computus fragment, the double value of *i* in much of Old Welsh, and the equation $y = i$ either in rare Greek words in rare Latin manuscripts or in Devonian Old English, could have recombined variables from the three to yield $y =$ obscure vowel, even without a known precedent for *y* in this value. This kind of juggling with letters as algebraic entities is roughly how the Chinese Communist government's mind worked in propounding a reformed system of romanization much of whose detail was alien to any existing tradition of use of the Roman alphabet. Scribes with a twentieth-century phonetic training could think in this way. Ones working at a place and time when even the most basic concepts of algebra were unknown are not likely to have done so. Close dependence on phonetic precedent is visible when we have the evidence to test for it, as with the versions of the runic alphabet, or Greek vowel-digraphs in Wulfila's Gothic, or even in the *alphabetum Nemnivi*. The likelihood of such an origin for *y* as an obscure vowel would in my opinion be overwhelming anyway, though the existence of the Cambridge Psalter as a particular model certainly enhances it.

Old English *y* in its late West Saxon secondary rôle for a clear sound had on occasion been borrowed earlier, as the isolated instance in the Computus fragment shows, but there is no reason to think such borrowing other than sporadic, for particular phonetic contexts as there. Welsh use of *y* as a general symbol for clear [ï] is not evidenced until later than the use for reduced [ə], and is likely to have begun later, by imitation or extension of the usage for the obscure sound. Whether the two standards held at first in the same centres or different centres is a nice question. My guess would be different ones. But the distribution of *e, i,* and *y* for these sounds in space and time in Middle Welsh almost certainly can be much elucidated by a disciplined statistical approach to extant manuscripts. I think Welsh scholars have much still to do on the topic, but I expect it to be productive work. I am not going to predict what they may find by way of detailed developments. Paul Russell is no doubt right to suggest (in conversation) that the developments for these sounds will have interacted with those centred on *u, w, wy* for which he has already produced some interesting results. His argument that manuscripts in an essentially 'Old Welsh' orthography, which avoided *y,* were still being written, specifically in north-west Wales, in the 1240s,[64] fits very well my picture of both clear and obscure *y* having entered Welsh principally from the south-east around 1100, the clear usage from 'late West Saxon' generally, the obscure from (a) particular centre(s) that may be Winchcombe.

I suppose the possibility is not excluded that the Welsh adoption of *y* into the standard alphabet was one of those ideas that are in the air at a particular time and have more than one point of origin and mixed motivation. Yet for the reasons already stated of phonetic distinctness and accentual need I think primacy of obscure *y* likeliest, and suspect the brand of Old English usage I have presented, either the Cambridge Psalter's own from Winchcombe or wherever, or some close congener(s) from other unevidenced (or unrecognized) south-west midland centres, really was the source from which Welsh orthographers took *y.*

---

64 Russell, NLWJ xxix.169, cf. 165 etc.; CMCS xxxvii.92, cf. 85, 95–96; *Introduction* 117–8.

Two developments in medieval literary Welsh and their implications for dating texts

Simon Rodway

MIDDLE Welsh texts are notoriously difficult to date with any degree of certainty. The earliest extant Middle Welsh manuscripts date from the middle of the thirteenth century (glosses and some longer fragments in Old Welsh exist in Latin manuscripts from the ninth century onwards) and these provide a *terminus ante quem*, but it is clear that many of the texts that first appear here were composed considerably earlier.[1] In the case of the prose and the anonymous poetry the absence of externally datable references means that an analysis of the language is the only guideline available towards a reliable composition date. In order to establish a rough chronology for developments in the language we turn to those texts which can be fairly accurately dated on external evidence, and then apply the results to the otherwise un-datable texts. The obvious starting point is the work of the early Gogynfeirdd or Poets of the Princes (*c.* 1100–1300) which comprises the earliest corpus of Welsh literature to which reasonably accurate dates can be posited which is also sufficiently large to allow meaningful linguistic analysis. The majority of this poetry is dedicated to aristocratic patrons most of whom can be identified and dated by reference to the chronicles and genealogies, and some of the poets themselves are also attested in the genealogies,[2] so we have a relatively firm chronological framework for this body of work. Although there

---

1   See Huws, *Llyfrau Cymraeg 1250–1400* (also published in NLWJ xxviii (1993–4); now translated as chapters 3 ('Welsh vernacular books 1250–1400') and 4 ('Table of Welsh vernacular medieval manuscripts') in Huws, MWM 36–64).

2   For example Einion ap Gwalchmai, his father Gwalchmai ap Meilyr and his grandfather Meilyr Brydydd; see EWGT 112–13.

is often a gap of up to two centuries or more between the composition date of a poem and its earliest manuscript attestation,[3] the complexity of the metrics employed in court poetry tends to discourage scribal alteration of the type that is often assumed to have occurred in medieval prose texts.[4] In the following study, I have also referred to the poetry attributed to the Cynfeirdd Aneirin and Taliesin,[5] the saga *englynion* and the other poems contained in Book of Aneirin (Cardiff, South Glamorgan Library, MS 2.81), the Book of Taliesin (Aberystwyth, National Library of Wales, Peniarth, MS 2) and the Black Book of Carmarthen (NLW, Peniarth, MS 1), all of which are universally agreed to predate the work of the Gogynfeirdd, although the matter of by how much remains contentious to say the least. I have not considered the irregular verbs *bod* 'to be', *dyfod* 'to come', *myned*, 'to go' and *gwneuthur*, 'to do, to make' here: they deserve a study in their own right.

I have previously established that a dramatic change occurred in the 3 sing. preterite indicative of the regular verb towards the end of the thirteenth century, both in prose and in poetry, with the innovative form *-awdd* almost entirely displacing the previously standard *-w(y)s*.[6] The latter has survived to the present day in some south-eastern dialects,[7] but it is noteworthy that by the fourteenth century, even Glamorganshire poets such as Trahaearn Brydydd Mawr and Casnodyn consistently used *-awdd* in their poetry, whatever they may have said at home.[8] In other words, a universal literary standard appears to have been set, one which embraced both poets and prose writers and copyists and

---

3   Some of the poems of the early twelfth century poet Llywelyn Fardd I, for instance, first appear in the Red Book of Hergest (Oxford, Jesus College, MS 111) which dates from around 1400, some two hundred and fifty years after their author's *floruit*; see CBT II, 3–5. For Llywelyn Fardd's dates and the probable existence of two poets of this name, see CBT II., p. 3; for the dating of the Red Book, see Gifford Charles-Edwards, NLWJ xxi.246–56. The situation is even more extreme in the case of some of the work of poets such as Cynddelw Brydydd Mawr and Dafydd Benfras, the earliest extant versions of which are contained in manuscripts copied from lost medieval exemplars by Renaissance scholars such as John Davies of Mallwyd; see CBT III, 8; CBT IV, 13–15; CBT VI, 25, 26, 28–31.

4   T. M. Charles-Edwards, *The Welsh Laws.*

5   Who are famously dated to the sixth century in one version of the *Historia Brittonum* (Harleian MS. 3859, fol. 188b); see Morris, *Nennius: British History and the Welsh Annals*, 78.

6   Rodway, CMCS xxxvi.

7   See Thomas and Thomas, *Cymraeg, Cymrâg, Cymrêg*, 67.

8   On Trahaearn's provenance, see *Gwaith Gruffydd ap Dafydd ap Tudur et al.*, p. 8; for Casnodyn see *Gwaith Casnodyn*, pp. 1–2.

which was different in at least one respect from that which had gone before.[9]

Is this change reflected in other developments at the same period? I turn now to 3 sing. imperfect indicative, of which three forms are attested in the medieval period: *-ei* (> Mod.W *-ai*, the only form that has survived until today), *-i* and *-(i)ad*.[10] I have found no evidence to suggest that the last ever strayed beyond composites with *bod* and as such it lies beyond the remit of my present survey.[11] Following Graham Isaac's hypothesis that the form *-ei* developed from a misanalysis of imperfect forms in *-i* (< *-iye* < *-eye*) of the irregular verbs *myned* (*e-i* < *egi*), *dyfod* (*de-i* < *degi*) and *guneuthur* (*gwne-i* < *guregi*),[12] we would expect to find a high incidence of *-i* in early works being superseded by *-ei* in later ones. The statistics are as follows (the figures below the percentages represent the number of instances in each text and those in brackets represent forms confirmed by rhyme; see also Figure 1 for a graphic representation):

EARLY GOGYNFEIRDD

	1st half 12th cent.	2nd half 12th cent.	1st half 13th cent.	2nd half 13th cent.
-ei	70% (56%) 21 (9)	93% (87%) 103 (54)	89% (83%) 17 (5)	100% (100%) 20 (7)
-i	30% (44%) 9 (7)	7% (13%) 8 (8)	11% (17%) 2 (1)	0% (0%) 0 (0)

It can be seen that *-ei* increases from 70% in the first half of the twelfth century to 100% by the second half of the thirteenth century. If we compare the situation in the earlier poetry, however, we see that *-i* was never particularly common in the attested literature:

---

9   I believe that this chronological explanation of *-w(y)s* / *-awdd* distribution holds more water than Peter Wynn Thomas's dialectological one for the reasons set out above. For the latter, see P. W. Thomas, BBCS xl.

10   See Evans, GMW 121–2.

11   Contrast Koch, *Early Welsh Poetry*, 36–37 who interprets a number of forms in *-(i)ad* from the *Gododdin* and other early poems which could otherwise be construed as nouns or verbal nouns as 3 sing. imperfect indicative forms.

12   Isaac, ZCP xlvi.201–2; id., *The Verb in the Book of Aneirin*, 376–7. For an alternative explanation of the genesis of the form *-ei*, see Hamp, *Ériu*, xxv. 269; but note Isaac's criticism, *The Verb in the Book of Aneirin*, 373–74.

	BOOK OF ANEIRIN	BOOK OF TALIESIN	SAGA *englynion*	REMAINDER OF BBC
-*ei*	84% (85%) 104 (44)	79% (80%) 30 (12)	93% (50%) 39 (3)	100% (100%) 25 (11)
-*i*	16% (15%) 20 (8)	21% (20%) 8 (3)	7% (50%) 3 (3)	0% (0%) 0 (0)

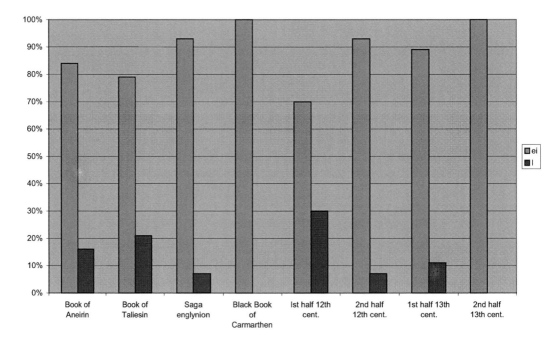

Therefore, if we envisage that at one stage -*i* was the only form taken by non-*bod* verbs, which is implicit in Isaac's attractive explanation of the development of the -*ei* ending, we must concede that this was at a stage in the far distant past, before the composition of any of the now extant literature. The ending -*ei* occurs even in the earliest poems of the Book of Taliesin (four times in the corpus of work ascribed by Sir Ifor Williams to the historical Taliesin; there are no examples of -*i* in this body of work)[13] and in the so-called most archaic

---

13   *rudei*, 'reddened' (CT/PT vi.21 = BT 68.3); *rodei*, 'gave' (CT/PT x.20 = BT 68.3); *cronyei*, 'collected, hoarded' (CT/PT x.21 = BT 68.3); *crynei*, 'shook' (CT/PT xi.21 = BT 30.8). Note that none of these examples are confirmed by rhyme, and that one

B2 text of the *Gododdin* (confirmed by rhyme).[14] However *-i* did survive as an acceptable alternative, in poetry at least, until the twelfth century. There are only two examples of it in the work of thirteenth century Gogynfeirdd, *rhoddi*, 'gave' from the work of Elidir Sais,[15] and *wynnoui*, 'stained' from a poem by Einion ap Gwalchmai.[16] It seems probable that these poets were brothers, part of a dynasty of poets,[17] and it seems possible that they may have inherited a propensity for forms which their contemporaries considered old-fashioned from their father Gwalchmai ap Meilyr and grandfather Meilyr Brydydd. There are two examples of *-i* in Meilyr's work,[18] and Gwalchmai was inordinately fond of it, using it seven times in his work compared to one example of *-ei*.[19] So essentially, I think that we can consider the presence of *-i* as a marker of pre- or early thirteenth century provenance, but its complete absence from the early BBC serves as a warning that 100% *-ei* does not necessarily indicate a late text.

The 3 sing. present subjunctive is another promising variable as once again we apparently witness a simple shift from one form (*-wy* (*-oe*))[20] to another (*-o*) through a regular process of simplification.[21] In the following statistics, I have not included irregular subjunctive forms such as *gwares*, 'deliver' and *duch*, 'take' (see also Figure 2 for a graphic representation).[22]

---

occurs in one of the Gwallawg poems (CT/PT XI) which have only dubious links to the historical Taliesin (although they are clearly old poems) while two more occur in 'Marwnat Owain' (CT/PT x), the early date of which has been questioned on metrical grounds (see CT, pp. xxxv–xxxvi = PT, pp. liv–lv; Morris-Jones, *Y Cymmrodor*, xxviii.188; Haycock, *Early Welsh Poetry*, 171).

14 For example *griniei*, 'pressed, thrust', CA l. 1229 (B2.34.9), rhyming with *drei*, 'broken' in the preceding line and *wanei*, 'pierced' in the following one. On the division of the *Gododdin* into three distinct texts (A, B1 and B2), see Isaac, JCL ii.87–89; id., CMCS xxxvii.56–57; Koch, *The Gododdin of Aneirin.*

15 CBT I, 15.24.

16 Rhyming with *dewi*, 'to be silent' in the preceding line and with the personal name *Beli* in the following one; CBT I, 26.7.

17 See CBT I, pp. 50-1.

18 *peri*, 'caused', CBT I, 3.21; *renni*, 'shared', rhyming internally with *ri*, 'king', ibid., 3.93.

19 *keri*, 'loved', CBT I, 7.7, 10.7; *tewi*, 'was silent', ibid., 9.82; *llochi*, 'sheltered', ibid., 10.8; *perchi*, 'respected', ibid., 10.24; *gotoli*, 'endowed', ibid., 10.25; *belli*, 'refused', ibid., 14.16; compare *lla6tei*, 'praised', ibid., 10.22.

20 On the origin of this form, see Morris-Jones, WG 339; McCone, *Indo-European Origins*,100, 104; Isaac, *Verb*, 365–7. On *ui* ~ *oi* in Old Welsh, see Sims-Williams, BBCS xxxviii.50–59.

21 See Morris-Jones, WG 113; Jackson, LHEB 380, 383.

22 See Evans, GMW 128. I see no reason to follow Nerys Ann Jones and Ann Parry

EARLY GOGYNFEIRDD

	1st half 12th cent.	2nd half 12th cent.	1st half 13th cent.	2nd half 13th cent.
~wy	73% (80%) 24 (16)	58% (70%) 42 (30)	15% (5%) 11 (2)	0% (0%) 0 (0)
~o	27% (20%) 9 (4)	42% (39%) 31 (13)	85% (95%) 61 (42)	100% (100%) 33 (19)

We can clearly see a dramatic increase in the incidence of ~o in the work of the early Gogynfeirdd with it completely supplanting ~wy by the second half of the thirteenth century. Once again, however, the evidence from the earlier poetry is not so clearcut:

	BOOK OF ANEIRIN	BOOK OF TALIESIN	SAGA *englynion*	REMAINDER OF BBC
~wy	75% (100%) 3 (2)	50% (39%) 24 (9)	0% (0%) 0 (0)	50% (56%) 12 (9)
~o	25% (0%) 1 (0)	50% (61%) 24 (14)	100% (0%) 5 (0)	50% (44%) 12 (7)

There are only four examples of the 3 sing. present subjunctive in the Book of Aneirin, including one of ~o (*gaffo*, 'get, obtain, achieve' from the most innovative A-text), but it should be noted that Sir Ifor Williams proposes emendation to *gaffwy* in order to obtain internal rhyme with *wy*, 'they' in the same line.[23] Thus we could consider this to be a 100% ~wy text, but in any case there are really too few examples here for the safe deployment of statistics. In the Book of Taliesin and the BBC, the two forms are more or less neck and neck. It should be noted that there are no instances of the 3 sing. present subjunctive at all in the earliest poems from the Book of Taliesin. The

---

Owen in interpreting the form *rod* in a poem by Cynddelw Brydydd Mawr (CBT IV, 16.147) as a 3 sing. present subjunctive form, 'give'. The form (which is confirmed by an internal rhyme with *vod*, 'will, pleasure' in the same line) would be unwarranted, as the editors allow (ibid., p. 293), and I see no problem with Lloyd-Jones's interpretation of it as a noun, 'gift' (*Geirfa* 20 s. v. *am*).

23   CA, p. 224. The instance is at line 615 (A.49.8).

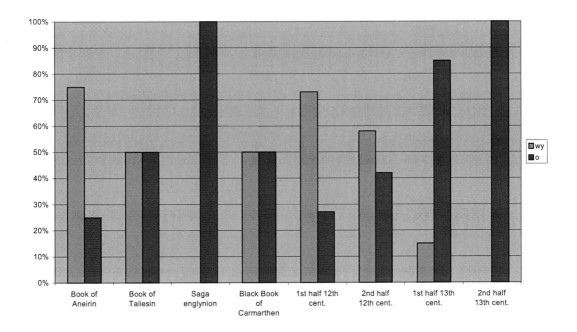

ending *-o* is the only form to be found in the saga *englynion*, but we are only speaking of five instances, none of which are confirmed by rhyme. On the whole, therefore, it would appear that a high incidence of *-wy* is a fairly safe indicator of early provenance in the case of poetic texts at any rate.

The situation is somewhat different with regard to prose. Graham Isaac notes that *-o* was consistently employed in prose texts even as early as the twelfth century *Braint Teilo* from the Book of Llandaf (NLW MS. 17110).[24] In fact, to my knowledge, the form *-wy* only occurs in one prose text, *Culhwch ac Olwen*,[25] and even there it is in a minority: three examples (only one in the Red Book) against 28 examples of *-o*. Perhaps we should consider the use of *-wy* by the poets as an archaism that had died out in other forms of literature by the beginning of the Gogynfeirdd period if not long before that. Its unexpected appearance in *Culhwch ac Olwen* mirrors other apparent archaisms in the White

---

24   *Verb*, p. 367. For the text, see Wendy Davies, BBCS xxvi.123–37. The Book of Llandaf is dated to a little before 1130 by J. R. Davies, CMCS xxxv.7–11.

25   *crettwy*, 'believe' (CO line 484); *dyccwy*, 'take' (ibid., lines 768 and 774 (Red Book: *dycko*)); contrast *dycco*, ibid., lines 91 and 269. I would like to thank Mlle Catherine Piquemal for drawing my attention to these forms.

Book of Rhydderch (NLW, Peniarth, MSS. 4 and 5) text, such as the problematic forms *amkawd, amkeudant* which, like two out of the three instances of
-*wy*, were modernised by the Red Book scribe.[26] Thus we should be cautious
about applying criteria drawn from the poetic tradition to contemporary
prose. The correspondences that have already been noted as regards the
adoption of the innovative preterite form -*awdd* show that comparison can be
useful, but in general it would seem that the poets, as perhaps is to be expected
were willing to use archaic or unusual forms to a far greater extent than prose
writers (many of whom, like the Red Book copyist of *Culhwch ac Olwen* were
prepared to modernise the language of the texts which they were transmitting).
This seems to reflect a conservatism among professional poets, who were part
of a somewhat backward-looking tradition as is attested by the frequent
echoes of their predecessors in the work of the early Gogynfeirdd,[27] and was
probably also encouraged by the strictures of rhyme.

I suggest, therefore on the basis of these three variables, the existence of a
standard literary language in Wales that changed substantially towards the end
of the thirteenth century, a time of great political upheaval which had far-
reaching implications for the literary establishment. The language of the poets
was not identical to that which is found in the prose, but there is evidence to
suggest that both experienced dramatic changes at around the same time. I
propose a picture of a reasonably homogenous literary language before *c.* 1300
in which poets had the liberty of using some forms which had died out
elsewhere in the language where it suited the metrical constraints of their work
or their own conservative nature. After this watershed, another standard was
set, one every bit as homogenous as the foregoing one in which these
archaisms were no longer acceptable, and in which the innovative preterite
ending -*awdd* replaced the traditional -*w(y)s*.

---

26   On *amkawd* and related forms, see GPC 82.
27   An explicit example of this would be the obvious debts owed by Owain Cyfeiliog's
      'Hirlas Owain' (CBT II, 14) to the *Gododdin* (see, for example, T. Gwynn Jones, *Y
      Cymmrodor*, xxxii). On the possibility that Cynddelw Brydydd Mawr was in fact the
      author of this poem, see G. A. Williams, *Beirdd a Thywysogion*, 180–201.

The structure and typology of prepositional relative clauses in Early Welsh

G. R. Isaac

B Y relative clause I mean subordinate clauses which have attributive function relative to a noun or noun phrase, and in which that noun or noun phrase has a role as an argument within the subordinate clause. This noun or noun phrase is the antecedent of the relative clause. By prepositional relative clause I mean those relative clauses in which the antecedent, whether explicit or implied, has a role in the clause which is syntactically dependent on, or governed by, a preposition. Such roles are those which may be called oblique with respect to the predication of the relative clause, or, in another terminology, peripheral to the proposition of the clause. The distinction between restrictive and non-restrictive relative clauses will play no part in my argumentation, since, as far as I can tell at this stage, this distinction is not reflected by identifiable syntactic distinctions internal to the relative clause itself.[1]

A. STANDARD INSULAR CELTIC PREPOSITIONAL RELATIVE CLAUSES

In this section, I give examples of prepositional relative clauses of the familiar types in the Insular Celtic languages.

---

[1]   Though I cannot rule out the possibility that a more subtle analysis might bring such distinctions to light.

1. MW

> y gwaywy   dywawt y   vorwyn du   ymdanaw
> the spear ptl. spoke the maiden black about-it(masc.)
> 'The spear the black maiden spoke about.'
> (*Peredur* 58.12–3)

2. MB

a) nep   a   vezo trech   oarnezaff e   pechet
   someone ptl. be   stronger on-him his sin
   'He whose sin is stronger than him.'
   (Lewis/Piette, LlLlC 28)

b) homan e 'n bro   maz vezo den   enhy   goac   maguet
   this is the country ptl. be   man in-it(fem.) tender raised
   'This is the country in which a man is tenderly brought up.'
   (LlLlC 29)

3. MCo.

> the lesky peyth   a yl den   orto bewe
> to burn thing   ptl. can man by-it live
> 'To burn something by which a man can live.'
> (Lewis, LlCC 33)

4. Mod.Ir.

> áit   a   dtugann siad An Lag air
> place ptl. give   they A. L. on-it-masc.
> 'A place they call An Lag.'
> (Ó hEinirí, *Scéalta* 24)

5. OIr.

> is   torbe namáa tra ar-a-tobarr   labrad   ilbelre
> cop. Profit only   then for-ptl.-give-pres.pass. speaking many-languages
> 'It is the only benefit then for which speaking many languages is given.'
> (Wb. 12d29)

The most widespread type is that in which the relative clause is preceded by various particles, and the role of the antecedent in the clause is defined by the appropriate preposition in its pronominal form, the pronoun being coreferent with the antecedent. In the case of Welsh and Breton, this type is still the one used in the modern languages, but in conformity with the medieval theme of the colloquium, I have taken medieval examples throughout. The Modern Irish example 4 is the obvious exception. In comparison with the Brittonic examples already given, this Irish example shows precisely the same structural features with precisely the same functional distribution. Old Irish, however, shows a quite different structural type, as in example 5.[2] This is a type which survives marginally in Modern Irish,[3] but remains usual in Scots Gaelic.[4]

In the context of a discussion of relative clauses in early Welsh, it is striking that I have not given any Old Welsh examples of this type of relative clause. The fact is that no clear examples of such relative clauses are attested in Old Welsh or in Old Breton.[5] But in the end I hope that the comparative evidence I do discuss is sufficient to allow some meaningful statement, however vague, to be made about the constructions in question in Old Welsh, and about their origins and about their developments.

B. TYPOLOGY OF RELATIVE CLAUSES WITH PERIPHERAL ANTECEDENTS

I believe it is important first of all to be aware of the wider cross-linguistic functional context of these constructions. As in so many other subsystems of Celtic grammar, so in the realm of prepositional relative clauses too, the Celtic languages present structures which deviate in interesting ways from the structural types familiar in the less exotic European languages, and in the standard languages dealt with in Indo-European studies. But, again, as in other areas of grammar, what is deviant from a European or Indo-European standpoint is not necessarily so when viewed in a wider perspective. To this end I present in this section a survey of various strategies for forming this type of relative clause in a selection of languages irrespective of their genetic affiliations. From the types represented I have omitted entirely that which uses relative pronouns in various oblique cases to form the clauses. This is the common strategy of most European languages, so the type is familiar enough.

The simplest formal strategy to code relative clauses with peripheral antecedents is, as in many grammatical constructions, to be seen in Chinese (Manda-

---

2　This is the standard type for Old Irish, though there are early traces of the other type, Thurneysen, GOI §507.

3　Ó Siadhail, *Modern Irish*, 313.

4　E.g. *am fear ris an robh mi a' bruidhinn* 'The man to whom I was speaking' (Gillies, *Celtic* 219, cf. Watson, *Stair* 697). The two types are also found side-by-side in Manx (Broderick, *Celtic* 280, cf. Williams, *Stair* 731).

5　But cf. below note 40.

rin), examples 6. The relative clause simply contains a full unmodified proposition syntactically connected to the head-noun by the subordinating particle *de*.

6. a) *wǒ māile   zhèi-běn shū   de   nèige shū diàn*
      [I   buy-perf. this   book ptl.] that bookshop
      'That bookshop I bought this book in.'
      (Reichardt and Reichert, *Chinesisch* 139)

   b) *wǒ māi shū   de   qián*
      [I buy book ptl.] money
      'The money I bought the book with.'
      (ibid.)

The Chechen example 7a shows simple deletion of a dative argument in a preposed relative. Though this undoubtedly falls under the heading of a
peripheral argument this is not quite the situation I am dealing for Celtic,
since Chechen would not have an adposition in this instance. More interesting
is the example from the closely related Ingush of 7b, in which the role of the
head-noun is again deleted from the relative clause, but this time leaving the
required postposition *juxxie* simply hanging. This is postposition stranding,
an SOV type mirror image of preposition stranding in English.

7.
a) *as   q'amel   dina   stag*
   [I-erg. (ø-dat.)$_i$ conversation did-converb] person$_i$
   'The person I talked to'
   (Nichols, *Caucasus* 65)

b) *so   juxxie leattaa   vʃašterdea   c'a:*
   [I-nom. (ø.dat.)$_i$ beside having-stood] built-together house$_i$
   'The building I stood beside.'
   (Nichols, *Caucasus* 132)

The Maasai example 8, also, is not structurally closely comparable to the
Celtic data, as the peripheral role in question, the goal of motion, the 'village',
is coded without preposition, but it does show how this type of syntactic
relation can be coded in the relative clause by special relative morphology of
the verb, *nátorikó*.[6]

---

6   Tonal pattern supplied from Maasai 175, 179, 217, 227, 228: ' high, ` low, ^ falling,

8. *K-ɛ-taan(á)*   *ɛ́nk-âŋ*   *n-á-to-rik-(ó)*   *ól-tʊŋáni*
   aff.-3sg.-is-near fem.-village [rel.fem.-1sg.-past-lead-past masc.-person]
   'The village to which I led the man is near.'
   (Tucker and Mpaayei, *Maasai* 114; transcription adapted)

The Egyptian examples 9 (Middle Egyptian) and 10 (Coptic, Akhminic dialect) show structures entirely compatible with the Celtic strategy with prepositional pronouns.

9. *ḥr wꜣ.wt*   *nfr.wt*   *ḫpp.wt*   *jmꜣ ḥ.w*   *ḥr=sn*
   on ways-fem.-pl.ᵢ beautiful-fem.-pl. [go-rel.-fem.pl. deceased-pl. on=themᵢ]
   'On the beautiful ways on which the dead go'
   (Loprieno, *Egyptian* 204)

10. *neï*   *et-k-na-bōk*   *achoun* *ara-u*
    thoseᵢ [rel.-2sg.-fut.-go into   to-themᵢ]
    'Those to whom you will go.'
    (Till, *Koptische Dialektgrammatik* 87)

In both cases the prepositional role of the antecedent in the relative clause is made explicit by the preposition itself, governing a resumptive pronoun which refers to the antecedent. This is the standard Insular Celtic type, which I will refer to as the 'resumptive strategy'. It is to be seen not only in VSO languages like Celtic and Egyptian, but also in the SOV type Persian of example 11, though here one would regard the construction as arising by contact with Arabic.

11. *farrāshi*   *keh* *kaqez-rā* *besh*   *dādam*   *kojā*   *raft*
    messengerᵢ [ptl. letter   to-himᵢ gave-1sg.] where went-3sg.
    'Where did the office-boy I gave the letter to go?'
    (Elwell-Sutton, *Persian* 53; transliteration adapted)

In contrast to the standard resumptive type of Insular Celtic, we also have the Old Irish type, in which the prepositional role of the antecedent is coded directly on the verbal complex, in combination with a relative particle indicating subordination. This, too, is a type to be found in other languages, as seen in the Bella Coola (Salishan, British Columbia) examples of 12.7

---

mid tone unmarked; bracketed vowels elided in speech). In the glossing, 'aff.' (K-) denotes an affirmative particle.

7   Glossing, d. = deictic prefixes/suffixes, per. = relative prefix, antecedent with peri-

12.

a) $q^{'w}\chi$-is   ti-ʔimlk-tx ti-lulusta-tx x-ti-q'^{w} tuc-tx
   carve-he/it d.-man-d. d.-mask-d. prep.-d.-knife-d.
   'The man carved the mask with the knife.'
   (Davies and Saunders, *Bella Coola* 101)

b) ti-q'^{w} tuc ti-s-q$^{'w}\chi$-is   ti-ʔimlk-tx ti-lulusta-tx
   d.-knife [d.-per.-cut-he/it d.-man-d. d.-mask-d.]
   'The knife the man carved the mask with.'
   (Ibid.)

c) ʔapsuɫ-ɬ   ʔal-a-cimilt-ʔac
   reside-we prep.-d.-valley-d.
   'We live in this valley.'
   (Davies and Saunders, *Bella Coola* 104)

d) wa-cimilt wa-si-ʔapsuɫ-ɬ-c
   d.-valley [d.-per.-reside-we-d.]
   'The valley we live in.'
   (Ibid.)

In the 12b the verbal complex *tisq'^{w}χis* contains the deictic marker *ti-* indicating the reference of the relative clause to its antecedent, and the prefix *-s-* indicating the nature of the oblique role of the antecedent in the clause, corresponding to the preposition *x-* in the non-relative 12a. Similarly in 12d, *-si-* in *wasiʔapsulilc* codes directly on the verb the locatival role expressed by the preposition *ʔal-* in the non-relative 12c. These parallel the Old Irish incorporation of the preposition in a special form in the verbal complex itself. Example 13 shows the same strategy in reverse order in the SOV-type Amele language (Papua New Guinea).

---

pheral role in relative clause. The verbal ending *-is*, glossed 'he/it' is bivalent, denoting a 3sg. Agent of an event which acts on an 3sg. Patient.

Grammatical notes: deixis (only forms occurring in the examples, not exhaustive for the language!): prefixes: *ti-*, proximal, masculine; (*w*)*a-*, proximal, plural. Suffixes: *-tx*, proximal, non-demonstrative, masculine; *-c*, proximal, non-demonstrative, plural; *-ʔac*, proximal, demonstrative, plural (extended spatial entities like 'valley' have plural marking).

Relative prefixes (antecedent peripheral with respect to proposition): *-s-*, proximal with respect to event; *-si-*, distal with respect to event.

13. Jo   uqa sab mane-na   eu   na tone-i-a
    [house [3sg. food cook-3sg.pres ptl. in]] fall-3sg.-today's past
    'The house she cooks food in has fallen down.'
    (Roberts, *Amele* 52)

The relative clause ends with the verbal complex *mane-na eu na*, consisting of
the verbal form *mane-na* 'cooks', followed by the subordinating particle *eu* and
the locative postposition *na* (e.g. *jo na* 'in the house'), indicating the nature of
the role of the antecedent in the relative clause. I shall refer to such cases
where all the information about the connection between the relative clause and
its antecedent is coded in the verbal complex itself the 'verbal complex strategy'.

In the case of Celtic then we are dealing not with language-specific phenomena, but with phenomena with a definable typological context. I maintain
that this context should be borne in mind in further investigation of the developments of, and relationships between the relativising strategies of Celtic.[8] I
will not claim to analyse these issues exhaustively here.

C. A RARE TYPE IN MIDDLE WELSH

While Middle Welsh overwhelmingly uses the resumptive strategy in prepositional relative clauses, it has been pointed out that there are also traces of the
verbal complex strategy found in Old Irish,[9] as in examples 14, 15 and, in a
cleft sentence, 16.

14. *gwelet y bed   a uynnei trw   yt gaffei   wreicca*
    see   the grave ptl. wanted through ptl. get.ipf.subj. get-wife
    'He wanted to see the grave by which he would be allowed to seek a wife.'
    (CO l. 27)

---

8   Contrast the dismissive comment of Calvert Watkins, *Celtica* vi.25: 'The preposition-
     al relative sentence is an Irish innovation, the direction of which is predictable in
     general linguistic terms', as if the construction is thereby to be excluded from further
     discussion (which it was by Watkins in the article cited). The present paper suggests
     that the verbal complex strategy of prepositional relative clauses is far more
     widespread in Celtic than Watkins thought.

9   Isaac, *Verb* 422–3.

15. *ac   ar   bara   ddyn bynnac   ar   y   syrthiau   y   tri   dafn   hyn*
    and   on   what   man ever   on ptl.   fall.ipf.subj.   the three drops these
    'And on whatever man these three drops would fall.'
    (YT 66.32–3)

16. *wyneb gared   eryt(h)uaccei   diryeit*
    face   love   by-ptl.-nurture.ipf   warriors
    '(It was) love of honour with which he used to nurture warriors.'
    (BA 32.16–7, Williams, CA 46.1149–50)

As in Old Irish these instances show the preposition defining the oblique role
of the antecedent and a subordinating preverbal particle (of varying form) incorporated into the sentence initial verbal complex.

   Examples 17 and 18 I regard as instances of the same construction, with the
preposition *yn* 'in', having developed in the direction of a conjunction 'where'.

17. *Sew   fort   y   ffoesiti.   Inytoet   aradur   in eredic   tir*
    cop.-it   way   ptl.   fled   to-it(fem.)   in-ptl.-was   ploughman ptl. ploughing land
    'This is the way he fled, where a ploughman was ploughing land.'
    (BBC 44.5–6, Jarman, LlDC 21.56–7)

18. *ynyterev   tonnev tir.   yg karrauc.   bet   gwallauc hir*
    in-ptl.-strikes   waves land   in C.   grave   Gw.   tall
    'Where waves strike the land in Carrog, (is) the grave of Gwallog the Tall.'
    (BBC 63.13–4, LlDC 36.22–3)

There is an identically formed conjunction *ene* with the meaning 'when', as
seen in example 19.

19. *ene   klywei awr*
    when   heard   shout
    'When he heard the battle-cry.'
    (BA 1.11, CA 1.23–4)

Identity of conjunctions meaning 'where' and 'when' is of course unproblematic, and Henry Lewis[10] long ago argued that MW *ene* 'when' was the

---

10   BBCS i.9–12.

cognate of the Old Irish conjunction *a* 'when' (example 21), and that the meaning 'where' was derivable from it.[11]

20. *a-rro-mbu   ercheltae*
    when-perf.-was removed
    'When he was taken away.'
    (Ml. 53b14)

However, in view of the fact that Old Irish also uses the preposition *i-* 'in' in a relative construction in the meaning 'where' (example 21), I suggest that in Welsh two originally distinct constructions have fallen together.

21. *ar i mbiat smachta   ni   biat caiche*
    for in are   requirements neg. are penalties
    'For where the legal requirements are (met), there are no penalties.'
    (CIH i, 64.27)

D. THE TYPE PREPOSITION + PARTICLE + VERB
WIDESPREAD IN EARLIER BRITTONIC

As I have shown, the verbal complex strategy is attested in a very few Middle Welsh instances, showing that the strategy existed side by side with the resumptive. But on this meagre evidence it is difficult to be more specific about the earlier occurrence of the constructions. There is, however, another source of information on this matter. That is, the prepositional interrogatives of the type *pam* (*paham*), *pyr, pa rac* 'why', *py ar* 'on what',[12] e.g.

22. *neu reitheu dewi pyr y-torrassant*
    or laws   D.   why ptl.-broke.3pl.
    'Or why they broke the laws of Dewi.'
    (BT 15.5, Williams, AP 1.140)

23. *Neur byt   bei syrthei.   py   ar   yt g6ydei*
    or-the world if fall.ipf.subj. what on   ptl. fall.ipf.subj.
    'Or the world, if it were to fall, what would it fall on?'
    (BT 80.10–1, Haycock, BBGCC 60.9–10)

---

11   GOI §890.
12   Evans, GMW 77, Morris-Jones, WG 293, Pedersen, VKG 203, Williams, BBCS xxiii. 217–33. NB: the type MCo. *py gansse* . . . , Mod.Ir. *Cé leis* . . . , is distinct.

24. *pa   rac   nam   kyueirch*
   what for neg.-me greets
   'Why does it not greet me.'
   (BBC 50.4, Jarman LlDC 27.42)

The grammars which discuss these forms deal with them simply as combinations of the interrogative *py, pa* and the preposition. While this is no doubt the simplest account, I suggest the reality, historical certainly, possibly also synchronically, is a little more complex. I analyse these prepositional interrogatives rather as the Welsh equivalent to Old Irish questions like example 25,

25. *Cid   ara   n-eperr   Crith Gablach*
   what for-ptl. say.pass. C. G.
   'Why is it called *Crith Gablach?*'
   (Binchy, *Crith Gablach* 1)

Syntactically precisely, *cid* = *cia* + cop. 'what is (it)?'. Therefore, literally, 'What is it because of which C. G. is said?', i.e. a cleft sentence, and therefore containing precisely that type of prepositional relative clause as I have been discussing. I suggest that the Welsh interrogatives too, *py, pa*, must be understood as 'What is (it)?'. Thus, in example 23, *py ar yt gổydei* 'What is it on which it would fall?'. This is seen outside of the prepositional constructions, e.g.

26. *Pa   roteiste   o-th-olud*
   what gave.2sg. of-your-wealth
   'What did you give of your wealth?'
   (BBC 20.7–8, Jarman LlDC 8.42)

Pace Simon Evans,[13] *pa, py* in such constructions is not 'substantival' ('what?'), but copular with a following relative clause, i.e. in cleft syntax, *pa roteiste otholud* 'What is it which you gave of your wealth?', so parallel to *py ar yt gổydei* 'What is it on which it would fall?'; cf. the stressed variant *pwy*, e.g.

27. *dayar pổy   y   llet.   neu pổy   y   thewhet*
   earth what-is her breadth or what-is its thickness
   'The earth, what is its breadth, or what its thickness.'
   (BT 20.23–4)

---

13   GMW 76.

28. *ac na wydat pwy ae lladei*
and neg. knew who-is ptl.-3pl. killed.ipf.
'... and (because) he did not know who it was who was killing them'
(PKM 46.5–6, *Branwen* 16.419)

The prepositional interrogatives are also familiar in Breton and, to a more limited extent, in Cornish, as in examples 29–31.

29. *pe dre ez eu antraet*
what through ptl. is entered
'How has he entered?'
(Lewis/Piette, LlLlC 31)

30. *perac ... na sarmonez*
what-for neg. preach.2sg.
'Why do you not preach?'
(Ibid.)

31. *prag om-gwysketh*
what-for me- strike.2sg.
'Why are you striking me?'
(Lewis, LlCC 36)

And they also occur in derived function as relative markers in these languages, the examples 32–6.[14]

32. *ma maestr ... pe dre aman ez ouf manet*[15]
my master what through here ptl. am remained
'My master ... through whom I have remained here.'
(Lewis/Piette, LlLlC 29)

33. *nep pe da ez reif me an bara gluibyet*
someone what to ptl. give.1sg. I the bread damp
'He to whom I give the damp bread.'
(Ibid.)

---

14 It is argued in LlLlC 28 that the resumptive strategy is the older in Breton, but this does not take account of the overwhelming comparative evidence for the verbal complex strategy discussed in the present paper.

15 This example shows a further development in the syntax of the construction in that the adverb *aman* 'here' splits up the verbal complex *pe dre ... ez ouf*.

34. *doe   pegant   ez   out   croeet*
    god   what-by ptl. are.2pl. create
    'God, by whom you have been created.'
    (Ibid.)

35. *vn sacrament   eu pe   dre   heny ez   roet   an puisancz dan   belegyen*[16]
    one sacrament is what through that ptl. was-given the power   to-the priest
    'It is a sacrament through which power was given to the priest.'
    (Ibid.)

36. *reson   prag   y   fe prynnys*
    reason what-for ptl. is bought
    'The reason for which (why) it has been bought.'
    (Lewis, LlCC 33)

It can be agreed, therefore, that early Brittonic showed the verbal complex
strategy of forming prepositional relative clauses much more frequently than
would appear by a superficial examination of the language of the transmitted
texts. How early and how frequently are still open questions. The fact that the
strategy has been shown to be common to Brittonnic and Goidelic would at
first sight appear to speak for considerable antiquity. However, it is plain that
the constructions in the two branches differ in non-trivial ways, specifically in
the nature of the particle with which the prepositions is combined in relative
syntax. In order to gain clarity on the earlier development of the construction,
I turn to consideration of its origin in Old Irish.

E. ORIGIN OF THE TYPE PREP. + PTL. + VB.

In Old Irish, the various prepositions are incorporated into the verbal complex
(the verb taking conjunct flexion or the prototonic form), in combination
with what has generally been taken to be a form of the neuter article (all forms
nasalising): *a* ⟹ *asa-*; *ar* ⟹ *ara-*; *co* ⟹ *cosa-, cos-*; *do, di* ⟹ *dia-*; *eter* ⟹ *etera-*;
fíad ⟹ *fíada-*; *fo* ⟹ *foa-, fo-, fua-*; *for* ⟹ *fora-, forsa-*; *fri* ⟹ *frisa-, fris-*; *i* ⟹ *i-*;
íar ⟹ *íarsa-*; *imm* ⟹ *imma-*; *la* ⟹ *lasa-, las-*; *ó* ⟹ *oa-, ó-, ua-*; *oc* ⟹ *oca-*; *re* ⟹
resa-; *tre* ⟹ *tresa-, trisa-*; *sech* ⟹ *secha-*; *tar* ⟹ *tara-, tarsa-*.

---

16   The example shows a later development in which the construction is extended by the
      addition of the demonstrative pronoun *heny*.

As is seen in this list, several of the forms which show the -s- have by-forms in certain contexts without the vowel -a-,[17] e.g.

37. ni   fris-tarddam ar-n-áthius
    something to-give.1pl. our-acuteness
    'Something to which we apply our acuteness.'
    (Thes. ii.293)

McCone[18] has suggested that the construction in question is a relatively late development internal to Old Irish itself, arising by combination of the prepositions with the demonstrative (s)a- (i.e. the same form as appears in Classical Old Irish as the neuter article).[19] For the use of a demonstrative pronoun/adjective in relative constructions he cites the typological parallels of English, German and Ionic Greek. But in the latter two at least it is a fully declined demonstrative that is used, not as a particle, but as a relative pronoun.[20] If the Old Irish construction was formed on this typological model with the demon-

---

17   GOI §492.

18   *Ériu* xxxvi.96–7, developing views similar to those previously expressed by Calvert Watkins, *Celtica* vi.24–5, cf. note 8 above. He also suggests that the resumptive and verbal complex strategies may have had a dialectal distribution, resumptive in the south and (innovative) verbal complex in the north; but this speculation depends on McCone's own views on the origin of the verbal complex strategy: the typological and Brittonic comparanda given in the present paper cast doubt on that analysis.

19   Breatnach, *Ériu* xxxi.1–9, had shown that, in Archaic Irish, relative verbal forms alone were capable of introducing relative clauses with antecedents in oblique functions, particularly that of the independent dative. McCone, *Ériu* xxxvi.96, in turn took this as evidence that the verbal complex strategy of prepositional relative clauses was a late development. However, while the independent dative was undoubtedly a stylistic device based on pre-Classical Old Irish usage, it is not itself evidence that Primitive Irish lacked prepositions. Most Old Irish prepositions continue well-attested Indo-European models, and are therefore fully attributable to Primitive Irish and Proto-Celtic. The fact that the prepositions could be omitted in certain stylistic contexts in, say, seventh-century Irish is therefore no evidence that they were not the grammatical norm for coding certain syntactic relations in that or any immediately preceding era, whether in relative or non-relative clauses.

20   Modern English uses the historically neuter demonstrative *that* undeclined in relative construction. But it is noticeable that amongst the range of constructions which English does allow in prepositional relative clauses, a parallel to the Old Irish construction is not found: *The man I got the money from*, *The man that I got the money from*, *The man who I got the money from*, *The man from whom I got the money*. The only permutation to parallel the Irish construction properly would be **The man from that I got the money*. But precisely that is not possible in English.

strative or article (s)a-, then it is surprising that it is not declined in relative construction: it always ostensibly has the neuter nominative/accusative singular form, regardless of gender and number of the antecedent, and regardless of the case-government of the preposition involved. There is no trace of relative clauses of the form **ind eich forsnaib-sedat ind fir 'the horses on which the men are sitting (recte fora- or forsa-), or **in fid assin-bert-som a crann 'the wood out of which he carried the tree' (recte asa-). These would have represented the correct typological parallel of the German and Ionic constructions.

Another factor speaks against the idea of late innovation. McCone was arguing on the basis of the attestation of the construction in Old Irish alone. However, it has been seen above that it is a pan-Insular-Celtic phenomenon: the fact that it is common to all three attested Brittonic languages, and there mainly in more or less lexicalised remnants (in the interrogative constructions), does suggest that the construction is of considerable antiquity, and unlikely to have arisen independently in the individual languages. Clearly, the origin of the constructions in question must be sought in an earlier phase of the language(s) than McCone envisaged.[21]

Even on the assumption that the particle really was the article (or the same form in its earlier demonstrative function), the forms tresa- (trisa-) and forsa- must be analogical, since the initial s- of the article could not be reflected by

---

21   It must be noted that Schrijver, Studies 106, like McCone, sees a reflex of pronominal forms in the construction, though in a different way. Schrijver regards -(s)a n- as a reflex, originally declined, of 'an old antecedent'. Since Schrijver's observation is made in passing, quite incidentally to his arguments in the cited passage, he provides no syntactic detail of the analysis he is thinking of. In particular, I do not understand in what sense it can have been an 'old antecedent': since the particle follows the preposition, which is itself syntactically and semantically part of the predication of the relative clause, it is unavoidable that the particle itself is part of the clause, therefore, by definition, not the antecedent. This is formally corroborated by the fact that the complex prep. + -(s)a- is followed by the conjunct or prototonic form. Schrijver develops the comments in GOI §510, p. 324 (cf. also §479), in which Thurneysen suggests that the conjunctions ara-, dia- and co- 'really belong to the principal clause', so that the conjunct and prototonic verbal forms following them, and prep. + -(s)a-, are analogical to the patterns of lexical compound verbs (on this analogy, cf. note 36 below). But here too, the issue of the syntactic structure and development of the clause types in question is left untouched. I will not speculate on how these arguments might be developed by other scholars. I believe that I provide necessary syntactic and typological context for a different analysis in the present paper. (Recall that none of the other analyses mentioned in the present footnote takes account of the Brittonic data.)

an Old Irish -s- in this position.[22] So there is a clearly attested tendency for the -s- forms to spread within Old Irish. Furthermore, the preposition i- 'in', in combination with a Primitive Irish neuter article *san, should have reflexes with -s- in this construction in Old Irish.[23] But it does not. We are therefore faced with a situation where there are forms where there should be no -s-, but there is one, on the one hand, and at least one form which is exactly where we should expect an -s- to appear, but it does not, all on the assumption that the particle is indeed the neuter article. There are clearly analogical forces at work, and we must investigate what it is they are doing, and where they are coming from.

In this connection it may be opportune to note that of those prepositions whose relative forms contain -s-, fri shows a surprising s in another part of its paradigm, in its general pretonic form in verbal compounds, fris- (e.g. fris-gair), and the analogical influence of as- (e.g. as-beir) has been mooted here.[24] Since there is, then, in any case, uncertainty as to the extent to which the relative forms of the prepositions were originally characterised by -s-, and since there is doubt as to the validity of the syntactic analysis of -(s)a- in these forms as the neuter article, I propose the following revision. The particle involved in these constructions was, originally, PIr. *ya < *yo, found unproblematically in other Old Irish relative forms,[25] attested for Brittonic also[26] and for Gaulish,[27] und ultimately reflecting an Indo-European relative pronoun,[28] still in fully declined form in Celtiberian.[29] Assuming Primitive Irish combinations

---

22   PIr. *trē-san- > OIr. **tría- or **tre-, PIr. *wor-san- > OIr. **worr-.

23   PIr. *in-san- > OIr. **is-. The parallel adduced by Watkins, Celtica vi.24, n. 2, between the Old Irish use of i- without particle in relative clauses and the Greek usage of ἐν- with the infinitive, is not relevant here. The relative constructions of the Insular Celtic languages are typologically bound up with verb-initial syntax: the Greek infinitival construction is something quite different.

24   GOI §893.

25   Cf. bertae < *beronti-ya 'who (pl.) carry', as-beir < *eχs-ya-beret 'who says', as-mbeir < id. 'who says'/ 'which he says', for-chain < *wor-ya-kanet 'who teaches', for-cain < id. 'who teaches/whom he teaches'. McCone, Ériu xxxi.10–27, and Ó hUiginn, Ériu xxxvii.33–88, have shown how the nasalising relative clause arose in Old Irish itself through analogy, so that there is no need to reconstruct, with Breatnach, Ériu xxxi.1–9, an 'accusative' form *yan < *yom of the relative particle in these constructions. Schrijver, Studies, has now argued at length for a more complex origin of the various relative constructions, in which the nasalisation has a segmental, not an analogical origin.

26   E.g. MW yssyd < *esti-yo 'who/which is', etc.

27   Alise-Sainte-Reine dugiiontiio, Chamalières toncsiiontio.

28   PIE *yos, *yeh₂, *yod, otherwise attested in Indo-Iranian, Greek, Slavic, and Phrygian.

29   E.g. from Botorrita IA, ios nom. sg. masc., ias acc. pl. fem. < *yeh₂ms, iomui dat. sg.

of the prepositions with *ya, for the prepositions ar, imm, and a, regular phono-logical developments would give Old Irish relative forms as follows:[30] *are-ya- > OIr. ara-, *imbi-ya- > OIr. *imma-, *eχs-ya- > OIr. *as-.[31] In the former two cases, the outcome is the attested form: on the latter case, see below.

These forms are the model for analogical developments which gave rise to the attested forms of the prepositional relatives. One proportion was respon-sible for the forms of those prepositions whose basic forms had consonantal auslaut in Old Irish:

ar : ara-, imm : imma- :: oc : X, eter : X, for : X, tar : X, sech : X, fíad : X

X = oca-,[32] etera-, fora-, tara-,[33] secha-, fíada.-[34] Another proportion is respon-sible for the relative forms of prepositions whose basic forms have vocalic auslaut:[35]

a : *as- :: co : X, la : X, fri : X, tre : X, re : X

X = cos-, las-, fris-, *tres-, *res-. The forms *as-, *tres- and *res- are unattested

---

masc. < PIE *yosmōi (cf. Skt. yasmai).

30 With nasalisation arising in the developments leading to nasalising relative clauses in general, cf. note 25.

31 The purely segmental development here is identical to that in compounds with the relative infix, as in the examples as-beir, as-mbeir in note 25.

32 If oc < *onkus (as McCone, Stair 190), then oca- < *onkus-ya- would be the regular in-herited outcome in the relative forms (note that *onkus-san- > **ocsa- would not give the correct outcome).

33 If tar < *tares (GOI §854), then tara- < *tares-ya- would be the regular inherited outcome in the relative forms. Tara- has the variant tarsa-, which could have been the reflex of *tares-san-, if there were not other evidence against *san. Tarsa-, like forsa- and possibly íarsa-, will have arisen by later analogy: tara- and fora- are earlier attested than tarsa- and forsa-, and while *íara- is not attested, íarsa- itself is only attested from Middle Irish on.

34 Secha- and fíada- too could be inherited, from *sekwā-ya- and *wēdū-ya- respectively, if these etymologies for the prepositions are correct. I hesitate to include all the pos-sibly inherited forms from this and the preceding notes in the model for the analogy, precisely because the etymologies are not absolutely certain (though likely), but it can at least be seen that even if only some of them are correct, then the inherited base becomes broader.

35 As in the proportion for vocalic auslaut, there may be more inherited forms in the model than are given here, if la < *lets, relative *lets-ya- (McCone, Stair 190; but cf. the doubts expressed in GOI §845). Similar looking, but differently motivated pro-portions have been proposed by Russell, Ériu xxxix.119; cf. Russell, TPhS lxxxvi.160.

in this function, due to chance absence in the fragmentary sources of the earliest period: *cos-*, *las-*, and *fris-* at least are attested. All forms in *-s-* were then subject to further levelling, to give uniformly vocalic auslaut in the relative forms:[36]

ara-	*as-	ara-	asa-
imma-	cos-	imma-	cosa-
oca- vs.	las- ⇒	oca- vs.	lasa-
etera-	fris-	etera-	frisa-
fora-	*tres-	fora-	tresa-[37]
tara-	*res-	tara-	resa-
secha-		secha-	
fiada-		fiada-	

The relative forms of *fo* 'under' and *ó* 'from' were subject to specific developments: PIr. **wo-ya-* > **wo-a-* > **wō-* > OIr. *fó-* ~ *fúa-*; PIr. **ō-ya-* >

---

36   The fact that the analogical influences analysed in these paragraphs only affected the prepositions in relative construction, but not the pretonic preverbs in compound verbs, although, in a majority of cases, preverbs and prepositions were identical, is traceable to the functionally quite distinct syntactic domains of the two classes of words. Though there can be no question of the formal identity of the preposition *as-* in *as-a-mbeir* 'out of which he carries . . .', and the preverb *as-* in *as-mbeir* 'which he says', they are performing two completely different functions from the point of view of the grammar of the language as an instrument of communication. In *as-beir* 'says', the preverb is part of a lexical unit of meaning, syntactically separable in various ways, but semantically inseparable. While we have no difficulty in identifying the preverb *as-* with the preposition *a* etymologically, and while it is not unlikely that an Old Irish speaker who cared to think about it would realise the same thing, there is no question of speakers explicitly accessing the analysis 'out-carries' of *as-beir* while using the form in actual communication: *as-beir* in all its syntactic and morphological variants, is, as a whole lexical unit, 'says' etc. On the other hand, in *as-a-mbeir*, the form *as-* is a syntactically conditioned variant form of the preposition *a* 'out (of), from', with its own paradigm, and range of functions, as a preposition. While there are certainly instances in which the etymological meanings of compound verbs are more transparent than in the case of *as-beir* 'out-carries' > 'says', the fact remains that prepositions and lexical preverbs belong to quite different subsystems of the grammar. There is thus no reason to suppose that analogical forces affecting the forms of prepositions in relative construction would have any effect on the forms of preverbs in lexical compounds. (The semantic and lexical differences between the constructions discussed in this note also constitute an objection to the analogical forces proposed by Thurneysen in GOI §510, p. 324, cf. note 21 above.)

37   The by-form *trisa-* is early evidence of the analogical influence of *fri* on *tre*.

*ŏ-a- > *ŏ- > OIr. ó- ~ úa-. Both also appear in more transparent analogical forms as *foa-*, *oa-*. The high-frequency prepositions *do* 'to', *di* 'from', have the idiosyncratic common form *dia-*, and *i* 'in' appears without any evidence of the presence of a particle at all.[38]

F. CONCLUSIONS

Just as the particle that appears in the construction in Irish is not historically what it appears to be at first sight, so in Brittonic too, it is not to be taken for granted that the precise attested form of the construction is a faultless guide to its prehistory. In this case, the limited nature of the attestation limits also the discussion possible, but at least as a working model, I propose that, like the Irish, the Brittonic constructions can be derived from a proto-construction containing the particle *-yo-: parallel to the development PIr. *are-ya- > OIr. *ara-*, PIr. *imbi-ya- > OIr. *imma-*, etc., reanalysed in Irish as prep. + neuter article, the development in Brittonic followed a similar path, Brit. *are-yo- > *ar-y(ð)- ~ *er-y(ð)- ~ *yr-y(ð)-, *ambi-yo- > *em-y(ð)-, which were reanalysed according to the Neo-Brittonic system of preverbal particles as *ar y, ar yt, yr y, am y*, etc. in their Welsh guise, *dre ez*, etc. in Breton.[39]

The presence of a few isolated instances of prepositional relative clauses with the verbal complex strategy in Middle Welsh sources, together with the evidence of the prepositional interrogatives in Welsh, Cornish and Breton, in varying states of lexicalisation, should be sufficient to justify the conclusion that, like Old Irish, Brittonic too at an early stage used that strategy far more than is apparent from the attested sources, and that its replacement by the resumptive strategy, seen in Irish in historical times, took place at an earlier period in Brittonic. Just how much earlier is not to be said with certainty. But the following considerations might be relevant. If we only had the interroga-

---

38   PIr. *in-ya- > OIr. *in-, nasalising like the rest of the prepositions in this construction (note 25): the minimal difference between non-relative *i* + nasal. and relative *in-* + nasal. (neutralised before vocalic anlaut) was levelled in favour of a generalised form *i*.

39   The negative forms of the construction would have been, e.g. Brit. *ambi-ne-yo-, PIr. *immi-ne-ya-, resulting in attested W (with the interrogative) *pam na...*, OIr. *imna-*.

   The ablatival interrogative MW *pan* 'whence' (as if **py ban*), OIr. *can* (< *kʷei san-yo- 'What is it from which...?'), would seem to be a very early instance of the lexicalisation of the construction, already in the immediate precursors of the attested languages, so that it was not affected by the various analogical forces operating in the historical languages. Note the lenition after the Welsh form, accurately reflecting the old vocalic auslaut.

tives as our evidence of the earlier strategy, we could not say much about the time at which the verbal complex strategy was still common in Brittonic: the interrogatives can be thought to have preserved the construction from any prior period. However, the fact that we have isolated instances of the pure prepositional relatives in Middle Welsh suggests that it cannot have been in the too distant past. Otherwise how could the construction be accessible for use in the 12th century and later? It would seem therefore, that if only we had more extensive and varied sources for Old Welsh and Old Breton, we should see the verbal complex strategy in full use there,[40] and that its all but complete replacement by the resumptive strategy is a development of precisely the Old Welsh and Old Breton period. This suggestion is by its very nature untestable. But I hope that as a model of the historical development of one aspect of Welsh syntax, it can be regarded as plausible, and that further investigation of some of the issues it raises, historical and typological, may bring more interesting phenomena to light, and enhance our understanding of this and other languages and grammars.[41]

---

40   There are two possible instances: i) *issit padiu itau gulat* (Codex Juvencus), and *passerenn pigurthet loyr* (Computus).

i) The Juvencus gloss would seem to be a more or less word for word translation of the Latin lemma *est cui regia* (*est* = *issit*, *cui* = *padiu itau*, *regia* = *gulat*), raising doubt as to whether it is to be construed as a well-formed Old Welsh sentence. Also rather than being *pa* + prep. *di*, *padiu* would seem to be better analysed as by Williams, BBCS xxiii.3.217–33, as the combination of *pa* and the verbal form *diw* 'is to'.

ii) It is possible that *pigurthet* in the Computus is to be read *pigurth[r]et*, segmented as *pi-gurth ret: pa-sserenn pi-gurth ret loyr* 'what star against which runs the moon' (Hamp, SC x/xi.65), with *pi-gurth* an example of the interrogative/relative construction discussed above in section D. But the interpretation depends on emendation, and other readings are conceivable.

In both cases, the uncertainty excludes using these instances as evidence for the arguments presented in this paper. If these arguments are upheld, then they may be able to contribute to the analysis of these Old Welsh clauses, but only if the latter are not made part of the arguments in the first place.

41   In conversation during the Oxford symposium, Dr. Stefan Schumacher informed me that he too, in his contribution on Middle Welsh to the forthcoming *Compendium Linguarum Celticarum*, identifies what I have here called the 'verbal complex strategy' in early Welsh prepositional relative clauses, and stresses the connection with various interrogative constructions. He kindly provided me with the relevant pages of his contribution. Justification for the independent publication of our results will easily be found in a comparison of our differing approaches, and, in any case, in the differences in detail between our analyses.

The dry-point glosses in
Oxoniensis Posterior

Alexander Falileyev

Paul Russell

A SCHOLASTIC colloquy entitled *De Raris Fabulis*, preserved in Oxford Bodleian Library MS 572 (S.C. 2026), ff. 41ᵛ–47ʳ, is usually dated on palaeographical grounds to the second quarter of the tenth century.[1] From the perspective of the history of the Brittonic languages it is an extremely important document as both the glosses incorporated in the text and the interlinear ink glosses contain side by side Welsh and Cornish words suggesting that the text may have had some contact with south-west Britain at some point in its transmission.[2] Craster published eight interlinear glosses which occur on fol. 42 (*recto* and *verso*), and which were scratched with a dry point not by the scribe of the text but by a different nearly contemporary

---

[1]   Madan and Craster, *A Summary Catalogue*, 170–4. This colloquy was edited by Stokes, 'Cambrica', 238– 44, and by Stevenson, *Early Scholastic Colloquies*, 1–11. The other colloquies in Stevenson have been re-edited in Gwara, *Latin Colloquies*, and in Gwara and Porter, *Anglo-Saxon Conversations*. Neither deals with *De Raris Fabulis* except in passing (see Gwara and Porter, *Anglo-Saxon Conversations*, 19–24); the latter also omits the Hisperic Colloquy (Stevenson, *Early Scholastic Colloquies*, 12–20)). See also Jackson, LHEB, 55–6. For comments on this text, see Lindsay, *Early Welsh Script*, 26–32 (esp. 28); de la Villemarqué, *Archives* v.245–8, and Plate 3 (following p. 272); Dumville, 'A Thesaurus Paleoanglicus?', 67; id., *English Caroline Script*, 142, n. 8; Charles-Edwards, 'The Uses of the Book'. For the suggestion of a ninth century date, see Dumville, 'A Thesaurus Paleoanglicus?', 66. The manuscript has now been digitalised in the Early Manuscripts Project at Oxford: http://image.ox.ac.uk/.

[2]   See Jackson, LHEB 56. The Cornish origin of this text was discussed by David Dumville in his lecture given at the Fifth International Congress of Celtic Studies (Penzance 1975). It unfortunately remains unpublished; cf. W. Davies, *An Early Welsh Microcosm*, 24, n. 3.

hand.3 Six of them, as noted by Craster, are Old English; Meritt added two more glosses to his list, and admitted that he could not decipher the one over *galmula* which is found in Craster's note.4 The two remaining glosses were considered by Craster to be Welsh: *lo* gl. *podi*, and *gili* gl. *secalium*. It is notable that most of these dry stylus glosses are found over the Latin words which are already glossed by ink glosses in a Brittonic language; this may simply be because these were difficult words for all concerned, whether British or English. The exceptions are *tin* gl. *stagnum*, the putative . . .*molc* gl. *galmula* (read below as . . .*ouol*), and the two glosses discussed here.5

Both these glosses which occur on fol. 42r are difficult. Discussing the first of them Jackson noted that 'in the present passage it is obvious that *podi* is used in the sense of 'monastery' or at any rate 'monastery lands;' hence we may suggest that *lo* is an abbreviation for *loc*, 'monastery,' as in *mynachlog*'.6 Indeed, *loc*, borrowed from Latin *locus*, is attested in the 'Computus Fragment', where it occurs eight times in the sense 'place'.7 The form, as it is printed by Craster, however, is problematic. Jackson notes that 'such suspensions are very common in the Old Breton glosses, and not entirely unparalleled in the Old Welsh'.8 But, recent examination of this gloss (13.5.1998) has shown that it should be read as *lo-*. This could be read as British *loc*, but it is far more likely that it should be understood as Latin *locus* (or better the genitive *loci* since it glosses *podi*).

The other gloss assumed to be Welsh is placed over the Latin word, *secalium* 'a kind of grain, rye, black spelt', and has been read as *gili*.9 The gloss, as

---

3   Craster, RC xl. For details, see the Appendix below.
4   Meritt, *Old English Glosses*, 57.
5   For details, see the Appendix below.
6   Jackson, *Journal of Celtic Studies*, i.71; for the Latin word see Davies, *An Early Welsh Microcosm*, 37–8, 121–2.
7   For this text see Williams, BBCS iii.
8   Jackson, *Journal of Celtic Studies*, i.71–2. Another problematic *lo*, which was sometimes considered to be Old Welsh occurs in Ovid's *Ars Amatoria* (Oxoniensis Prior, Bodleian MS. Auct. F. 4. 32, fol. 38a) glossing Latin *ipsa*. According to Lambert, ÉC xxiv.292, this should probably stand for Latin *Io*, the name of the mythological figure to whom *ipsa* refers. The *Io* in the Juvencus glosses (Stokes, 'Cambrica', 206) is the earliest attestation of the Welsh word for 'calf', and its form is unproblematic.
9   Craster refers to the entry *gilus* in Holder, *Alt-Celtischer Sprachschatz*, without any further comment on the form found in the manuscript. The collection of evidence presented by Holder s.v. *-gilum*, *-gilus* (p. 2021) is characteristically eclectic and linguistically controversial, and quite likely contains entries of different origin; though he lists a few plant-names there, he does not provide a translation. It therefore remains difficult to

published by Craster, looks as if it contains a case ending. But this could be explained by a spelling mistake; we may compare an interlinear ink gloss on fol. 43ª *guapeli* gl. *sudaris*, where the final *-i* stands apparently for the second *-l* (cf. Middle and Modern Welsh *gobell*, 'saddle, pad'); the word notably occurs on the same folio in the spelling *guopell* (glossing Latin *ultia*). In the case of *gili*, the reading is far from clear. The first three letters are definitely *gil*; the last one is a smaller sign, which looks like *b* or *h*. Unfortunately this reading of the gloss with a final *-b* or *-h* instead of *-i* does not make it any clearer. If we assume a Brittonic provenance, the only correspondence that could be envisaged is the connection with the words meaning 'sharp' (referring to the spikes of the grain?), which are attested already in Old Welsh, e.g., *gilb* gl. *foratorium* in the same manuscript (fol. 42ᵇ); compare also *gílbín* gl *acumine* in the Juvencus glosses,[10] and *gilbin* gl. *ostrum* in BN lat. 10290 (fol. 14b).[11] This interpretation would allow therefore to consider this gloss as ultimately Welsh in view of the corresponding Cornish form found in *Vocabularium Cornicum*, *geluin* gl. *rostrum* which shows the different vocalism.[12] Other possibilities would involve, for example, taking *g* to denote or alternate with [ɣ],[13] or taking the combination of *l* and *h* in the end of this word to represent /λ/ make little sense at all. On the other hand, the form could be interpreted as Old English: since the last (smaller) letter is uncertain, one may suggest a connection with Old English *gilp* 'powder, dust', or perhaps with *gilm* 'a yelm, a handful of reaped corn', either of which might give tolerable sense in the context. In other words, of the two possible Brittonic dry-point glosses in this manuscript one is almost certainly Latin, and the Brittonic character of the other is open to serious doubt.

A further issue is raised by these dry-point glosses. The interlinear ink glosses in this manuscript are to be attributed to the scribe of the main body of the text and were written at the same time. There is clear evidence for this on fol. 43ʳ where *sambuca et ultia* is written with a large space between *sambuca* and *et* to allow room for the long gloss to be written over *sambuca*, namely *.i. strotur gurehic*. Similarly, on fol. 42ʳ *sella* is written as *se lla* perhaps so that the

---

extract anything useful from this data to help us with the form in *Oxoniensis Posterior*.

10 Stokes, 'Cambrica', 221.

11 Lambert, ÉC xix.194.

12 For the Cornish form see van Tassel Graves, *The Old Cornish Vocabulary*, 219–20; Campanile, *Profilo etymologico del cornico antico*, 48. An Old Cornish form *gelb* could be expected, if these words go back to Common Brittonic *gulbyo-*; for *i*-affection in Cornish, see Jackson, LHEB 595.

13 Cf. *gerthi* gl. *iure* in the same manuscript in view of Middle Welsh *ierthi*, (*g*)*erthi*.

ink gloss *.i. struduguar* could be fitted over the top without overlapping the next word. Not only are the ink glosses in the same hand but were written concurrently with the text; that is, he did not go back and copy the glosses into his clean text afterwards but copied them as he was copying the main text. The glosses, therefore, were in his exemplar and so predate the 10th-century date of this manuscript.

The assumption is that the dry-point glosses post-date the ink Brittonic glosses. Careful consideration of the placing of the dry-point glosses confirms this: the dry-point glosses on the Latin terms, *incudo*, *baxus*, *colomaticus*, *metallum*, *aratrum*, *uomer*, *uoscera*, *rostrum*, and *dolabra*, have been placed in a gap between the ink gloss and the main text or in the margin.[14] The placing of the dry-point gloss only makes sense in relation to the placing of the ink gloss. There is one instance where Old English *bytel* and Brittonic *ord*, both glossing *malleus*, seem to be written one on top of the other. It is tempting to suppose that the ink *ord* was written over the dry-point *bytel* but that would go against the cumulative evidence of all the other dry-point glosses which were written after the ink glosses. If one goes down the line of thinking that the Old English or Brittonic glosses were written in more that one batch, matters become unnecessarily complicated. There is no evidence that the ink glosses were added at any other time than when the manuscript was being copied; if so, it does not make sense to think that an Old English gloss could predate the ink gloss. In the case of *bytel*, there is probably a simpler explanation. It does look as if *bytel* was written on top of *ord* for the simple reason that there was no convenient space around *malleus* or its ink gloss into which the dry-point gloss could be fitted.

Craster concluded his article with the following words: 'We now have evidence of a second glossator entering both Old English and Brythonic glosses, and the fact that he should have done so is a testimony to the bilingual character of certain districts bordering upon Wales in the tenth century'.[15] However, it is clear that the same hand is not responsible for the ink Brittonic glosses and the Old English dry-point glosses; the former are in the hand of the main scribe and were copied from his exemplar *pari passu* with the main text. The latter were squeezed in at a later stage between the main text and the ink glosses, and in one case over the top of the ink gloss. Since it now appears that the scribe responsible for the dry-point glosses need not be regarded as

---

14   For details, see the Appendix.
15   Craster, RC xl.136.

responsible for any glossing in Brittonic, it is no longer necessary to assume that the glosses were added in an area of bilingualism; the Brittonic glosses may have been added in a Brittonic speaking area and the Old English ones added subsequently after the manuscript had moved to an English speaking area.

The difficulties of the interpretation of the scratched glosses are well known.[16] If the readings presented here are correct, namely that *lo-* is to be read as Latin *loci*, and that *gil-* is at least as easily explained as Old English, the only two candidates for Welsh dry-point glosses should probably be removed from the dossier.[17]

APPENDIX

In view of the relative inaccessability and antiquity of the discussions of these dry-point glosses (for references, see notes 3 and 4 above), it may be helpful to list briefly all the dry-point glosses found in this text. Our most recent reading under good light conditions recovered more detail than was seen by Craster or Meritt. We read two glosses not noted by either Craster or Meritt; in the following list they are marked by *. Where it may be useful, an attempt is made to indicate the position of the dry-point gloss in relation to the ink gloss and the lemma (Latin text in italics, ink gloss in bold, dry-point in normal). In some instances scratches are visible but nothing can be made of them; they are given as .... in order to indicate the full extent of dry-point glossing.

fol. 42ʳ tin gl. *stagnum.*

fol. 42ʳ lo- gl. *podi.*   The gloss is probably to be read as *loci*; see the discussion above.

fol. 42ʳ gilb gl. *secalium.*   The last letter of the gloss is uncertain; see the discussion above.

---

16 See, for example, Page, *Anglia*, xcvii.28–29; P. Ó Néill, 'The Earliest dry-point glosses', 2–3.

17 Alexander Falileyev would like to acknowledge the support of the Alexander von Humboldt-Stiftung.

*fol. 42^r . . pvvi: gl. *colomaticus.* The first visible letter may be Þ. The arrangement of glosses is as follows:

.i. **barr** . . **pvvi:**
et colomaticus

fol. 42^r …ouol gl. *galmula.* Craster read …molc. The -c cannot be seen. Meritt, *Old English Glosses*, p. 57, commented, 'I cannot decipher these scratches'.

* fol. 42^r …c gl. *fordalium.* The arrangement of glosses is as follows:

…c**.i. lefet**
fordalium

fol. 42^v bil gl. *lignismus.* The arrangement of glosses is as follows:

.i. **uiidimm** bil
lignismus

fol. 42^v …. gl. *scapa uel rostrum.* The arrangement of glosses is as follows:

.i. **tarater**

. . . .

scapa uel rostrum

fol. 42^v …. gl. *rostrum uel clauum.* The arrangement of glosses is as follows:

.i. **epill**

. . . .

rostrum uel clauum

fol. 42^v …. gl. *dolabra.* The arrangement of glosses is as follows:

.i. **gebel** . . . .
dolabra

fol. 42^v Þec gl. *metallum.* The arrangement of glosses is as follows:

.i. **mas** Þec
metallum

fol. 42ᵛ hiwan gl. *incudo.*

The arrangement of glosses is as follows:
> .i. **ennian**
> hiwan
> *incudo*

fol. 42ᵛ bytel gl. *malleus.*

The Latin word is also glossed by an ink gloss **ord**. The two glosses are written one on top of the other. It is likely that the dry-point gloss was superimposed on the ink gloss; see the discussion above.

fol. 42ᵛ Þec gl. *baxus.*

The dry-point gloss is in the left margin. The arrangement of glosses is as:
> Þec .i. **creman**
> *baxus*

fol. 42ᵛ . .iu gl. *uoscera.*

The arrangement of glosses is as follows:
> i. **serr** iu
> *uoscera*

fol. 42ᵛ scaer gl. *uomer.*

The arrangement of glosses is as follows:
> .i. **suh** scaer
> *uomer*

fol. 42ᵛ sul gl. *aratrum.*

The arrangement of glosses is as follows:
> .i. **ara** sul
> *aratrum*

It is usually supposed that the Brittonic gloss should be *arater*; however, only *ara* can be read. Stevenson notes that *ter* seems to have been erased. The dry-point gloss is in the space where the end of the ink gloss would have been. If so, it is not clear why *ter* was erased to make room for the dry-point gloss; there is no other case in this manuscript of the ink glosses being erased (even partially) to make room for the dry-point gloss. Usually, the latter is inserted in any blank space in or around the ink gloss and the main text.

The Old Welsh glosses on Weights and Measures

Pierre-Yves Lambert

THE Old Welsh glosses on Weights and Measures are found in the manuscript called, since Zeuss, 'Oxoniensis Prior', by reference to a list of Oxford manuscripts with Old Welsh glosses published in 1707 by Lhuyd.[1] This is Bodleian Auctarium F.4.32, also called St Dunstan's Classbook, because the first page was decorated by the saint himself in Glastonbury Abbey in the second half of the tenth century.[2] In the introduction to the facsimile, R. W. Hunt gave a detailed analysis of the contents.[3] The codex is made up of four distinct parts, the first one being Breton (Eutyches, *Ars de Verbo*, with Brittonic glosses, in a Continental hand), and the second one Anglo-Saxon (an homily on the Cross in Old English); the third and fourth parts are Welsh: the fourth is a copy of Ovid, *Ars Amatoria*, Book I, with OW glosses, and the third is the Book of Commoneus, the owner of this part of the manuscript, according to a scribal note found on f. 19v: *Finit opus in Domino o thei quiri* (= $\tilde{\omega}$ Θεὲ κύριε) *altissimo, meo patre Commoneo scriptum simul ac magistro*, to be read very probably, with a dative sg. *meo patri Commoneo scriptum*, 'written for my father Commoneus, also my master as well'.

The *Liber Commonei* is a medley of didactical, exegetical and liturgical texts: the Alphabet invented by 'Nemniuus', an Easter table for sixteen years, probably written in 817, and other computistic texts, then f. 23 (recto and verso), the text on Weights and Measures, with glosses overflowing to the

---

1   Zeuss, *Grammatica Celtica*, 1090–91; Lhuyd, *Archaeologia Britannica*, 226.
2   Budny, '"St Dunstan's Classbook"'.
3   Hunt, *Saint Dunstan's Classbook*, v–xiii.

bottom of the preceding folio (f. 22v), with also the end of the last extract written in the margin of the next folio (f. 24r), and finally, liturgical texts and prayers in Greek and Latin (ff. 24–36).[4]

The author of the tract on Weights and Measures is Victorius or Victorinus of Aquitaine. He also wrote an Easter cycle, *Cursus Paschalis*, on the order of Pope Hilary in 457: the same Pope used to refer to him as the *calculator scripulorum*, a reckoner of small weights. This tract, often named *Calculus Victorii*, was attributed to Bede for some time (since the edition by Hervagius, Basel 1580; cf. *Patrologia Latina*, XL 677). However, Wilhelm von Christ, in a decisive study dated 1863, gave this text its right attribution.[5] The edition used here is that of Friedlein from a Bern manuscript.

Victorius certainly drew most of his materials from earlier sources. For example, the extract on weights of oil and honey has many parallels in Greek and Latin arithmetical tracts.[6] But what is most important from our point of view is that this tract is generally found with a commentary by Abbo, abbot of Fleury.[7] This is more than a coincidence since Abbo, a contemporary of Dunstan, came to England, and taught in the newly founded monastery of Ramsey, the abbot of which had been monk in Fleury. Abbo met Dunstan when he was archbishop of Canterbury. He dedicated to him some of his Insular writings (a Life of St. Edmund, etc.). We also have a letter of Abbo to Dunstan, asking him to send back manuscripts belonging to Fleury: it is very probable that the glossed Eutyches was one of them, since we know of the presence of Breton manuscripts in Fleury. Although we have no trace here of the commentary by Abbo, the simple presence of this text at Glastonbury might have a connection with him. Just as the great scholar of Fleury saved the *Calculus Victorii* on the continent, it might be thanks to his teaching that this extract was kept in Glastonbury.

As it is often the case with ancient texts, the first manuscript studied by modern scholars represented a mixed tradition: in 1863, von Christ had access only to the Bamberg ms. (Bamberg MS, H. J. IV 24, from the 10th c.), which contained essentially the commentary by Abbo. Von Christ nevertheless succeeded in isolating the beginning of the text as the beginning of the proper

---

4   For the last part, see the discussion by Breen, *Archiv für Liturgiewissenschaft*, xxxiv.

5   von Christ, *Sitzunberichte*, Jahrgang 1863, vol. 1.

6   Cf. the texts collected by Hultsch, *Metrologicorum Scriptorum Reliquiae*, especially, I, Prolegomena, pp. 100–101, 132–133, etc.

7   On Abbo, abbot of Fleury (Abbo Floraciensis), see Manitius, *Geschichte der lateinischen Literatur des Mittelalters*, II, 664; A. Guerreau-Jalabert, *Abbo Floraciensis*.

Calculus Victorii, and tried to rescue some other extracts from the quotations by Abbo. Better documents were later published by Friedlein, first from Bern Burgerbibliothek 250 and Basel O. II. 3., then from Vatican manuscripts (Reginensis lat. 766 and 1569).[8]

Several studies have already been devoted to the Old Welsh glosses: from the first edition by Johann Kaspar Zeuss to the important article by Ifor Williams,[9] we have benefited from a long series of contributions, ranging from textual discussions to etymological notes, by prominent Celticists, Stokes (who published a new edition), Thurneysen, Loth and Henry Lewis.[10] None of the editors tried to edit the whole of the text with all its glosses, the Latin as well as the Welsh ones.

There is no doubt that Ifor Williams achieved real progress: following a remark made by Henry Lewis concerning the OW text on bottom of f. 22v, he realised that this was a batch of glosses relating to f. 23r and f. 23v; he also paid considerable attention to the Latin glosses, which sometimes provide a clue about the understanding of the main text by the glossator. But Williams had no reliable edition of the main text at his disposal, because the text had not yet been identified (this was done by R. W. Hunt, the editor of the facsimile[11]), and therefore he did not try a complete edition of the fragment. He did, however, search far and wide for parsallel texts in the metrological literature, and managed to provide us with a solution for most of the riddles of these difficult glosses.

This edition is intended to be as close to the manuscript as possible. Some corrections have been suggested between brackets, either in the glosses or in the main text. Normally non-interlineary glosses are connected with their lemma by reference symbols, the existence of which has been indicated by <> at the beginning of the gloss. A few interlinear glosses written by the main hand have been incorporated in the main text between double brackets [[ ]]. For technical reasons, Roman symbols of measures have been replaced by bold capital letters, followed by their reading in italics (the correspondence between

---

8   Friedlein, *Zeitschrift für Mathematik und Physik*, xvi; see also Friedlein, *Bolletino di bibliografia e di storia degli scienze matematiche e fisiche*, iv (where he edited some Vatican manuscripts; I have not had the opportunity to see this).

9   Zeuss, *Grammatica Celtica*, 1090–91; Williams, BBCS, v.

10   Stokes, TPhS 1860–61, 237–8; Thurneysen, RC xi.203–6; Loth, *Vocabulaire*, passim; Lewis, BBCS iii.

11   Hunt, *Saint Dunstan's Classbook*, ix.

symbols and letters is given in Table 1). The Old Welsh sections are printed in bold.

Table 1: Key to the signs used in the manuscript

(f. 23 r.)
(Rubr.) Incipiunt pauca excerpta de mensurís calculi.
i. Olearia incipiunt.

Mensura centum sextarii.
omnes sextarii[1] himminae[2] duæ, quartarii[3] .iiii., octari[4] .uiii., chiati .xii.
Chiatus[5] olei **L** [[sescuncia]], **T** [[scriptulus]] iiii.
Octarius[6] **J** [[quaras]], **N** [[semiuncia]].
Quartarius[7] **H** [[quincus]].
Himmina[8] **C** [[distas]].
Sextarius[9] olei pendit libram[10] **A** [[assis]], **E** [[bi<ss>ae]].
Congeus[11] sextarii sex, olei pondo[12] .x.
Semodius[13] congei .iii. **H** *quincus.* sextarii .uiii., olei ponto[14] .xiii. **H** *quincus*
Modius[15] semodi duo, congei[16] duo[17] et .ui. **E** *bisse,* sextarii .xui., olei ponto[18]

I	<>.i. magnus sextarius et paruus sextarius. *scilicet* magnus bís xu uncias habet, paruus bís .x. <.i. olei>. Sextarius dictus de sexta parte congii.
2	<> Himina *dicitur* quasi semina, hoc *est* semis.
3	<> quartari .i. quarta pars sextari .i. u. unciae olarit*er*, mellarit*er uero* .uii. et semiunciam habet q*ui*a hoc est quartum xxx.
	et [duo] semis .uiii.–ua (= *octaua*) pars sextarii olei, *[octarius] *uero* mellis iiii. unciæ nisi una*m* quartam partem
4	<> octarii .i. octaua pars sextarii .x unciæ.
5	.xl. scrip*uli*
6	.i. lix scrip*uli.*
7	.i. u. unciæ.
8	.i. x. unciæ.
9	.i. qu*an*do d*icit* olei, uigilat mensuras mellis, de q*uib*us postea dicetur.
10	<> .i. pundus. libra *enim* aliquando generalis, ut *est* híc, aliquando specialis, q*ua*ndo idem signi*ficat* quod est assis .i. xii unciæ.
II	.i. **is** .i. cxx unc*iae*
12	.i. xii. unciæ, idem et assis.
13	.i. clx unciæ
14	unus pondus xii unc*ias* h*ab*et.
15	.i. cccxx unc*iae*
16	.i. ccxl unciæ
17	.i. assis
18	.i. idem *est* et assis .i. as

.xxui. **E** *bisse*.

Mensuras *propter* diuersitatem prouinciarum intellegendum esse diuersas:.

Anfora italica[19], modi .iii., semedi sex, congei .uiii.[20], sextarii .xl[uiii]., olei ponto lxxx:.

Anfora gallica[21], modi .iiii., semodi .uiii., congei .x. **E** *bisse*.[22], sextarii lxiiii, olei punto centum .ui. **E** *bisse*:.

(Rubr.) Incipiunt mellearia pundera

Chiatus[23] mellis pendit **J** *quadras*, **N** *semiuncia*
octarius **J** *quadras*, **N** *semiuncia*, **T** *scripuli* sex.
quarta(rius)[24] **F** *septus*, **N** *semiuncia*
himmina[25] **A** *assis*, **J** *quadras*
sextarius[26] mellis punto[27] duo **G** *semis*
congeus[28] sextarii sex, mellis pundo[29] .x.
semodius[30] congeus[31] et iiii. **D** *dodras*,[32] sextarii[33] .uiii., mellis punto .xiii. **H**

---

19 .i. dcccclx unciæ

20 *quia* unus congeus *habet* cxx uncias

21 .i. îcclxxx unciæ

22 .i. híc bise lxxx. significat *quod* conuenit eo *quod* octauum significat numer*um* .i. uiii. uncias tantum :.

23 Chiatus olei dualit*er* diuiditur et unius conmensura partis duab*us* partibus diuisís, huc *est* intigritati additur. Et [ita] chiatus mellis subpletur et h*æc* conuenientia in reliquís mensurís olei et mellis debet obseruari atq*ue* probari:.
in marg.: (chiatus .i. l)x scrip.*uli*, octarius [x]c scrip*uli*

24 i. uii. unciæ et semiuncia

25 .i. xu. unciæ

26 .i. xxx. unciæ

27 .i. olei.

28 .i. clxxx uncia*e*.

29 .i. xuiii uncias *habet*

30 .i. ccxl unciæ .i. mel*lis*

31 .i. clxxx .i. olei.

32 .i. ássis

33 .i. ccxl.

quincus.[34]

modius[35] semodi duo, congei[36] duo .ui.[37] **E** *bisse,*[38] sextari .xui. mellis [pondo] xxui. **E** *bisse.*

Anfora italica[39] modi .iii., semodi .ui., congei[40] .uiii., sextarii[41] .xluiii., mellis punto[42] .lxxx.

Anfora[43] gallica modi .iiii., semodi .uiii., congei[44] .x. **E** *bisse,* sextari lxuiii., mellis punto[45] centum .ui. **E** *bisse.*

---

34   hic **H** *quincus* significat semis. **F** *septus* semp*er* habet .uii. uncias

35   .i. cccclxxx unciæ

36   .i. ccclx unciæ

37   .i. assis mellis

38   .i. híc bisse mellis .i. xii uncias ha*bet*, ui. itaq*ue* ass*is* mellis et **E** *bisse* mel*lis* cxx unc*ias* ha*bet* i*n* mensura mellis

39   .i. ccccxl unc*iae* unusquisqu*e enim* mod*ius* cccclxxx uncias ha*bet* i*n* mensu*ra* mellis

40   clxxx unc*iae* in unoquoq*ue* congeo

41   .i. unusquisq*ue* sex*tarius* xxx unc*iae.*

42   .i. xuiiii unc*iae* in unoquoq*ue* pun*do*

43   .i. î dccccxx unciæ

44   <> [. . .] bisse híc cxx uncias ha*bet*, notandu*m* qu*od* c*um* bisse octinarium no*n* seruat nume*rum*, demedia pars addita ad mensu*ram* olei hanc ratione*m* efficit, si p*ro*bari oport*et.*

45   xu unciæ

Ad libram[46] mellis in libra[47] duo[48] tres quinque olei
in sextario[49] sex < quattuor quinque > ad sextarium[50]
centum[51] [[pondo olei sextari[52] lx., *centum*]] puntos mellis sextari .xl.[53]

Talentum[54] cuiuslibet mercidis pontos lxxx.
talentum[55] olei sextari xluiii. talentum mellis .xxxii. sextarii.

De geometrica[56] ratione.
Digitus[57] **N** *semiuncia* **P** *sicilicus,* [58]
palma **J** *quadras,*

---

46   **.i. di mesúr.**

47   .i. in mensura

48   (f. 22 v) <> Duo .u. (**int doú pímp**). In libra. .iii. u. (**ír trí .u.**) IN
libra. mellis (.i. **treán cánt mél**).
semp*er* sex (.i. u.) **hínt trí pímp**. in sextario (.i. **ín hestaúr mél**)
.i. is xxx há guorenníeu. guótig .iiii. u. (ir petguar. pímp) ad
libram olei
.i. ir. hestoriou oleu. is trimuceint hestaur. mel.
uerbi gratia, uas in quo mensura<n>*tur* xx unciae de oleo usq*ue* d*um*
plenu*m* fuerit, in ipso iterum remensurant*ur* xxx unc*iae* mellis usq*ue* d*um*
plenu*m* fuerit, *sed* distat in grauitate *et* in multitudine unciarum, quamuis
si melle uas impleat, non t*er*tia pars numeri sextariorum olei in mellis
sextarís continetur:.

49   .i. mellis

50   .i. ui. u. *fiunt* .iiii. u.

51   **hint c punt.**

52   .i. î cc unc*iae*

53   î cc unc*iae* simili*ter*

54   dccccxl unciæ .i. olei, mellis, auri et argenti

55   dccccxl unc*iae*

56   de geomet*rica* n*unc* loquitur et in manib*us* metitur.

57   .i. xuiiii scrip*uli*   [*leg.* xuiii]

58   .i. t*er*tia pars unciæ pollicis, **teir. petgúared párt** unciae mensura
pollicis **ír bís bichan** .i. **ámcibrét ir máut biheit hetham ír**
eguin hittoi ír húnc isit petguared pard guorfrit nímer ho
hinnoid guotan amcibfret ir bis hiri erguid si unc*iæ* pollicis xx
et demediu*m* unc*iae*.

cubitus[59] .i. **I** *treas* pedes   [= 1 + 1/3 feet]

gresús[60] .ii. **G** *semis* pedes   [= 2 + 1/2 feet]

passus[61] .u. pedes,

pertica[62] pedes .x.,

arripinnis[63] perticas .xii., passus[64] .xxiiii., pedes centum xx.

legua habet passus .îd., pedes .ûîî d., arripinnis .lxii. **G** *semis*, ictus[65] .lx.

stadium habet passus .c̄ d̄xxu., pedes dcc xxu.

Iugerum habet passus .xl.uiii, pedes .ccxl.

Sexdecim digiti[66] transuersi pés *est*, palma[67] quadras[68], bes[69].

cubitus[70], ulna[71] dodras.

duo et semis pedes gresus, .u. pedes. passus.

Achina .c. pedes, ictus .xxu. pedes in quadro[72]

| (f. 23v) xxiiii passus arripinnis proprie (*dicitur*), .ii. arripinnes iugerum, .î.d. pasus legua, .îîîî. passus.: < scinus siue parasanga >.

---

59   áb ulna usq*ue* ad ungulas

60   .i. xxx unc*iae* digiti

61   lx. unciæ

62   .i. cxx unciæ

63   î ccccxl unciæ

64   .i. accus*atiuus*

65   hic ictus circu*m* ut quadrata*m* figura*m* xxxi pedes et iiii digitos transuersos ex unoq*uoque* lateræ habens

66   xii uncias h*abet*

67   .i. **boscig:.**

68   .i. iii unc*iae*

69   .i. bisse .i. unciae .uiii.

70   <> **hor elín cihutún hi torr**. usq*ue* ad artu*m* pugni bes *est*. **hou boit cihitun ceng ir esceir. is moi hinnoid** .uiiii. unciæ.

71   <> ideo ulna d*i*cit ad discriptionem mensuræ a sinu intus incipientis bes *dicitur* usq*ue* ad artum pugñi utraq*ue* mensura extenditur:.

72   .i. pedes .xxu. .i. híc iatu (or iactu) á *priore aliter* decet mensurari, hunc ictum in quadro metitur. (*See Figure 1 below p. 116, for the design of a square*)

[DE PONDERIBUS]

Ouellus[73] minima pars mensuræ[74].

Dodras uiiii. uncias[75],

denarios .x.[76] numero,

pondeus[77] duo et semis[78].

sestertium[79] .u. sextarii.

gomer[80] .ui. modi[81],

medignum[82] sextula[83], sexta pars sextarii.

libra xii minas, libra greca[84].

.lx. librae aticae tallentum[85]:,

---

73   .i. demedium scripuli

74   <> .i. olei et mellis et in metallis.

75   .i. habet

76   .i. uncias *uel* scriptulos

77   <> (f. 22v) Pondeus. idem *est* et depondeus .i. duo scripuli et semis et in depondeo fiunt. Notandum cum Lucas dicit nonne .u. passeres depondeo ueniunt unusquisque passer obello conparatur. Nec huic Matheus contradicit dicendo nonné duo passeres ab asse ueniunt. as *enim* unus scripulus *est* qui dualiter diuisus bis. obellum redit, quibus duobus obellis .ii. passeres conparantur:.

Dou punt petguar. hanther. scribl prinit hinnoid .iiii. aues et .u. qui adicit Lucam **ní choilám hinnoid amser. is cihun argant agit eterin illúd. ir pimphet eterin diguormechís** Lucas hegit **hunnoid** in *pretium* benedictionis **hoid hoitou hou bein atar. ha beinn cihunn.** *reliqua* Matheus uero **dou eterinn cant hunnoid di assa** .i. **asse bichan.** unus scripulus *est* partire et fiunt duo demedii et *pretium* duorum auium:.

78   .i. obellus

79   **.i. hestaur.**

80   c. unciæ < o > (= *correct to gomor*)

81   .i. î dcccc xx unciae

82   .i. modi dignum

83   .i. iii. unciae et uii scripuli

84   .i. xiii unciae

85   (f. 22v) Cum dicitur lx librae aticae tallentum, híc aliquid *contrarium* uidetur, superius *enim* dixit tallentum pondo lxxx, hoc *est* unciae dcccclx, hic *uero* cum lx libras ad supplementum (. . .*one word erased* . . .) adscribsit.

De aliis mensuris aliarum rerum:,

Duo coclearia[86] clemę dicitur.
iiii (*read* iii) clemes[87] mistrum faciunt.
mister iiii <pars> chiati.
Chiatus[88] .iii. (*read* ui) pars chimminae.
Chimmina[89] medius sextarius *est*.
Ephi uel offa .iii. modi, quorum decima pars *est* quadrisextium[90] et chimmina[91] et semis[92].
Hin uero modius et .iii. sextarios, cuius quarta pars quadrisextum et chimmina et semis ęque, quia pars .iii. sextariorum quarta chimmina et semis.

Item de alia ratione[93] incipit.
ii. S *obellus* [*read* **M** *uncia*] Sextarius[94], himmina i **M** *uncia*. quartarius[95] **N'**

---

non dcccclx uncias *sed* dccxx uncias tallentum *continet* et ideo maius minusque tallentum fieri estimamus a*ut* libra atica et grec[i]a q*uae* mna nominatur .maior. *est* quam libra latina. libra *enim* grec[i]a xui h*abet* uncias, latina u*ero* .xii.

Notandum q*uod* cum *dicitur* gomor qui c*entum* uncias h*abet*, *deci*ma pars effi esse, cum*que* quadrisextium et himmina et semis, xc.ui. uncias efficiunt ho*c* *est* decimam effi et desu*nt* .iiii. unciae de **sé ni choilám immit cel ir nimer bichan gutan ir maur. nimer.** *uel* maior *est* gomor Ebreorum quae h*abet* c. unc*ias* quam Aticorum quor*um* sunt hii numeri.

86 coclerium scrip*ulus* et quarta pars scripuli
87 .i. duo scrip*uli* et demedium
88 xl. scrip*uli*
89 .i. x unciae
90 .i. .iiii. sextarii .i. lxxx unc*iae*
91 .i. x unc*iae*
92 .i. ui unc*iae*
93 Eandem mensura nun*c* (*or* h*ec*) nominationem ostendit et prima. Sextarius *enim* hoc modo sexta pars assis *est*. pondera haec numerantur in congeo ita et in asse.
94 .i. duæ unciæ
95 quarta pars unc*iae*

semiuncia, octarius[96] **P** *sicilicus.*

chiatus **R** *sextula.*

congeus sextarii .ui. **A** *assis*[97], *passus*[98] .x[[ii]] (*read* u ?)

lx librae[99] tallentum est . lxxx puntos[100] tallentum.

stater .xx. **S** *scripulos, sicel*[101] *et sicilicus*[102] .i. stater: [[duæ scriptulae]]

dragma[103] .ii. **S** *scripulos, ut alii iii* **S** *scripulos,*

dedragma[104] .ui. **S** *scripulos,* (xxiiii. **S** *scripulos* **M** *uncia*)

denarius .x. **S** scriptula et demedium scriptuli

trimessis: [[trimesis tres]] *soldus*[105] *est.*

tributum[106] .x. pars pecuniæ[107]

census[108] soldus ab unoquoque, denarios .x. Finit amen.

A	assis	xii uncias	
B	iabus	xi uncias	[? read *deunx*]
C	disdas	x uncias	[read *dextans*]
D	dodras	uiiii uncias	[read *dodrans*]
E	bisse	uiii uncias	[*bisse* or *bes*]

---

96 demedium *unciæ*

97 .i. xii unciae .i. unusquisque sextarius binas uncias habet

98 <> (f. 23v marg. sup.) .i. cum natura fit congei cxx uncias habere, hac uice in xii uncias passus est redigi. Aliter passus xii si soluas in uncias, numerum unciarum, efficiant quae lx librae .i. dccxx uncias et tallentum minus implent et ita hec mensura crescit.

xui digiti transuersi pedem efficiunt. pes uero xii uncias digiti habet, pedes .u. efficiunt passum. passus itaque xii.lx pedes, hoc est dccxx uncias.

99 .i. dcccclx unciae et hoc tallentum maius ut putatur.

100 <> librae aticæ ut predixi aut tallentum dualiter fit .i. paruum et minimum.

101 xiiii scripuli

102 .i. ui scripuli

103 .i. xx scripuli

104 .i. duæ dragmæ

105 .iiii scripuli et demedium

106 proprium nomen mensurae

107 .i. scripulus

108 proprium mensurae .i. soldus maior ut Cessari per totum mundum reddebatur.

F	septus	uii uncias	[read *septunx*]
G	semis	ui uncias	
H	quincus	u uncias	[read *quincunx*]
I	treas	iiii uncias	[read *triens*]
J	quaras	iii uncias	[read *quadrans*]
K	sextas	ii un*ciae*	[read *sextans*]
L	sesun*cia*	semis et uncia	[read *sescuncia*]
M	uncia	i uncia	
N	semiun*cia*	xii scripuli	
O	duæ sesclæ	uiiii scripuli	[read *duae sextulae*]
P	sicilicus	ui scripuli	
Q	sescla	iiii scripuli	[read *sextula*]
R	demedia ses.	ii scripuli	
S	obellus	i scripulus	
T	[scripulus]		

[Ianua Calculi]
bis media [sescla][109]

bis sescla	duae sescl̨e
bis sicilicus	semiuncia
bis duæ sesclae	semun*cia* et sescla,
bis semiuncia.	quadras
bis unciæ	sextas
bis sestuncia [read *sesc.*]	quadras
bis sextas	treas
bis quincus	distas
bis semis	assis
bis septus	assis et sextas
bis bisse	assis et treas
bis dodras	assis et semis
bis disdas	assis et bisse
bis iabus	assis et distas
bis as	dipondeus
bis bini	quaterni
bis turni [read *terni*]	seni
bis quaterni	octeni

---

109 <> duae unciae

bis quini	deni
bis seni	decus depondeus
bis septus	decus quartus
(f24r)<> bis octus	decus sextus
bis nonus	decus octus
bis deni	uigeni *uel* bie
bis bie	quadri *uel* quadrageni
bis trigeni	sexai uel sexageni
bis quadrai	octai uel octageni
bis quinai	cean
bis sexai	cean bies
bis septai	cean quadrai
bis octai	cean sexai
bis nonai	cean octai
bis cean	ducean
bis ducen	quadracen
bis tricen	sexacen
bis quadricen	octicen
bis quincen	cile
<> bis sexacen	cile ducean
bis septacen	cile quadricen
bis octacen	cile sexacen
bis nonacen	cile octacen
bis cile	discile.

Figure 1: A square *actus* (here *ictus*) is measured from its centre: 25 (*pedes*) from the centre to one angle. A side is: 31 *passus & 4 digiti transuersi.*

COMMENTARY

This text falls into seven divisions:

1. The weights of oil (*olearia*) = Friedlein, *Zeitschrift für Mathematik und Physik*, xvi.72.5–73.8.
2. The weights of honey (*mellearia*) (= Friedlein, 74.9–75.23); this ends with a short extract dealing with the correspondance between pounds of oil and honey.
3. Geometry, including both length units and surface units (= Friedlein, 74.24–75.9).
4. Money units, from *obellus* to *talentum* (= Friedlein, 75.10–75.21).
5. *De aliis mensuris*, (in other manuscripts: *de rebus liquidis*): liquid units (= Friedlein, 75.22–76.5).
6. *De alia ratione* (Friedlein: *de altera ratione*), on volume units and weights (= Friedlein, 76.6–76.18).
7. *De signis ponderum*: a table of the weights (from *as* to *uncia*, and from *uncia* to *scripulus*), together with their symbols; this extract is omitted by Friedlein who refers to Hultsch, *Metrologicorum scriptorum reliquiae*, II, p. 121.9–123.10, 133.14–135.6, but these are quotations from Isidore's *Etymologies*. We are unable to ascertain the authenticity of this extract.
8. Finally, a table of the 'doubles', beginning *bis media sescla, sescla,* ending *bis cile, discile*: this occurs in the counting tables (at the end: col. 128–130), under the title *Ianua Calculi* (a title here omitted); see Friedlein, 69.1–70.13.

Parts 1–6 (and possibly 7) provide us with one continuous extract of Victorius's *Calculus*. Part 8 is taken from an earlier part of the same work.

Parts 1 and 2: Weights of oil and honey.

This text is intended to give the respective weight of different volume measures, *chyathus, octarius, quartarius, hemina, sextarius, congeus*, etc., when they are filled with oil, first, and secondly when they are filled with honey. Williams was lead astray by the first gloss, referring to two different *sextarii*; he thought that, in the same way, one could distinguish between two series of volumes, the first one being used for oil, the second for honey. But this view is certainly unfounded. What is clear, however, is that two pounds are distinguished, the *pondus olei* and the *pondus mellis*. They do not have the same value in ounces; the ounce is therefore the only common/simple weight unit we can rely on: one *pondus olei* is twelve ounces, and one *pondus mellis* is eighteen ounces. It automatically follows that *pondus* is used here as a unit of volume and not of weight. The same proportion will be found with the other volumes: oil weights two third of the same volume of honey.

	OIL	HONEY
Chyathus	*sescuncia,* + 4 *scrip.* = 1 oz, 12 + 4 scrip. or 1 + 2/3	*sextans* + *semiuncia* = 2 oz, + 1/2 oz
octarius	*sextans, semiuncia* = 2.5 oz	*quadrans, semiunc., 6 scr.* 3 + 1/2 + 1/4 = 3.75 oz
quartarius	*quincunx* = 5 oz	*septunx, semiuncia* = 7.5 oz
hemina	*dextans (distas)* = 10 oz	*as, quadrans* 12 + 3 = 15 ounces
sextarius	*pondus* = *as, bisse* = 12 + 8 = 20 oz	2.5 'pond. olei' 12 x 2.5 = 30 oz
congeus (6 *sextarii*)	10 'pond. olei' = 12 x 10 = 120 oz	10 'pond. mellis' (18 oz) = 10 x 18 = 180 oz
semodius (8 *sextarii*)	13 'pond. olei' + *treas* 156 + 4 = 160 oz	13 'pond. mellis' + 1/3 (13 x 18) + 6 = 240 oz
modius	26 'pond. olei' + *bisse* (26 x 12) + 8 = 320	26 'pond. mellis' + 2/3 (26 x 18) + 12 = 480
anfora italica	80 'pond. olei' = 960 ounces	80 'pondera mellis' = 1440 ounces
anfora gallica	106 'pond. olei' + *bisse* = 1280 ounces	106 'pond. mellis' + 2/3 = 1920 ounces

Disparities with the model edited by Friedlein concern mainly the place of certain glosses, or the change of numbers or symbols. There are traces of misinterpretations and of later corrections in the main text, as we shall see. As Friedlein chose to incorporate the text of the glosses into the main text, it is not always clear whether we are faced with a gloss or not. It is furthermore possible that many explanations go back to the author himself.

Wilhelm von Christ remarked that in many cases Abbo's commentary was supposing the same weight for oil, and for water or wine: as we are not at present dealing with this commentary, we shall refrain from entering this discussion.

I have kept in the main text, between double square brackets [[ ]], the glosses by the main hand on the symbols of weight which seem to be limited to the first occurrence of each symbol. Among them, I interpreted *sescuncia*, supposing a ligature -*sc*-.

Glosses 1 to 4 are in the upper margin. The merging of these glosses has brought about some confusion about where in the main text they belong.

Gloss 1. Also in Friedlein. The punctuation should fall between *paruus* and *sextarius*, as in Friedlein.

Gloss 3 is the conflation of two different glosses, one on *quartarius*, the second one (beginning with *et [duo] semis*) on *octarius*; this later one should have been written as a continuation of gloss 4. Read: *[octarius] uero mellis iiii. unciae nisi*, etc.

After *octarius*, (*duo et semis unciae*), in the main text, we would expect the symbols *sextans* (= *ii unciae*) and *semiuncia*, as in Friedlein, instead of *quadrans - semiuncia* (which may have been imported from the next paragraph, on honey measures).

Gloss 6: read lx (60) instead of lix (cf. Friedlein). Gloss 6 should go with gloss 7, and explain *quartarius*.

Gloss 9, about *uigilat* in Late Latin commentaries, and particularly in Celtic countries, see my note, *Ériu* xxxvi.

Gloss 10 is also in Friedlein.

In the definition of *sextarius olei* (main text), we find a form *binae* for *bissae* (interlinear gloss by the main hand).

Gloss 11 contains the OW copula: **is**, first identified by Williams (BBCS v.228). As is obvious from Old Irish or Old Breton texts, the copula is generally used, in reckoning, before the result of an operation, as in current English: 'two fours *are* eight'; parallel to this, the article can be used before the subject of the copula sentence.

Examples from OBr. glosses: Angers 477, 13b33, *is doudec*, 59b17 *is dou<hou>ceint*; 59a30 *is tricont seith. . . i(s) seith uith. .* ; with the article: 14a1, *partire* *per nouem, nouies quini* = *quadrais quinquis*, glossed: *in pem-nau, in* (read *int*) *pemp guar dou u<ce>int* 'the five nines are forty-five'.

Examples from OIr. glosses: BCr 33a3–4, *partire per septem: septies trigeni : ducenti decus, .i. it secht trichit inna deich ardib cétaib* (the division has been transformed into a reversed multiplication: 'the 210 are 7 x 30'); 42c1 *quater centeni, .cccc., it chethir chét* 'they are 400' etc.

The proportion of *semodius* against *congeus* is not exact: *congei .iii. quincus*. If, as I suspect, this formula is giving the difference between *congeus* and *semodius* in ounces, the value in ounces of *.iii.* (supply *asses*) would be 36 oz; there remain 4 ounces, that is *triens* (here, in this ms., *treas*). So the text should have read: *Semodius, congeus* (+) *.iii.(asses)* (+) *triens*. With *quincunx* instead of *triens*, we are given one ounce too much. Friedlein's text has the same error. We will find similar deviations about *semodius* and *congeus* later on in *mellearia pondera*.

For the number of pounds in the semodius: *olei ponto .xiii. quincus* : here again, *triens*, not *quincus*, would have been the precise fraction (XIII pounds = 156 ounces, only four are wanting).

Modius is said to be equivalent to *congei duo et .ui. bisse*; Friedlein has, *congei II et .VI. semis*. The difference between *modius* and *duo congei* is reckoned by the normal value of *as* / pound. Our text is thus the better one; for the difference of 80 ounces is exactly equivalent to VI (*asses*) + *bisse* (that is, (6 x 12) + (2/3 x 12). The same formula occurs in the corresponding phrase in *mellearia pondera*.

However, an interlinear gloss in Friedlein gives another reckoning: *CCXL unc. unum asses et (bisse) LXXX unc. efficiunt*. Here *bisse* is interpreted as the eight-twelfths, not of the *as*, but of the *congeus*. This could refer to another version of the main text, *modius, congei duo et bisse* (that is, 240 + 80 = 320 ounces). In the glosses, however, the explanation by *as* (originally above *congeus*) clearly indicates the entire unit of which *bisse* is a fraction.

Olei ponto .xxui. bisse is exact (26 x 12 = 312, 8 are left = *bisse*). The end of gloss 19 (*.i. as*) was certainly intended as a different gloss, for the cypher xxui.

anfora gallica . . . congei .x. bisse: here *bisse* means the two thirds of one *congeus*, that is 80 ounces.

olei punto centum ui. bisse is right: here *bisse* is the two thirds of a pound, 8 ounces, plus one hundred and six pounds (106 x 12 = 1272), this is 1280.

chiatus mellis: the same error as in *octarius olei* above (see after gloss 3), with *quadras* instead of *sextans* (*.ii. unciae*).

Gloss 32 and main text *et .iiii. dodras*: the difference between *semodius mellis* (240 ounces) and *congeus mellis* (180 ounces) should amount to *.u. asses* (60 oz). But *iiii. dodras*, with an *as* = 12 ounces, gives (12 x 4) + 9 = 57. Or, if we are dealing with a *libra* = *as* of 18 ounces, then *iiii. dodras* would amount to (18 x 4) + 13.5 = 85.5 when we expect (18 x 3) + (18 x 1/3), that is, *.iii.* + *triens*.

Gloss 34: *hic quincus significat semis.* What is expected is a fraction equivalent to six ounces (the difference between 13 x 18, and 240), that is, a third of the *libra mellis* (18 oz). So *quincunx* should here again (see gl. 11) be replaced by *triens*, understood as a third of the *libra mellis*.

Gloss 38: between *modius* (480 ounces) and two *congei* (360 ounces), we have a difference of 120, here written *ui. (assis mellis et) bisse.* Actually (6 x 18) + (18 x 2/3) = 108 + 12 = 120. This gloss is intended to draw attention to the use of *bisse* as a fractional number in the pound of honey.

Gloss 39 is wrong: read the first number as *îccccxl* (1440) instead of *.i. ccccxl* (440).

Gloss 42: *xuiiii* (19) should be corrected to *xuiii* (18).

Gloss 46, the second Welsh gloss (first noticed by Lewis, BBCS iii.1), offers no difficulty: preposition **di** 'to', = Mid. W. *y.* But the real purpose of this gloss is to comment on *libra* (the prep. being automatically translated with the noun). By paraphrasing *libra* with **mesur**, 'measure', the glossator probably refers to its use as a volume unit, not as a weight. A parallel gloss occurs in the manuscript used by Friedlein: *ad mensuram*, glossing *ad libram*, but displaced into the preceding line (p.74, l.12). Gloss 47 is still another example of this interpretation.

Gloss 48 (on the bottom of f. 22v). The proportion observed when passing from oil to honey is expressed by the three numbers, *duo, tres, quinque.* Though we cannot understand exactly the exact process involved, *quinque* is not the sum of the preceding two numbers, but rather a multiplicandum common to both of them: 'three fives become two fives'. This is what is implied by the Welsh translation, where the starting point is distinguished by the article (**ir tri .u.** 'the three fives'), and the result, when switching to oil, by the copula (**int dou pimp** 'this is two fives').

As Williams already demonstrated (BBCS v.248, in an additional note (and probably as an afterthought)), **trean cant mel** means 'a third (more) for honey', ('traean ychwaneg i'r mel'). Previous interpretations were inclined to read *cant* as the number. I have developed arguments in favour of Williams' final thoughts in CMCS viii.

But the three fives (of honey) become six fives (thirty ounces), when it comes to a bigger volume, the *sextarius*. The sequence of Latin and Welsh words is here difficult to parse, as to whether they are appositive translations or first hand syntagms. We would have been happier with a text like, *semper sex (.i. u)* (= *hint [huech pimp] ir]* *tri pimp in sextario (.i. in hestaur mel)*. We might have had an haplology or a leap from *hint* to *[ir]*. Or it might be simply a confusion with the preceding sentence, *tri pimp* creeping here again in the place of *huech pimp*. Williams (BBCS v.231), after Henry Lewis, argued for this second solution: a simple error with *tri* instead of *hueh*.

hestaur, is the Welsh borrowing from Lat. *sextarius*. Mid. E. *sester* has also been borrowed into Mid.W.

In the following sentence, the translation *ir petguar pimp* is a sufficient basis to read the preceding number (rather uncertain, one of the stroke being aligned with a stroke of the preceding line) as *.iiii. u*, not *.iii. u.*. Now *guorennieu* can be interpreted in two different ways: either a plural substantive preceded by the partitive prep. *há* (= Mid. and Mod. W *o*), or a subjunctive pres. 3 sg., preceded by the direct relative particle *ha*. This second solution is more attractive: the partitive prep. *a* is a Breton variant[1] (already by Old Breton times), and the plural ending is *-ou* in the next sentence (*hestoriou*). Amongst others, Jackson noticed how strange was this plural ending in such an archaic text.[2] The verbal use is known through the compound OBr. *doguorennam* gl. *perfundo* (Lux.). For the ending, cf. OBr. *digurbonneu*. This interpretation was first sketched by Zeuss, but all subsequent writers chose the first solution: a substantive meaning 'fractions'.[3]

---

1   There might seem to be some evidence of a 'Breton dialectal colour' in some parts of this batch of glosses. But when carefully examined, the possible Breton features turn to be just archaisms: *trean* instead of *treian / traian* (OBr. *troian, troean*); *hanther* for *hanner*; *guotig* instead of *guetig*, *hagit* instead of *hegit* are similar archaisms (through lack of vowel-infection). On the contrary, OW innovations are plenty: the *au-* diphthong (*hestaur, maut*), the article *ir*, the vowel reduction to *-i-* (*amcibret, diguormach*), the reduction of prep. **tu/*to* to *di-* (*di asse, di mesur*), and yod-epenthesis (*-uceint*). Characteristicly OW is the combination *gutan* (Mid. W. *odan*).

    A sign of an early date is the fact that the diphtong *-ui-* is still written *-oi-* : *hinnoid, hunnoid, hittoi* (probably the copula); in *coilam* we have the (later) *-oe-* diphtong, as in *hoit oidou*.

2   Jackson, LHEB, 370 n.

3   Loth, *Vocabulaire*, 145; Thurneysen, *RC* xi.203; Lewis, BBCS iii. 3; Williams, BBCS v.231, who even translates it as *unciae*.

The dossier for a substantive is certainly worth examining: we actually have a measure name on the stem *renn-*, (= *rand-* + vowel infection), both in Welsh *rhennaid* (quoted by Williams, BBCS, v.231; see also CA 384) and in Mid. Br. *renn*, a grain measure, Latinised *renda* (Redon Cartulary), with a derivative *rennat* (parallel to *rhennaid*), borrowed into French as *renée*.4 But the dossier lacks an important piece of evidence: there is no attested compound of *renn-* with the prefix **wo-*. Translate: 'it is thirty that he would pour, after the four fives in the pound of oil'.

The rest of the gloss refers to the next sentence of the main text, *centum [[pondo olei sextari lx., centum]] puntos mellis sextari .xl..* Here the main text has suffered from a severe lacuna, later filled by some scribe who might be the main glossator. Actually, we need not understand the Welsh words as one single sentence: there might be two distinct glosses, first *ir hestoriou oleu* (above *olei sextari lx.*), and then *is trimuceint hestaur mel* above *mellis sextari .xl.* As I have already argued (CMCS viii.37–42), *trimuceint* means 'sixty' (exactly, 'three twenties'), so that we can safely suppose this gloss to have been written on another type of text, that is, a text with another number, *mellis sextari lx..* This is precisely the text we find in Friedlein's edition, where 'hundred pounds of oil' and 'hundred pounds of honey' fill exactly the same number of *sextarii*, sixty. This would agree with what we already said about the pound or *libra*: at this point in the text it was meant to be a measure of capacity. In this occurrence, the OW gloss is referring to a better text than that which has been preserved in the manuscript and which has been restored by the corrector. A similar observation was made by Thurneysen.5

Here Williams (BBCS v.232) tried to defend the main text, arguing that hundred pounds of oil would fill sixty *sextarii*, whereas hundred pounds of honey would fill only forty. But these calculations cannot be accepted. Moreover, if the words of the main text have to be constructed into complete sentences, this is not necessary for the contents of the gloss.

The remaining Latin part of gloss 48 is exact, but for the very end: *quamuis si melle uas impleat, non tertia pars numeri sextariorum olei in mellis sextaris continetur.* In the *CMCS* article (CMCS viii.39–40) this sentence is divided wrongly. What would the implication of the negative *non*? That the number of *sextarii* of honey is less, or more than the third of the number of oil *sextarii*? Nothing

---

4   Cf. Ernault, *Glossaire*, 570; see also Loth, RC xli.400–403 (and xlii.372), quoting particularly haut-vannetais *renad* 'demi-pairée' (120 livres).

5   Thurneysen, RC xi.203–204.

comparable with 'a third of the oil-*sextarii*' is to be found in other glosses, except in one gloss edited by Friedlein (p. 74, n. 19): *MCC. similiter sunt, tunc tertia pars numeri sextariorum olei in mellis sextarium continetur.* Our glossator has probably attempted to contradict this gloss.

Note some linguistic archaisms: *trean*, later *traian* (*traean*); *guotig* with no indication of the internal *i*-infection, and spirant -*g*- still written.

Gloss 50: *ft*, with an abbreviation stroke: probably *fiunt* rather than *faciunt*.

Gloss 51 is written in continuity with the preceding gloss, but the meaning requires a different clause, with a different lemma: **hint c. punt**, 'they are a hundred pounds' with the copula 3 pl. *hint*, ought to gloss *centum pondo*. On the haplology in the main text, cf. the commentary to gloss 49.

Glosses 55 and 56 should present the same number, as in Friedlein (the right number is 960). The end of gloss 55 explains *cuiuslibet mercidis* of the main text (Friedlein has the same gloss).

Part 3 : De geometrica ratione

Gloss 57: read xuiii instead of xuiiii (cf. Friedlein). Eighteen scriples are the sum of *semiuncia* (12) plus *sicilicus* (6).

Gloss 58. *Digitus* is first defined as the third part of *uncia*. *Uncia* then is a length unit, as is clear from Isidore, *Etym.* XV 2 (. . . *uncia habens digitos tres*) (cf. English *inch*). Later, we find another equivalence: the measure of a thumb (or, the small finger), is three fourth of the ounce; this corresponds to the formula in the main text, *semiuncia* (1/2) + *sicilicus* (1/4). This refers to another definition of what is *uncia*. The following glosses will refer to two different *unciae*: *unciae pollicis* and *unciae digiti*. We have to content ourselves with this plain observation that different systems and different commentaries have been conflated in these glosses. It is important to bear in mind that we are dealing with the width of a thumb or of a finger, not their length.

The beginning of gloss 58 is rather obscure. Should we translate the succession of words as it stands, it would make no sense. *Digitus* is actually *tertia pars unciae*, but why is there *pollicis* after *unciae*? *Unciae pollicis* might refer to a particular unit, compare *uncia digiti* in gloss 60. Or, in a simpler explanation, *tertia pars unciae pollicis* is just a way of saying *tertia pars pollicis*.

The following OW words cannot be a translation of what preceeds since we now have to do with 'three-quarters of an ounce'. This is the width of a thumb: *mensura pollicis*. Then comes the OW for 'the small finger': is this an approximate translation of *pollex*? Or are we now dealing with still another unit?

amcibret is the 'total width', or 'total course': compound with *ambi- and *kom-, of a stem *s(t)r-(H)-to-, Lat. *stratus*, OIr. *sreth*. Cf. MBr. *queffret* 'together', W *cyffred* 'course; throw; society', Co. *cyffrys* 'as well as'. The compound *amgyffred* exists, as a verbal stem, in MW *amgyffredaf* 'I comprehend, understand'. The hesitation in spelling between *amcibret* and *amcibfret* recalls exactly that of the OBr. cognate *cobret / cofrit*, in the compounds *gucobret* ' (who) includes' / *dicofrit* 'sine cofrito' ('without community / without any division').

The word *guorfrit* could be another instance of the same stem. But it could as well have a spirantisation of -p- after *guor* (cf. *gorffenn* etc.). We could expect either a long or a short -i-. In the PN *Guorfrit* (Lib. Land. 215), we could suppose the word *pryd* 'form, beauty' (that is, 'excessive beauty'). The only other example of *gorffryd* in Welsh literature is Cynddelw's *kyghallenn dilenn orffenn orffryt* (CBT IV 17.34), translated into MnW '(Ein) hamddiffynwr [yng] ngwasgariad terfynol [ein] tranc', 'Our defender in the final conflict of our destruction'. But another possible meaning was indicated by Lloyd-Jones, *Geirfa* 568: 'gormod, tra mesur, rhagor, gweddill' (cf. OIr. *forcraid* 'excess, superfluity'). An alternative translation could then be 'power of destruction [through] the end of [any] superfluity'. In fact, Lloyd-Jones (*Geirfa* 568) compared OW. *guorfrit* to an OBr. gloss *gurprit[* on the Latin adj. *superstitiosa* (in the text of the *Canones Hibernenses*, in the Orléans ms.). This is not an abridged *gur-pritiri*, or *gur-brit*, as suggested by Loth and Stokes, but probably an abridged *gurprit[oc*, with an adjectival suffix to match the suffix of *superstitiosa*. 'Superstition' is the additional and superfluous belief, e.g. that of the Jews still adhering to older norms after Christ's revelation (*superstitia* is glossed with OIr. *for-banna*). The meaning, 'additional, superfluous'[6] would best suit the context : *uncia*, the ounce, is situated under the length of the long finger but above (*guorfrit* 'in excess') the 'number of this one' (referring to the already discussed thumb).

Our translation then is: 'The total width of the thumb up to the extreme point of the nail, this is what is the *unc* (= *uncia*), which is (one) fourth part above the number of this one (the normal thumb), (but) under the total width of the long finger, according to this'.

It would seem that there are two fingers and two thumbs: *digitus* is a third of

---

6   Or 'in addition', in 'excess': in my opinion, *guor frit* could be read as two words (prep + noun) or only one. I am not convinced that *guorfrit* belongs to the stem *ster-H-. It would rather include the already quoted *pryd*.

a thumb, itself the three fourth of an ounce. The OW sentence tries to give a realistic view of the ounce: it is a thumb width counted very generously, at the tip of the thumb, where it is the broadest. It is then superior by one fourth to the normal thumb. In the same way, a distinction occurs between small and long fingers: I suggest to read *ir bis hiri* (= *ir bis hir,*) instead of *hinn.*

Biheit hetham is probably to be understood as *bicheit heitham*; cf. Fleuriot and Evans, *Dictionary*, s. v. *bichit, bicit, becet* 'till' (prep. **kʷus,* = OIr. *co h-,* 'till, up to' + the equivalent of Mid. W. *cyhyd,* Mid. Br. *keid, *ko-situ-* 'as long as'). MBr. and Mn.Br. have *bete* 'till', a contraction of *bichet.*

   At the end of this gloss, *unciae pollicis xx et demedium unciae,* is probably a gloss on *cubitus,* here defined as *.i. treas pedes,* that is, 16 dig. + 16/3, approx. 21.33 (but *cubitus* is defined as *.i. quadras pedes* in Friedlein, that is, exactly 16 + 4 = 20 *digiti*).

Gloss 59: read *ad ungulos. Ungula* is a hoof.

Gloss 65 and text: *ictus* is for *actus.*

Gloss 67: **bos-cig** is a compound of *bos,* the noun for 'palm' (OIr. *bas*); the second element might be equivalent to *ceinc* 'branch' (compare a similar closing in the Mid.Br. derivative, *quinquis*); or to *cig* 'flesh'. See also *ceng* in gl. 70 below. It should be remarked that the reading could equally be *bosug* (= *bos-wnc* ?): It appears that *palma* is equivalent to the ounce as defined by Isidore: three *digiti.*

Gloss 70: 'From the elbow up to the muscle, as far as the juncture of the fist, this is *bes;* (but) if it is as far as the straight of the fore-arm, this is longer: 9 *unciae* (instead of 8)'. *Ceng,* 'straight', 'thin', probably related to *cyfyng,* cf. OIr. *cumang; cihitun / cihutun,* also attested in OW and OBr. charters (*cihitan* in Lib. Land. 122, *cohiton* in two Redon charters), is an expanded form of *cyhyd,* Br. *keit. Esceir,* as Br. *esker* (*div-esker*) normally refers to the shin; here it refers to the forearm. In *torr* we might have read the native word for 'belly'; cf. a Breton parallel used for 'the calf of the leg': *cof ar c'har.* But it seems more convenient to read *torr* as a borrowing from Lat. *torus* 'fore-arm'.

   At the end of the extract on Geometry: 'scinus siue parasanga', in a late hand, refers to (Egyptian) *schoenus,* and (Persian) *parasanga*; cf. Isidore, *Etym.* XV, 16.1.

Gloss 77: *Depondeus* and the price of sparrows.

   We are now presented with a discussion on the value of ancient coins, with exegetical implications. *Dupondius* originally means 'two pounds', but was currently used to refer to a special coin, worth two *asses* (Latin *as* is then considered as a money unit, not a weight measure). This was worth half a *sestertium*, and a quarter of a *denarius*. The exegetical problem arises from a clear discrepancy between the Gospels of Luke and of Matthew about a saying of Jesus: in Luke XII.6 he says, *Nonne quinque passeres ueneunt dipondio, et unus ex illis non est in obliuione coram Deo?* 'are not five sparrows sold for a *dupondius* (two *asses*), and (nevertheless) no one of them is forgotten before God', and in Matthew X.29, *Nonne duo passeres asse ueneunt, et unus ex illis non cadet super terram sine Patre uestro?*, 'are not two sparrows sold for one *as*, and (nevertheless) no one of them will fall on the ground without (the consent of) your Father'.

Modern writers have insisted on the fact that sparrows, used as sacrificial victims by the Jews, were certainly the cheapest animals available for that purpose.[7] Others have tried to take the two different prices at their face value: supposing that the two evangelists did not write at the same time, there might have occurred an inflation of prices, linked to a devaluation of the *as*, between the time of Mathew and that of Luke. Actually, a sparrow is worth half an *as* according to Mathew's Gospel, but two fifth of an *as* according to Luke: prices have increased by a tenth between Luke and Mathew (in this (abstract) chronological order, which is not the true order of succession)[8].

Many historians drew attention to the price of sparrows given in the Diocletian edict: the devaluation led to sell 10 sparrows for 16 copper denarii, which would put one sparrow at the price of 6.4 *dupondii* or 12.8 *asses*.

Early commentators were more concerned with theological interpretations. Ambrosius simply gives a symbolic meaning to these numbers: the two sparrows are the two constituents of a human being, soul and body; the five coins are the five senses. Such developments reoccur in Jerome's writings. On the discrepancy of prices, Ambrosius only remarks *alibi asse ueneunt, alibi dupondio, quanta uilitas delictorum! mors enim uilis, sed pretiosa uirtus.*

Here we are fortunate enough to be able to quote two Hiberno-Latin witnesses: first, what has been called, since Bischoff's leading study on Hiberno-Latin biblical exegesis, 'Das Bibelwerk', an enormous exegetical compilation, and secondly, a gloss in the Harleian Gospels.

---

7   See, for example, Deissmann, *Licht vom Osten.*

8   Specific studies on this particular subject: Findlay, *The Expositor* vii (considers Luke's version as more exact). Stolz, *Verbum Domini* xiv. M. J. Lagrange, *Evangile selon saint Luc* (Paris, 1921), 353–4 refers to peculiar explanations by Harnack (the falling of sparrows price) or Godet (the Evangelists consciously introduced this kind of discrepancies. . .).

1. *Das Bibelwerk*: we used the text of ms. Paris BN Lat. 11561, f° 153rv. We have tried to distinguish the different components and to trace them to their respective sources:

a. *Nonne duo passeres asse ueneunt. Hieronimus dicit. si parua animalia et quae non uiuunt post mortem non pereunt sine D(e)i prouidentia et uoluntate, quanto magis qui aeterni [estis]. uos non debetis timere quod sine D(e)i uiuentis prouidentia mala sustinere (. . .)*
(cf. Bede, *In Matthaei Euangelium Expositio*, PL 92 col. 55; *In Lucae Euangelium Expositio*, PL 92, col. 488)

b. *Item. duo passeres corpus et anima, quinque uero secundum Lucam, id est quinque sensus corporis significat. . .*
(cf. again on fo 167vb ; cf. Ambrosius PL 14/15, col. 1726–29; other Hiberno-Latin commentaries refer to this explanation: see an anonymous Commentary on Luke, Joseph F. Kelly, *Scriptores Hiberniae Minores*, CCL 108 C, Turnhout 1974, on Luke XII.6; and Sedulius Scottus himself; cf. Bengt Löfstedt, *Sedulius Scottus, Kommentar zum Evangelium nach Matthäus* (2 vol., Freiburg, 1980, 1991), I.298–299).

c. *Item nonne duo passeres. Heret nolite timere.*
(*baeret*[9] commonly used in Hiberno-Latin commentaries to refer to the preceding context, 'it sticks to. . .'; cf. OIr. *toglenamon.*)

d. *Station in Greco, passer in Latino. sed non idem sunt quia illi magni, isti parui.*
(read στρουθίον, 'sparrow', or possibly στρουθίων, which gave Lat. *strutio*, whence 'ostrich'; στρουθός had the two meanings; the big species referred to is certainly the *strutiones*, ostriches).

e. *Asis Grece, quadras in Latino. Quadrans enim dicitur .iiii. pars nummi id est viii^a pars denarii quod hic conuenit. iii asis sunt: minimus quarta pars denarii, medius .viii. de/narii, maior .xii. uncias.*

f. *Item secundum Lucam, Nonne quinque passeres depondio ueniunt. Dipondio nomen mensure .xx. denarios. Sic concordant Matheus et Lucas, ut assis secundum Matheum, viii. denarios.*

g. *Alii dicunt sicut minimus assis de argento passer conparatur, si uero medius assis de aere, si maior de pane ueniunt. Id est in uenundationem.*

(e), (f), and (g) agree in supposing two (f) or three (e-g) different asses. But, by mistake, *uiii. denarii* (= *octaua pars denarii*) is reinterpreted as *uiii denarios* in (f), and possibly already in (e), where *uiii. denarii* is presented as bigger than

---

9 Abridged 'hêt', an abbreviation often wrongly developed into 'habet'. For an example of misinterpretation see *Bethu Phátraic*, line 670, where (ms.) *beret* becomes 'habentur et'. See De Bruyne, *Palaeographia latina* v.48–49, and vi.67–68.

quarta pars denarii. Unless we take *maior* 'bigger' as referring to the size of the coin, as indicated in (g). The values indicated in (f), *.xx. denarios, .viii. denarios*, would be acceptable by Diocletian's time. But the idea itself that *denarius* would be a subdivision of the pound cannot have occurred to any mind before the creation of the Carolingian pound, valued twelve (instead of ten) *denarii*. Finally, (g) supposes three *asses* of different value according to the metal, *de argento / de aere / de pane* (read *de stanno* or *de raudo?*).

(a), (b), (c) and (e) reoccur (in another order) in one of the sources of this Bibelwerk: the *Liber Quaestionum in Evangelios*, cf., for example, MS. Orléans 65 (62) p. 127, on "Canon V: Mt XCIII/Lc CXLV". We should also refer to a passage of *Breues euangeliorum glossae secundum canones*, Vienna, Vindobon. Palatinus Latinus 940 (f. 76v) on the extent of divine providence.

2. In the Harleian Gospel (London, BL Harleian 1802, f. 28a), we have the following gloss on the text of Mathew[10]:

nonne duo passeres asse ueniunt (*.i.* **renaiter** 'they are sold') (top marg.) *quomodo congruit hoc quod dicit Lucas, nonne .u. passeres dupondio ueniunt, id est .u. passeres pro dupondio. cuius magnitudinis est dupondius ? idem est et duo silli, sillus autem est unus scriptulus et quarta pars scriptuli.* **inna da sill is da scripul co leth** ('The two *silli* are 2.5 scruples') *et sic conuenit quod dixit Lucas dupondium .i.* **coic lethscripuil .h. ar coic eonu** ('five half scruples, then [h. = autem: read *dano, didiu*], for five birds'), *.ii. uero minuta dicit Marcus* (xii.42) *quia .iii. scriptuli in minuto, .ui. in duobus minuti(s) sunt.*

This commentary introduces new (small) units, the *sillus*, worth half a *dupondius*, or two scriples and a half, (is it the Hebrew *siclus?*) and the *minutum*, mentioned as the smallest coin in Luke XII.59, here exemplified with Mark XII.42, where *duo minuta* are said to be equivalent to one *quadrans*. The value of *dupondius*, 'two scriples and a half' is the same as in our gloss 77, both in the Latin part (*depondeus .i. duo scripuli et semis*) and in the Welsh part:

The Welsh part of gloss 77 reads as follows:

dou punt = a paraphrase for *dupondius*, 'two pounds', followed in apposition by **petguar hanther scribl** 'four half-scruples'; this equivalence agrees with what has just been said in the Latin part of the gloss concerning Mathew: two sparrows are worth one *as* (or *scripulus*), each *as* or *scripulus* is divided in two obols; *petguar hanther scribl* would be equivalent to four obols.

---

10   The gloss was edited by Stokes, RC viii.367–368.

As is well known, the Welsh borrowing from Lat. *scripulus*, *yscribl* (with the reflex of long *-i-*), came to mean 'cattle' exactly as Bret. *saout* 'cattle' comes from the Lat. coin name *sol(i)dus* > OBr. *solt*.[11]

prinit hinnoid *.iiii. aues*, 'this (a demonstrative referring to *dou punt*) buys (or can buy, will buy) four birds'.

All the following sentences are built in the same way, with a *nominatiuus pendens* followed by a complete sentence, where the pronoun in coreference with the *nominatiuus pendens* is a demonstrative:

et .u. qui adicit Lucam **ní choilám hinnoid** : probably to be corrected into *et quintum quem adicit Lucas*, with a confusion of case. 'And the fifth which Luke adds, I cannot understand this one'.

amser is cihun argant agit eterin *illud*: 'since this bird is worth (literally 'goes for') as much money / the same amount of money'. This subordinate clause depends on the preceding clause. The verbs *agit* and *prinit*, are absolute forms of the 3sg. indicative present, from the stems *ag-* 'to go' and *pryn(a)-* 'to buy'. A form with the yod-infection occurs in the next sentence (but Mid. and Mod. W. *a* 'goes', Br. *(y)a*, are the modern reflexes of a form without infection).

ir pimphet eterin diguormechis Lucas, begit hunnoid in pretium benedictionis boid boitou hou bein atar ha beinn cihunn **reliqua** 'The fifth bird which Luke added, this one goes 'for the price of a blessing' for ages of ages, if they were birds that were the same value etc.' Here again, a *nominatiuus pendens*, in coreference with a demonstrative in the core of the sentence.

Eterin is now *aderyn*, a singulative of *adar* 'birds'. **Diguormechis**, with *i*-infection, is an *s*-preterit 3 sg. on the stem *diguormach-* 'to add', a stem used in OBr. in relation with the name of the 'adjective', *diguormach* gl. adiectionem, *doguormaheticion* gl. adiectis, gl. adiectiua (all found in the Priscian Paris BN Lat. 10290).

In pretium benedictionis: it comes as the price of a blessing, it is given for a blessing. Any exchange would involve not only a payment for merchandise or a service, but also a sort of 'tip', something graciously added to what is due, just for pleasing the merchant or the craftman. We could just call it 'gratifica-

---

11   Cf. valuable studies by Loth, *Revue de l'Histoire des Religions*, xxxiii.371 and Vendryes, RC xlii.393.

tion', in its etymological meaning: making someone thankful. And *in pretium benedictionis* could just be translated 'for the price of a thank you', since a blessing is exactly what Breton used to mention when saying 'thank you': *bennoz Doue!* But 'thank you' is perhaps a too pedestrian translation. What is wanted here is a real blessing; the customer might fear the merchandise bought or the arrangement obtained could have been 'cursed' by the partner.

Paul Russell has drawn my attention to something similar in the Old Irish legal tract *Cóic Conairi Fuigill* 'The Three Paths of Procedure', in reference with *duil-chinne* (§89): '*duilcinne gacha aice,* full payment for every manufactured object, means a certain object (*duil*) which must be given for every tool or object: *duilchinne* is a tenth of (the value) of every product, and it is given in food and drink. And this is equally consumed by the good and the bad craftman, because they are equally able to deliver a blessing. And (*dúilchinne*) must be paid after the full payment of the tool price. And if (the buyers) do not give any *dúilchinne*, there is no fine for them, but the partners (litt. the other part), will not deliver their blessing on the tool as long as the *dúilchinne* is not paid to them'.[12] As Thurneysen observed, a fine could punish the refusal of a blessing.

hoid oitou, without a preposition, is certainly an equivalent of *in saecula saeculorum*, what is now expressed by Mod.W. *yn oes oesau*. The graphic difference between *hoid* and *oit-* might point to a real lexical variation, between *hoidl* (mod. *hoedl,* Mid. Br. *hoazl,* *saitlo-*) and *oit* (mod. *oed,* Br. *oad*). The absence of a preposition is not uncommon for a temporal complement (particularly for a certain length of time).

bein, beinn are certainly the 3pl. *beint,* the verb 'to be' in the past subjunctive (3sg. *bei*). *Hou* is an OW. graph for the prep. *o* used as a subordinating particle. *Ha* is a late graph for the direct relative particle *hai* (probably connected with Gaul. *sosio*).

End of the gloss: *Matheus uero* **dou eterinn cant hunnoid di assa .i. asse bichan** *unus scripulus est* 'Mathew, however, this one has two birds for an *asse*: a small *asse* is equivalent to one scriple'. This is just a paraphrase. *Di* could be either the prep. Mid. W. *y* 'for', or (less probably) the prep. corresponding to Br. *di,* 'from'. This small *asse* can be interpreted as a reference to the coin, as opposed to the weight measure. On the devaluation of the bronze *as,* cf.

---

12 See *Cóic conara fugill,* text §89 p. 48–49, and note 44 p. 72 ('Die Verfertiger des Gerätes müssen ihren Segen über es sprechen, damit es nicht schaden kann (*AL* I 132.5)).

Williams, BBCS v.235. Note that *partire* is a deponent imper. 2 sg. and translate the last sentence: "divide (it), and it makes two halves and the price for two birds".

Gloss 80 has a letter *o* intended as a correction above the *-e-* of *gomer*, which is consequently to be read *gomor*. The end of the gloss, *.c. unciae*, is probably displaced, see below.

Gloss 85: correct *grecia* to *greca* (the adjective). The Welsh passage begins, seemingly, with the last word of the sentence *desunt .iiii. unciae de sé*. *Sé* is certainly a demonstrative particle, here employed as a pronoun. It has been kept in Breton. *de se* means 'from this' (Latin prep. *de* + OW *se*). It would also be possible to read this syntagm as the beginning of the following sentence. *Si*, in *erguid si*, gloss 58, is probably a variant of the same particle.

ni choilam, as in gloss 77: 'I do not understand'.

immit-cel ir nimer bichan gutan ir maur nimer, 'the small number is hiding under the big number'. The glossator is trying to make out the value in ounces indicated by the phrase *quadrisextium et himmina et semis*: this amounts to 96 ounces, 4 ounces too short to reach the value indicated for *gomor* in gloss 80: 100 ounces. How he came to consider this as a *gomor*, is still unclear to me (see point 3 below). A few points of certainty may be established:

1. Obviously the definition of *gomor* is variable: we have seen above that it was equivalent to *sex modii*, or 1920 ounces (gloss 81); Isidore, on the other hand, considers it weights as much as sixteen *modii*.

2. In gloss 80, 100 ounces is certainly displaced from *sestertium* (*.u. sextarii*): five *sextarii* would exactly make 5 x 20 = 100 ounces. This dislocation of a gloss might be the source of the glossator's error, when he considers 100 ounces to make a *gomor*.

3. Anyway, to remain in agreement with the main text, the glossator should not have considered *gomor* (= *vi. modii*) as equivalent to *decima pars effi*, but rather *effi* (= three *modii*) as equivalent to *demedia pars gomor*. It is clear that *effi*, or 960 ounces, is ten times 96 ounces, not 100.

The archaism of *immit-cel* lies in the infixation of a particle *-it*, seemingly similar to what is suffixed to the verb in the absolute *agit / hegit*, or in the relative (indirect) *isit*. The common relative form of the copula, *yssydd* (< *esti-yo-*) would have been written in Old Welsh as *issid*. The use of *-t* in *isit* might refer to a different suffix, parallel to the verbal particle *yt*, and to the suffix of the absolute forms in the 3 sg. It seems possible here to distinguish three places for this *-it*:

1. before the simple posttonic copula, *itt-oi*.

2. after the simple conjugated verb in the 3 sg., *agit*, *hegit*.

3. infixed after the first preverb in the compound, *immit-cel*.

Diguormechis exhibits no particle, however (curiously enough, Gaulish *deuorbuetid* (Lezoux), with the same preverbs, seems to be resistant to infixation).

It is possible that this *itt/it* is a particle related to Gaul. *-utu*, *-uton*, *-utan*, (Larzac) suffixed to verbal forms; and to Old Irish *-d-*, characterizing the class C of infixed pronouns; and that from the first use described above, *itt* developed into a verbal particle (Mid. W. *yd*, Br. *ez*). Consequently, we can justify the use of 'absolute forms' as apodotic, or completive verbal forms: *hegit* comes after a *nominativus pendens*, *agit* comes after a complement focalised with the copula (and *agit* being intransitive, the complement cannot be considered as a direct object). On the contrary, *diguormechis* is preceded by a direct object: the relation is a direct one, and was expressed just by lenition (here falling on the *m-* of *mechis?*). The implication of all this is that the so-called 'absolute' forms are not independent verbs in this collection of glosses, but rather dependent verbs, and *immit-cel* is probably marked as the object of *ní choilam* 'I do not understand that . . . it hides itself': *immit-cel* = Mid. W. *yd ymgel*, with the reflexive prefix *imm-*. It would be interesting to extend this line of research; even in the Llywarch Hen englynion, the absolute form is not always at the beginning of a clause: *tonn tyruit* (CLlH 4.20), *deil cwydit* (CLlH 24.13).

Gloss 90: *quadrisextium* should obviously be explained as equivalent to four *sextarii*, not three.

I shall leave the remaining glosses without commentary.

This small piece of *diguonimereticaeth* (the OBr. word for 'arithmetic') gives some place to *cemaruuidtit* (the Old Breton word for '*peritia*, competence, science'), but is overloaded with *hencassou* (the Old Welsh word for 'traditions'). It remains far from clear that a more scientific approach to the text of *Calculus Victorii*, relying on more manuscripts, will really clarify the situation; our main concern has been the Old Welsh glosses and we have tried to understand the errors of our Welsh glossator, rather than to emend the text of Victorius. This is not the final edition of these glosses. There remain many uncertainties here and there which, I hope, will appeal to other commentators. What should be emphasised in this conclusion is the boldness of our Celtic glossators, ready to use their own mother tongue for scientific purposes. True, the Welsh glossator uses preferably his own language to express his doubts: was he afraid to be understood by too large an audience? I would prefer to think that, when his mind is reaching a higher level of reflection, when he is resisting a Latin scholastic teaching, when he is refusing slavishly to copy a wrong model, then he unconsciously returns to his own language. He has tried to understand what he was copying, and this intellectual tension has naturally been expressed in the most familiar language.

Are there elements of non-standard language in the work of the *Gogynfeirdd*?

Peter Busse

WELSH medieval poetry has generally been considered to be a quite monolithic entity, at least at a more superficial level. While ignoring the late attestation of the Cynfeirdd and the hiatus between the tenth and twelfth century, scholars like the late J. E. Caerwyn Williams and others,[1] drew a direct line from the *Cynfeirdd* to the *Cywyddwyr*. More recent research has shown the situation to be more complicated.[2] The style of these poets, namely the *Gogynfeirdd*, was considered to be very difficult and esoteric, and its language to be incomprehensible and elaborate.[3] If one looks closer, a more complex picture emerges. The *Gogynfeirdd*, mainly in the early period, the twelfth century, did indeed refer to their predecessors, but their tradition left them enough scope for innovation and stylistic experiment. This does not only concern formal criteria of the poems, but also concerns the language the poets use. Interestingly, on the one hand, one finds in their corpus many examples for forms of 'non-standard' language, that is elements, which hint at the spoken language of the time as well as dialectal variants to the standard used by the Gogynfeirdd. On the other hand, many archaisms tend to be used in the texts. The term 'non-standard' thus involves not only 'low register'-forms, dialectal forms but also attempts to adopt a high literary style

---

1   G. Williams, *Introduction*; Williams, BWP; J. E. C. Williams, *The Poets of the Welsh Princes*; *The Court Poet*.
2   E.g. CBT III, 55–7.
3   J. E. C. Williams, *The Poets of the Welsh Princes*, 64 ff.

oriented at the language mostly of the *Gododdin*. All of these differ from what could be called 'classical' Middle Welsh as it is found in the Four Branches of the Mabinogi. The intention of this study is to consider the relationship between language use and the formal paraphernalia of Gogynfeirdd poetry in order to try and establish whether there were any rules by which they were operating.

Which linguistic criteria can be identified as belonging to a lower register?

Colloquial elements in Middle Welsh literary language are

a) affixed personal subject pronouns with the finite verb and conjugated prepositions.[4]

b) the use of *bod* and *taw* for expressing subordinate clauses.

Dialectal elements are

a) the presence or absence of stem-forming <y> in verbal nouns and plurals e.g. NW *peidyaw* vs. *peidaw*

b) the stem-forming <th> /ð/ vs. <t> /t/ in the 3. Sg. of the conj. prepositions *gan* and *rhwng*: NW *ganthaw* vs. SW *gantaw*

c) the use of the 3 sg. pret. in *-wys* vs. *-awd*.[5]

These elements are considered by Thomas as shibboleths of Middle Welsh dialects whereas an increased use of <th>, <y> and *-awd* are judged as North Walian dialectal features. Further dialectal elements could be the use of the abnormal sentence.

Reading the *Gogynfeirdd* one can easily identify a relationship between types of lyric, metrical and linguistic form. According to Rhiain Andrews six different types can be distinguished: *mawl* (eulogy), *marwnad* (elegy), *cerddi crefyddol* (religious poems), *bygwth/dadolwch*, *cerddi i ferched* (love poems, "amour courtois") and others (e.g. *gorhoffedd* etc.)[6]. Each of these types seems to have its characteristic form and the language use seems to depend on the context and the sub-type. The range of subjects and topics is far more elaborate than in the case of the *Cynfeirdd*. Gwyn Williams has considered even the simple fact of writing love-poetry to be remarkable and innovative: 'Like Gwalchmei he (sc. Cynddelw)

---

4   Evans GMW 57; Andrews BBCS xxxvi.
5   Thomas, 'In Search of Middle Welsh Dialects', 292
6   Andrews BBCS xxxvi.16

broke away from the epic severity of conventional poetry to write in praise of a woman.'7.

The examination of formal criteria shows that eulogies tend to be written in *awdl*-metres such as *cyhydedd naw ban, toddaid* etc.[8] In contrast, elegies are more often written in *englynion*. There seem even to have been traces of different regional 'schools' of composition.[9] This might be illustrated with the poems which the young Cynddelw wrote in Powys on his patron Madog ap Maredudd and the poems he wrote in Gwynedd on Owain Gwynedd which are different in style and in language. The language used in Powys is less elaborate, less sophisticated and more comprehensible[10].

As for the linguistic criteria of the Gogynfeirdd, their language is characterized by a tendency towards grammatical archaism. This may have been a way of 'showing off', i.e. the poet appears to be trying to impress the audience with obsolete, complicated forms. Note for example Cynddelw's use of the obsolete impersonal forms in *-ator, -itor* etc. *gwelhator, clywitor* etc. in *Arwyrain Owain Gwynedd* 2[11].

Old absolute endings are used:

Torressid gormes yn llyghessaбc '**He destroyed** the sea-born invaders. or: **He destroyed** the enemy (who was) a seafarer' (Meilyr Brydydd, *Marwnad Gruffudd ap Cynan*, l. 80 (CBT I, 3))[12]

Occasionally the old future in *-awt /-awd/* can be found:

*Cathyl cywystraud, kyvan volaud, **cluttaud** attad* 'an adorned song, a complete praise **he will bring** to you' (anonymous, *c.* 1100, *Mawl Cuhedyn Fardd*, l. 7 (CBT I, 2)).

Archaic verbal forms like *yssym* ('is for me') are also used by the Gogynfeirdd:

Yssym ut aryfrut, kystut kedyrn '**He is for me** a lord with blood-red arms troubling the mighty' (Einion ap Gwalchmai, *Mawl Llywelyn ap Iorwerth*, 1 (CBT I, 25)

---

7   G. Williams, *Introduction*, 79
8   G. Williams, *Introduction*, Appendix 1
9   Busse, *Cynddelw Brydydd Mawr*, 31–34.
10   Cf. *Arwyrain Madog ap Maredudd* (CBT III, 1–8) with *Arwyrain Owain Gwynnedd* 1–3 (CBT IV, 1–43)
11   CBT IV, 20.20, 27
12   Cf. also J. E. C. Williams, *Gruffudd ap Cynan*, 179, 184 (different translation: 'with his fleet he quashed the enemy').

Very often constructions with infixed pronouns are used:

A'th yolwyf, ry-m-purwyf kyn no'm poeni 'I shall praise thee, I should purify **myself** before my wounding' (Meilyr Brydydd, *Marwysgafn Meilyr*, l. 18 (CBT I, 4))

In nominal composition the work of the Gogynfeirdd is characterized by an enormous range of new formations—a substantial part of Welsh vocabulary is first attested in the twelfth and thirteenth centuries. Poets try to surpass their rivals in creating more elaborate and imaginative compounds, as evidenced by a pronounced nominal style; both elements combined with the metrical need for alliteration, make the texts obscure and sometimes incomprehensible. Compare the passage in *Breudwyt Ronabwy* on the poet Kadyriaith:

Ac ar hynny nachaf ueird yn dyuot y datkanv kerd y Arthur. Ac nyt oed dyn a adnapei y gerd honno, namyn Kadyrieith ehun, eithyr y uot yn uolyant y Arthur. 'And thereupon, lo, bards coming to chant a song to Arthur. But never a man was there might understand that song save Cadyrieith himself, except that it was in praise of Arthur.' (BrRh 20, Transl. Jones/Jones)

A remarkable feature in the work of the *Gogynfeirdd* which seems to contradict the characteristics mentioned above is the frequency of affixed subject pronouns after verbs and conjugated prepositions. Their use, even in Modern Welsh, is considered to be colloquial style. I quote from a modern Welsh novel:

Stampiodd *ei ffordd at y llwyfan. . . 'Gwarthus! Cywiluddus!'* **gwaeddodd** *yn sydyn.* '**He stomped** his way to the stage. . . 'Disgraceful! Shameful!' **he shouted** suddenly.'[13]

This is an illustration that even in contemporary written language insertion of the personal pronoun is not obligatory, but its omission is considered to be superior style. In the corpus of the Cynfeirdd these are similarly very rare. Several examples are to be found in Canu Llywarch Hen. One example from the elegy on Maen (CLlH IV 4b) will suffice here:

oedwn i *dywal galanas* 'I was fierce in slaughter'

In the works of the *Gogynfeirdd* verbs, conjugated prepositions and constructions with infixed pronouns are frequently found, which support a suffixed pronoun as well, although the syntax does not require them:

---

13   M. Williams, *Diawl y Wenallt*, 2, ll. 17–20.

*Pan **gaffwyf-y** gan glein glan gyfloga6d.* 'If I got from the Saints a holy abode'
(Meilyr Brydydd, *Marwnad Gruffudd ap Cynan*, l. 7 (CBT I, 3))[14]

*Tr6m **arnaf-y** eu lletkynt* 'Heavy on me (is) their sadness' (Llywelyn Fardd I,
Marwnad Cedifor ap Genillyn, l. 30 (CBT II, 4)

*Rex radeu urno, **ry-n-bo-ny** garda6d* 'King of high blessings, let mercy be with us'
(Meilyr Brydydd, *Marwnad Gruffudd ap Cynan*, ll.71, 3 (CBT I, 3))[15]

In spite of Simon Evans's assertion that 'these forms are used as auxiliaries,
and from an early period appear to have been more commonly employed in the
spoken than in the literary language.' (GMW 57), many Welsh philologists have
tried to explain this as being due to metrical considerations. In this context
Rhiain Andrews's observations on suffixed pronouns may be cited:

> Yn ystod y ganrif hon y mae golygyddion canu'r Gogynfeird (a'r Cynfeirdd)
> wedi tueddi gweld y rhagenwau ôl yn elfennau i'w gollwng neu eu cadw ar sail y
> nyfer o sillafau sydd yn y llinell, fel pe bai'r rhagenwau yn dyfiant damweiniol.
> Os bydd deg sillaf mewn llinell o gyhydedd naw ban ac un o'r rheini yn
> rhagenwau ôl, awgrymir yn fynych hepgor y rhagenw er mwyn adfer y llinell i'w
> 'phurdeb' naw-sillafog.'[16]

She further identifies the texts in which the pronouns occur and outlines their
distribution among the different metres as follows:

englyn	95 poems	16 (17%[17])
cyhydedd nawban, toddaid, cyhydedd hir	61	38 (62%)
mesur un cyfuno 3 a 4 curiad	40	21 (52 %)
cyhydedd fer, toddaid byr, traeanog	32	15 (47 %)
rhupunt	5	3 (60 %)
arall	2	—[18]

---

14   Cf. also J. E. C. Williams, *Gruffudd ap Cynan*, 176, 183.

15   Cf. also J. E. C. Williams, *Gruffudd ap Cynan*, 176, 182.

16   Andrews, BBCS xxxvi.13–29 (at p. 13): During this century the editors of the poems of
the Gogynfeirdd (and the Cynfeirdd) have tended to see the affixed pronouns as
elements to be deleted or kept according to the number of syllables which are in a line,
as if the pronouns were something occuring accidentally. When there are ten syllables
in a line of *cyhydedd naw ban* and one is an affixed pronoun it was frequently suggested to
leave out the pronoun in order to restore its nine-syllable 'purity'.

17   The percentage denotes the percentage of poems containing affixed pronouns.

18   Andrews BBCS xxxvi.15

Furthermore she examines the distribution of suffixed pronouns in different types of poems:

mawl	89	20 (23%)
marwnad	70	23 (32%)
crefyddol	32	23 (72%)
bygwth/dadolwch	12	7 (58 %)
i ferch	10	8 (80 %)
arall	22	12 (55 %)[19]

From this survey it emerges that the more formal the context, the less often suffixed pronouns are used. In texts where a closer link with the spoken language may be presumed such as in love poems, satires and nature poems (e.g. *gorhoffeddau*) and also in religious poetry the percentage of affixed personal pronouns is much higher. This seems to have something to do with the fact that many (not all) religious poems seem to belong to a 'lesser' category than *moliadau* or *mawnadau*. But even in religious poems differences in the register can be observed. If *Canu Tysilio Sant* (CBT III, 3) and *Canu i Dduw* (CBT IV, 16) by Cynddelw are compared with *Canu i Dduw* (CBT IV, 17) by the same poet, more elaborate compounds, Latin loanwords and fewer affixed pronouns are found in the former and less elaborate vocabulary and more affixed pronouns in the latter.[20]

As for the usage of affixed personal pronouns, the pronoun of the 1 sg is by far the most frequent: it is used after the finite verb, conjugated prepositions and constructions with infixed pronouns, but also with archaic forms like *ysym*:

*Ac **yssym-i** Duw a diwykwyf—o'm drwc* 'And God it is for me who reward for my misery.' (Gwalchmai ap Meilyr, *Awdl i Dduw*, 63 (CBT I, 14))

The second most common is the 2 sg pronoun after the imperative and in questions:

*Beth a **dewi di**, dec y gostec?* (Hywel ap Owain Gwynedd, *Awdl i ferch*, l. 10 (CBT II, 8))

Less frequent are the 1 pl pronoun after infixed pronouns and the 2 pl pronoun in questions.

The forms mentioned above must be analysed according to their metrical context. That is to say, one has to examine whether the metre allows emendation. For example, *Rhieingerdd Efa ferch Madog* by Cynddelw Brydydd Mawr

---

19   Andrews BBCS xxxvi.16
20   P. Busse, *Cynddelw Brydydd Mawr*, 65–69 (Affixed pronouns), 70–92 (Compounds).

(CBT III, 5) contains a large number of affixed personal pronouns such as *tremyn y treitồn-y* (1. 11), *pan dreiteis-y* (1. 13), *llawen y carwn-y* (1. 17), *cany wney-di* (1. 32), etc. If one counts the syllables of every line a certain irregularity emerges. A *cyhydedd naw ban* should self-evidently contain nine syllables. However, it frequently contains eight to ten syllables. More importantly, these irregularities do not only occur in lines which contain suffixed personal pronouns: for example,

A dywed yno eniwed—ohanaf (1. 51) (11 syllables)

Petestric yolit pa hyd y'th yolir (1. 134) (10 syllables).

When various copies of this poem are compared, it emerges that the earlier manuscripts contain the pronouns, while later ones do not. One problem confronting us is the fact that a particular suffixed pronoun is rarely attested in the corresponding place in the two earliest manucsripts of the poem, Llawysgrif Hendregadredd and the Red Book of Hergest. A comparison of the poem's syntax with Cynddelw's praise-poetry shows that it is much easier and more transparent than his four praise poems to Owain Gwynedd. The context of the poem has to be taken into consideration as well. It shows continental, mainly French or Provençal influences, and its context is a rather non-formal one. Ceri M. Lewis suggested, that it might have been written by Cynddelw in his function as *bardd teulu* and not as a *pencerdd*.[21] By comparing these examples with direct speech in MW prose texts (e.g. Pwyll), one can see that these forms are used in spoken language—the prose itself does not contain them.[22] This phenomenon can still be observed.[23]

   Suffixed pronouns are statistically more frequent in the twelfth century as for example in the works of Meilyr Brydydd, Hywel ab Owain Gwynedd, Cynddelw in his less formal poems. In the later poems they are not used anymore. Moreover, in the early texts they are used mainly in non-formal poems, i.e. love-poems, *gorhoffeddau* etc. In contrast, praise-poetry and elegies rarely contain them, and where they do, they can be frequently emended by reference to the metre.

   Other elements of colloquial language can be found. Two poets, Llywelyn Fardd I and Hywel ab Owain Gwynedd use the stem *gant- /ganồ/-* instead of *ganth- /ganð/-* with the conj. preposition *gan*:

Duồ gantut eu but parth ac atann (Llywelyn Fardd I, *Canu Cadfan*, 1. 168 (CBT II, 1))

---

21   *A Guide to Welsh Literature* I, 138 f.
22   Cf. the passage from *Pwyll* quoted by Andrews BBCS xxxvi.27
23   Cf. the example quoted from M. Williams.

Hoet yrddi, a mi genti yn gas. (Hywel ab Owain Gwynedd, *Awdl i ferch*, l. 8 (CBT II, 11))

This can be considered as a dialectal feature, an assertion which seems to be supported by the fact that Llywelyn Fardd I was closely associated with Merionethshire, where this feature occurs (as Dr Ann Parry Owen has pointed out to me). Moreover it would be surprising if Hywel ab Owain Gwynedd as a nonprofessional poet did not enjoy the liberty of using 'lesser' forms.

Another element of colloquial language or of dialect seems to be the use of the 3 sg preterite in *-awd*. Its usage seems to suggest a hint of the language of Medieval Wales. The work of P. W. Thomas, Awbery et al., as well as that of Ingo Mittendorf, Simon Rodway,[24] Stefan Schumacher and my own M.A. thesis would suggest that the 3 Sg pret. in *-awd* which spreads rapidly, first in MW prose, later in poetry as well, seems to be a north-western dialectal feature which spreads to the dialects of the NE and SW. In SE dialects we still find *-ws*, the old *s*-preterite.

The work of the Gogynfeirdd shows a highly conservative use of *s*-preterites; *-awd*-preterites are very rarely found. They occur in love poetry as exemplified by the line

*Ny mad **gyrchawd** gỽenn gỽely Eidic* (Cynddelw, *Awdl i ferch anhysbys*, 8 (CBT III, 4))

and other poems of stronger emotional character like *Marwnad Llywelyn ap Gruffudd* by Gruffudd ab yr Ynad Goch (CBT VII, 36) where we find the line

***Gwascarawd** alaf, gỽisgaỽd bop gaeaf* (Gruffudd ap yr Ynad Goch, *Marwnad Llywelyn ap Gruffudd*, 12).

In religious poetry they are also comparatively frequent, as for example in

*Mat **gyrchaỽd** garchar alltuded* (Cynddelw, *Canu Tysilio Sant*, 21 (CBT III, 3)).

The use seems to be permitted by the context, and supported by the rhyme-scheme.

Stem-forming <*y*> with verbal nouns and plurals is regularly used. Exceptions have not yet been identified.

The use of affixed personal pronouns may be related to the use of dialectal features as well as alternating stems of conjugated prepositions and verbal forms. The more personal the context, the more frequent are postponed pronouns and

---

24   Rodway, CMCS xxxvi; Mittendorf, *Akten des 2. deutschen Keltologensymposiums*; Schumacher, *Akten des 2. deutschen Keltologensymposiums*; Busse, ZCP lii.

the 3 sg pret. in *-awd* (even if these are still extremely rare).

What trends can be observed?

a) The postponed personal pronouns are found in poems of less formal character like love-poetry, religious poetry etc. They are used to strengthen the verbal form, mostly in the 1 sg or the imperative 2 sg or pl. They are used to reinforce infixed pronouns. It seems that these fell out of use during the Early MW period (mostly with prefixed *ry-* and *dy-*) and were supported by double-marking, i.e. infixation and suffixation.

b) The 3 sg in *-awd* is quite rare in the language of the Gogynfeirdd of the 12th-13th century. It is used where grammatically required (for example *lladdawdd*), and in texts with a more personal context such as religious poetry, love poetry and elegies. In prose an exponential increase can be observed in the 13th century. From the 14th century on, it is also used in poetry.

c) Stem-forming <*y*> with verbal noun and plurals is the normal situation; <*t*> for <*th*> with the conj. prep. *gan* is rare but it occurs in a handful of poems. Other factors which distort our picture of the poetic tradition are the existence of different scribal schools, and the diverse origins of the scribes.

I hope to have shown that despite being written in a high register one can indeed find elements of spoken language in much of the work of the Gogynfeirdd. Following P. W. Thomas's criteria, they seem to indicate a Northern or even North-Western dialect. These colloquial features are restricted to poems of a more personal nature. The concentration of these forms in the 12th century shows, that the Gogynfeirdd were not only highly conservative poets. Together with the metrical experiments in this period, for example of Meilyr Brydydd and his school, as representatives of a national literary renaissance they took up influences from outside. Blending both the traditional with the new they created something fresh which had an enormous impact on the development of Welsh poetry.

The Progressive in
Ystorya Bown de Hamtwn

Erich Poppe

1. THE PROGRESSIVE IN MIDDLE WELSH

IN a recent paper Ingo Mittendorf and I (Mittendorf and Poppe, *Celtic Englishes*) have attempted to outline some typological and functional characteristics of the so-called progressive in Middle Welsh, i.e., of periphrastic constructions consisting of an inflected form of *bot* 'be' plus *yn*[1] plus a verbal noun. Here I want to test further and refine our findings by analysing the uses of this construction in the Middle Welsh *Ystorya Bown de Hamtwn*.

Our previous discussion was based on the examples of the progressive in six Middle Welsh prose texts, *Culhwch ac Olwen* (CO), the four tales of *Pedeir Keinc y Mabinogi* (PKM), and *Buched Dewi* (BDe). We concluded that the basic semantic image conveyed by the progressive in these texts is processivity, i.e., a dynamic state presented as a series of identical intervals without a defined beginning or end. This process may have a temporal point of reference in some superordinate event, and we termed this the (syntactically) dependent use. It is typically found in preposed temporal clauses introduced by conjunctions meaning 'while/when' which temporally contain the event described in the main clause. In independent use, i.e., used without an explicit or implicit

---

[1] This aspectual *yn* and the local preposition *yn* 'in' are homophones. The latter, however, triggers the nasal mutation, whereas aspectual *yn* is followed by the unmutated consonant. T. A. (BBCS xviii) suggests that local and aspectual *yn* are etymologically the same word; Isaac (JCL iii) derives aspectual *yn* from *wnc/wng* 'near, close by', a local preposition cognate with OIr. *oc* 'at', Mod.Ir. *ag*, Sc.G *ag/a'*, Manx *g–/Ø*, which are used in the progressive constructions in the Goidelic languages. For some further considerations see now Gensler, *Language* lxxviii.751–7. The derivation of progressives from locative expressions has good typological analogues (see Bybee et al., *The Evolution of Grammar*, 129).

temporal point of reference, the periphrastic construction adds a processual, dynamic dimension to the verb's meaning, and this often, but not necessarily, results in a focus on the verbal event. The latter is an option available to writers in order to express specific stylistic and pragmatic nuances, and it requires a sometimes subtle interpretation of the context and the writer's communicative intentions.

Our findings thus agree with Mezger's earlier view that *yn* plus verbal noun (both in the progressive construction and as sub–predicate) has two typical functions, to mark an action either as highlighted or as ongoing ('entsprechend bezeichnet *yn* + Verbalnomen teils die Handlung, die besonders hervorgehoben werden soll, teils die, die eben vor sich geht', Mezger KZ lviii.241), which correlate with our pragmatic and aspectual features respectively.

After our discussion had gone into press, Mac Cana (*Celtica* xxiii) appeared, and we were therefore unable to refer to his discussion. He sets out 'to essay a brief overview of the periphrastic [present tense] forms in several Middle Welsh prose texts for the light they may throw on earlier stages of the functional rapprochement between the two forms of the verb' (*Celtica* xxiii.157), i.e., periphrastic present and simple/synthetic present, with a focus on the 'emergence of the periphrastic construction as a general, non–progressive present' (*Celtica* xxiii.161). On the basis of examples from PKM, CO, *Owein*, and BRh, he suggests the following functions for periphrastic constructions, in both present and non–present tenses: progressive,[2] durative or continuative,[3]

---

2   Mac Cana's examples are in Mittendorf and Poppe's corpus nos. (8.6), (8.2), (9.2), (9.19), (9.37/9.44), (9.45), (9.25). The following example was inadvertently omitted in Mittendorf and Poppe: *Sef dial a wnaethant, gyrru Branwen o un ystauell ac ef, a'y chymell y bobi yn y llys, a pheri y'r kygyd, gwedy **bei yn dryllyaw** kic, dyuot idi a tharaw bonclust arnei beunyd* (PKM 37.26–38.1) 'This revenge they took, they drove Branwen from the same room with him and compelled her to cook in the court, and they made the butcher, after he had been cutting meat, to come to her and to give her a box on the ear every day'. The subjunctive is conditioned by the clause–type, a generalizing temporal clause, and the progressive denotes duration and habituality.

3   Mac Cana's examples are in Mittendorf and Poppe's corpus nos. (9.48) and (9.32). We did not include the following example because we read *yn* plus verbal noun as sub–predicate, rather than as coordinate with *y maent*: *Eu rannu ym pob lle yn y kyuoeth, ac y **maent** yn lluossauc, ac **yn dyrchauael** ym pob lle, ac **yn cadarnhau** y uann y bythont, o wyr ac arueu goreu a welas neb'* (PKM 36.26–29) '"I distributed them everywhere in my realm, and they are numerous, and prospering everywhere and fortifying wherever they have been, with the best men and arms anyone has seen."' If one accepts Mac Cana's syntactic interpretation, the progressive could be said to denote duration and habituality here. Note that Mittendorf and Poppe did not consider non–finite

stative (with *eisted* and *seuyll*),[4] prospective,[5] as well as 'a modal of intention meaning approximately "is in the process of/proposing to/about to"' (*Celtica* xxiii.160).[6] Mac Cana does not consider the syntactic environments of progressive constructions (our dependent versus independent uses), and he analyses the periphrastic construction solely in terms of what he calls aspectual and modal functions (*Celtica* xxiii.161). It is therefore difficult to correlate his findings with our suggestion that the periphrastic construction combines aspectual and pragmatic features.

2. YSTORYA BOWN DE HAMTWN

Ystorya Bown de Hamtwn (henceforth YBH) is the Welsh version of the Anglo–Norman *Geste de Boeve de Haumtone*, which according to Watkin (YBH lix) was translated around the middle of the thirteenth century; it is thus 'probably the earliest example of the translation of a secular French narrative into Welsh' (Lloyd–Morgan 'Late medieval Welsh Grail traditions', 81). The oldest manu-

---

expressions of the periphrastic construction in their corpus.

4   Mac Cana's examples are in Mittendorf and Poppe's corpus nos. (9.3) and (9.15).

5   Mac Cana's examples are in Mittendorf and Poppe's corpus nos. (9.49), (9.31), and (9.21). I do not think that a prospective interpretation, as suggested by Mac Cana, is contextually warranted for the following example: *Y guyr hynny a'y godiwawd, ac a ouynyssant idaw, pa darpar oed yr eidaw, a pha achaws yd* **oed yn mynet** *e ymdeith.* (PKM 32.20–2) 'These men overtook him and asked him what his intention was and why he was going away.' Matholwch has already left the court and is in the process of going away, which is indicated by the fact that the messengers overtake him, and the periphrastic construction simply marks the processivity and the temporal extension of his going away. In the case of *Pan doethant, yd oed y guyr hynny* **yn mynet** *y gymryt kynghor.* (PKM 72.6–8) 'When they came, these men were going to take counsel' the context does not appear to be unambiguously in favour of either the progressive reading (i.e., 'in the process of going') or the prospective reading (i.e., 'about to go').

6   I am not quite clear whether Mac Cana wishes to subsume the 'instances [of periphrasis] with verbs of perception, thinking or emotion [...] as well as those indicating an action continuing up to the present' (Mac Cana, *Celtica* xxiii.160) under this modal use, which his connecting phrase 'One might include here' seems to imply, since at least perceptions and emotions are generally viewed to be quite independent of conscious agenthood and thus incompatible with modal intentionality. Mac Cana aptly draws attention to the cognitive closeness between prospectivity and intentionality. His example for the modal use appears in Mittendorf and Poppe's corpus as no. (9.50), and his examples with verbs of perception, thinking, or emotion are nos. (9.1), (9.42), (9.43), (8.5). His example for an action continuing up to the present is Mittendorf and Poppe's no. (8.4).

script in which YBH is found, *Llyfr Gwyn Rhydderch*, has been dated by Huws (CMCS xxi.2 (= MWM 228)) to around 1350. *Llyfr Gwyn Rhydderch* contains two different beginnings of YBH (YBH 1–49, 50–132),[7] the first of which is abandoned towards the middle of the second column of the first page, which is then left blank. The first 21 lines of the two beginnings are identical (YBH 1–21 = 50–73); these and the remaining text from line 73 onwards agree with the version of YBH in *Llyfr Coch Hergest*.

Watkin (YBH xxxiii–xlii) argues in favour of the dependence of *Llyfr Coch*'s version of YBH on the one in *Llyfr Gwyn*, and one of his strongest points is perhaps the form which lines 3457–3458 of *Llyfr Coch* have in *Llyfr Gwyn* (YBH xxxix). Jones ('Rhagymadrodd', vi), however, does not accept his arguments. It appears to be scholarly consensus now that at least the other texts in *Llyfr Coch* are not copied from *Llyfr Gwyn*, but that both derive from a common exemplar.[8] It may be relevant in this context that YBH takes up separate quires, viz. 10 to 14, in *Llyfr Gwyn* and that this is the only contribution of YBH's scribe, scribe C, to the manuscript,[9] so that the texts of YBH in *Llyfr Gwyn* and *Llyfr Coch* need not have the same relation to each other as the other texts. Be that as it may, it is tempting to associate the first and abandoned beginning of YBH in *Llyfr Gwyn*, and especially the unique text of lines 21 to 49, with another, now lost adaptation of the *Geste de Boeve de Haumtone*.

Roberts (*Guide to Welsh Literature* 236) suggests that the 'translator [of YBH] has a wealth of vocabulary which he uses to effect in passages of abuse, dialogue and fights, and which may well have derived from the colloquial idiom'; Watkin notes some traces of the spoken language in the morphology and the syntax.[10]

---

7   All references are to the line–numbers in the edition of YBH.

8   See, e.g., Jones, 'Rhagymadrodd', vi, and Gereint, xi–xiv. In this context it would be important to identify mistakes in the text of YBH which may be due to copying from a written exemplar. Cases in point may be *y doeth ef* corrected to *yd yttoed ef (yn kerdet)* (859), *ac vn a gymerth* (923) for *ac ef a gymerth* as in *Llyfr Coch Hergest* (see YBH 99: 'o ragweld *ac un* 924 y daeth *un yma*') and *(achub) y sore* (3365) for Anglo–Norman *Ysoré* (Boeve de Haumtone, l. 2925) with confusion of transitive and intransitive uses of *achub*.

9   See Huws, CMCS xxi.4, 10–12 (= Huws, MWM 231–2, 239–40).

10   YBH cxviii, cxx, clxxii, and compare his examples for *fy* > *y* (p. cxx), *-eu*, *-e* (p. cxx), *-af* > *-a* (p. cxxiii), *-nt* > *-n* (p. cxxiv); see also Thomas BBCS xl.22 on the occurrence of *taw* in YBH, which he argues was non-standard in Middle Welsh, as it is still in modern (southern) Welsh. GPC, s.v. *braf*, gives YBH as the only literary source for the meaning 'big, huge' of *braf* and notes that this meaning is still current in spoken northern Welsh. Thomas BBCS xl.41 thinks that the text may have originated in what he calls 'an

3. THE PROGRESSIVE IN *Ystorya Bown de Hamtwn*

3.1. FORMAL RANGE

The progressive in YBH is attested with the following tenses and moods of *bot*: in the indicative with the present, consuetudinal present (as narrative present in subordinate clauses only), preterite (including one example with *ry*), imperfect, and pluperfect; in the subjunctive with the present and imperfect. The uses of the preterite and pluperfect and of the present and imperfect subjunctive are not mentioned by Evans (GMW) and Richards (*Cystrawen*) in their descriptions of periphrastic constructions; all are—with the exception of the present subjunctive—also attested in the corpus analysed by Mittendorf and Poppe. The present and imperfect indicative occur with the highest frequency in all texts analysed so far, as can be seen from Table 1. Syntactically, the periphrastic construction is used in YBH in main and subordinate—i.e., adverbial, adjectival, and noun—clauses.

TABLE I: ATTESTED TENSE–MOOD–COMBINATIONS WITH THE PROGRESSIVE

MOOD	TENSE	FREQUENCY OF THE PROGRESSIVE					
		CO	PKM	Bde	YBH	abs.	%
indicative	present	3	21	5	19	48	33%
	cons. pres./future	1	4	0	2	7	5%
	imperfect	5	21	14	28	68	48%
	cons. past	0	3	0	0	3	2%
	preterite	2	0	2	5	9	6%
	pluperfect	0	1	0	4	5	3%
subjunctive	present	0	0	0	1	1	1%
	imperfect	0	2	0	3	5	3%
imperative		0	0	0	0	0	0%
		11	52	21	62	146	

historical transition zone between south-western and northern areas' and also does not want to rule out scribal interference if the manuscript, Llyfr Gwyn Rhydderch, was produced in Strata Florida as has been suggested by Daniel Huws CMCS xxi (= MWM 227–68).

TABLE 2: VERBS OCCURRING IN THE PROGRESSIVE IN YBH IN
FINITE AND NON—FINITE CONSTRUCTIONS[11]

amouyn 'look for'

arwein (2) 'carry/lead'

brathu 'bite'

cadw 'guard'

cael/caffel (2) 'receive'

canu 'strike [of a bell]'

karu 'love'

keissaw (3 + 2?) 'look for'

kerdet (4) 'go'

colli (2) 'loose'

credu (2) 'believe'

crynu (2) 'tremble'

kymryt (+ yn) 'take (upon)'

kysgu (4 + 1?) 'sleep'

kytgyscu 'sleep together'

damunaw 'wish'

darestwg 'subdue'

dial (?) 'revenge'

diffeithaw (3) 'harm'

dwyn 'carry'

dyuot (2 + 1?) 'come'

dywedut 'speak'

edrych (4) 'watch'

eisted (1 + 1?) 'sit'

gofalu (2) 'annoy'

gorchymyn 'command'

gwarandaw 'listen'

gwarchadw 'guard'

gwassanaethu 'serve'

gwediaw 'pray'

gwneuthur (1 + 1?) 'do'

gwneuthur (kewilid a sarhaet)
'make (shamed and disgraced)'

gwneuthur (y ewyllus) 'satisfy (his
passion)'

lledratgaru 'love secretly'

llad (2) 'kill'

llosgi (2) 'burn'

llywyaw 'rule'

mynet 'go'

nofyaw 'swim'

presswylyaw 'dwell'

rodi 'give'

rwystraw 'prevent'

ryuelu 'wage war'

swperu 'take supper'

triciaw (3) 'stay'

tybygu 'think'

tywyssyaw 'command'

ymddidan (2) 'converse'

ymdirgelu 'hide'

ymgreinaw 'roll around'

ymlad 'fight'

ymlit 'follow'

---

11   The number of occurrences, if more than one, is given in brackets; a question mark
indicates occurrence in doubtful contexts (see § 3.3., exx. 64–74).

Table 2 lists the verbs which are used in progressive constructions in YBH, in both finite and non–finite constructions. Various semantic sub–classes are represented here, but the majority of verbs belongs to the class of atelic process verbs, as is typical for progressive uses on the basis of cross–linguistic observations. Atelic verbs are 'those which do not have to wait for a goal for their realization, but are realized as soon as they begin' (Garey *Language* xxxiii.106). A number of telic verbs, which describe an action or event directed towards a goal and require for their realization that this goal is reached (compare Garey *Language* xxxiii.106), occur in the progressive as well, such as *cael, colli, llad, rwystraw,* and *ymdirgelu.* However, as Nehls has pointed out in relation to uses of the progressive in Modern English, it is not the semantic difference between verbs which conditions the grammaticality or non–grammaticality of a progressive, but the semantic difference between predications:[12]

> In telischen Aussagen tritt die Verbalform in der NEF [i.e., non–expanded form] auf; setzt man statt dessen die EF [i.e., expanded form], so wird die Aussage atelisch. Der Kontext, in dem die in Satz (14) [i.e., *The last time I saw him he was dying; today he is well again*] vorkommt, erfordert, daß die Verbalaussage atelisch ist. (Nehls 'Kontrastive Anmerkungen', 179)

A semantic classification of isolated verbs therefore cannot provide conclusive insights into the uses of the progressive in Middle Welsh. However, it will be useful to consider the meaning of individual verbs in interaction with their contexts in the analysis of some of the examples below.

3.2. FUNCTIONAL RANGE

I shall begin with what appears to be the clearest functional domain of the progressive, its dependent use as a temporal frame for another verbal event which is contained within this frame's temporal extension. The temporal extension remains unspecified, its beginning and end fade out. Dependent use is typically, but not necessarily, associated with subordinate syntactic status of the frame: the frame is provided by a preposed temporal clause, the framed event is given in the main clause. The relevant examples are given under (1–6).

(1) A ffan **vyd** ef ddydgweith **yn kerdet** y kyfarfu ac ef marchawc. (1458–60) 'And while he was travelling one day, a knight met him.'

(2) A ffan **vyd** yvelly **yn nofyaw**, ef a wyl llog yn agos idaw. (2392–4) 'And while

---

12   Note also Garey's remarks (*Language* xxxiii.107–9) on the interaction of the semantics of the verb and its complement in defining the aspect of the complete verbal phrase.

he was swimming thus, he saw a ship near him.'

(3) Eissoes, tra **yttoed** Bown **yn ymdidan** a'r brenhin y marchogyon a raculaenassant tri gyrua march ymblaen Bown. (2895–8) 'However, while Bown was conversing with the king, the knights outstripped Bown by three furlongs.'

(4) A phan welas eu tat wynt yn dyuot mynet yn eu herbyn a oruc, a phan **yttoydynt yn mynet** ef a deuth Sabaot at Bown y erchi kennat. (3831–5) 'And when their father saw them coming, he went to meet them, and while they were going, Sabaot went to Bown to ask permission.'

(5) Ac yna yd aeth y'r llong a dyrchauel hwyl a dyuot y Hamtwn a oruc pan **yttoydit yn canu** kloch hanner dyd. (3851–3) 'And then he went to the ship and set sail and came to Hamtwn while it was striking midday.'

(6) '[...] vrdaw Bown yn marchawc vrdawl ac ef a wna nerth mawr it a chanhorthwy, kanys y dyd arall yd **oedwn** o ben y twr **yn edrych** arnaw pan y hachubawd dec fforestwr [...].' (515–20) '"dub Bown a knight and he will give you great strength and help, because the other day I was watching him from the top of the tower when ten foresters struck him."'

I have not found in YBH any obvious examples of the use of a synthetic verbal form in a preposed temporal clause where the meaning of the clause would lead one to expect a progressive.[13]

In three further examples (7–9) the frame is a complex expression consisting of a noun phrase qualified by a relative clause; in all the examples the noun phrase functions as a temporal adverbial.[14] In (9) this expression frames the verbal event of the preceding main clause.[15]

13　I have found no instances of synthetic imperfect forms of verbs other than *bot* in such clauses. The preterite is typically used in preposed temporal clauses with verbs of perception; here the completed act of perception precedes the verbal event of the main clause, compare, for example, 3301, 3302–3.

14　This is typically the case, but compare the following example with a locative expression as antecedent: *Pan dyuu y thymp idi, ef a dyuu y iawn bwyll iti. Sef y dyuu myn yd oed meichad yn cadw kenuein o uoch.* (CO 6–8) 'When her time came to her, her right sense came back to her. It came back where a swineherd was keeping a herd of swine.'

15　The use of the concept 'frame' here is different from the one employed in the functional analysis of Middle Welsh word order, where it is used to distinguish between the pragmatic functions of pre–verbal and post–verbal adverbials respectively (see Poppe, SC xxiv/xxv, *Untersuchungen*). The contrast between (7–8) and (9) indicates that temporal frames are typically also pragmatic frames (or 'settings'), as in (7–8), but need not be so. In (9) the temporal frame functions pragmatically as 'specification' (see also Firbas *Brno Studies in English* xiv.41 for this concept).

(7) Y petwyryd dyd yd **yttoed** ef **yn kerdet** y gwelei palmer yn eisted dan vric pren ac yn kymryt y giniaw. (858–62) 'And on the fourth day he was travelling he saw a pilgrim sitting under a branch of a tree and eating his food.'

(8) A nosweith yd **oed** ef **yn kysgu** y doeth pryf gwenwynic, a Cholubyr oed y enw, a'y vrathu ygnhewillin y tal. (1010–4) 'And one night he was sleeping, a venomous snake—and Colubyr was its name—came and bit him in the middle of the forehead.'

(9) Ac yna yd oed Ermin gwedy drigyaw y ben y twr yr amser yd **oedynt yn dyuot** ac arganuot Bown yn dyfot a phymthegmil y gyt ac ef o wyr aruawc. (3520–4) 'And then Ermin had climbed to the top of the tower while they were coming, and he saw Bown coming and fifteen hundred armed men together with him.'

The majority of the examples, however, show an independent use of the progressive and are more difficult to interpret since aspectual and pragmatic features interact in a rather more complex fashion. I want to look first at the instances of the progressive with forms of *bot* in the imperfect in auctorial narrative. The contexts indicate that here the aspectual feature would appear to be predominant. The relevant examples are given under (10–16).

(10) Sef gwreic a vynnawd, wreic ieuank tu draw y vor, a honno a **oyd yn karu** gwr ieuank arderchawc a oed amherawdyr yn yr Almayn. (6–10 = 56–60) 'This woman he desired, a young woman from overseas, and she was in love with a young and noble man who was ruler in Germany.'

(11) [. . .] ac ymhoylut dracheuyn tu a'r llys a wnaeth ef yn llawen. Ac yd **oed** Iosian **yn edrych** ar y gyfranc, ac yna y dywot hi. (462–5) 'and he went back again happily to the court. And Iosian was watching the incident, and then she said.'

(12) Sef yd **oydynt yn gwarandaw** arnaw y ddeu wr a oedynt yn y warchadw. (1091–3) 'So the two men who were guarding him, were listening to him.'

(13) A gwedy gwisgaw racdun y kerdyssant tu a chastell Sebawt a'e llu a ranyssant yn ddwy vydin, a brenhin Prydein a **oed yn tywyssyaw** y vydin vlaen a'r amherawdyr y vydin ol. (2639–45) 'And after they had armed themselves, they marched towards Sabaot's castle, and they divided their host into two armies, and the king of Britain was commanding the army in the front and the emperor the one in the rear.'

(14) Yn yr eol honno yd oed amylder [o nadred] a cholubyr a ffryuet ereill gwenwynic, a'r pryuet hynny **oedynt yn y ofalu ac yn y vrathu** yn vynych. (986–9) 'In this prison there was a multitude of serpents and snakes and other venomous animals, and these snakes kept annoying him and biting him

frequently.'[16]

(15) Ac o'r castell hwnnw y dygei Sebaot a'e allu kyrcheu y gyfoeth yr amherawdyr gweith[eu] hyt dyd gweitheu hyt nos, ac ywelly yd **oedynt yn diffeithaw** kyfoeth yr amherawdyr yn fenedic wychyr. (2193–9) 'And from this castle Sabaot and his troops made inroads into the emperor's realm, now during the day, now during the night, and thus they kept destroying the emperor's realm boldly and fearlessly.'

(16) Mawr uu y vrwydyr a balch a mawr yd **oed** Bown a Therri **yn darestwg** onadunt, a Sabaot nyt oed lwfyr canys y neb a drawei marw vydei. (3706–10) 'Great and splendid was the battle, and Bown and Terri kept subduing them mightily, and Sabaot was not cowardly since the one he would strike would die.'

The only sentence I have found in which one of the verbs of (10–16) occurs as a synthetic imperfect, is (10'), with a synthetic imperfect of *caru*:

(10') A mawr y karei Bown yr vnbennes uonhedic. (3396–7) 'And Bown loved the noble lady greatly.'

The intended difference between (10) and (10') is difficult to capture, but could perhaps be related to a somewhat greater detachment of the description in (10').[17] In (14–15) the progressive conveys an additional nuance of habituality;[18] note the adverb *yn vynych* in (14). *Brathu* 'bite' is a verb with punctual meaning which in combination with the progressive conveys a habitual, or an iterative, image; *diffeithaw* 'destroy' and *darestwg* 'subdue' are telic verbs which loose their telicity in a progressive construction.[19] In (16) the emphasis on the duration and the iterativity[20] of the fighting adds a dynamic dimension to the description.

In (17) the selection of different aspects, perfective versus imperfective, for the christian and the pagan acts of praying could be intended as a comment on the success of the respective prayers: the christian god will fulfil the promise, as is shown by Bown's subsequent victory, whereas the heathen god does not, in

---

16 See Watkin (YBH 101) for the proposed emendation.

17 Compare Mittendorf and Poppe's discussion of a similar contrasting pair in BDe 9.5–7 versus 8.29–30.

18 'Habitual situations are customarily repeated on different occasions' (Bybee et al., *The Evolution of Grammar*, 127).

19 Note the contrast between non–progressive *y dygei* [...] *kyrcheu* and progressive *yd oedynt yn diffeithaw* in (15), which is paralleled in the present in non–progressive *y dwc kyrcheu* and progressive *y mae yn diffeithaw* (2300–3), quoted below as (29).

20 'Iterative describes an event that is repeated on a particular occasion' (Bybee et al., *The Evolution of Grammar*, 127).

spite of extended and repeated prayers implied by the use of the progressive.[21]

(17) A gwedyaw a oruc Bown ar Duw yr hwnn ny dywawt kelwyd, ac Iuor a **oed yn gwediaw** ar Mahwn ac Apolin. (4073–6) 'And Bown prayed to God who did not lie, and Ifor was/kept praying to Mahom and to Apolin.'

In the next group of examples (18–19) the aspectual image of the event's temporal extension would appear to blend with the pragmatic feature of high-lighting this event within its narrative context. Rodefon becomes the centre of narrative interest in the immediately following fighting scene, and the fact that Bown and Iosian were watched kissing each other will significantly influence the development of the plot.

(18) Adaw y dref a wnaythant ac yn y herbyn y doeth Bradmwnd a chan mil o perchen meirych gyt ac ef, a Rodefon **oed yn arwein** y ystonderd ef o'r blaen. (579–83) 'They left the city, and Bradmwnd came against them with a hundred thousand knights, and Rodefon was carrying his banner in front.'[22]

(19) Sef a wnaeth ynteu yna, kyuodi yn eiste a dodi y dwylaw am y mynwgyl hi a rodi kussan idi. Sef yd **oydynt yn edrych** arnun yn ymgussanu y ddeu wr a rydhayssei ynteu o garchar Bratmwnd. (798–803) 'This he did then, he stood up and embraced her and gave her a kiss. Now the two men he had saved from Bradmwnd's prison, were watching them kissing each other.'

In subordinate clauses a purely aspectual image of an event's unspecified tempo-ral extension is realized by the progressive in a number of relative clauses (20–23).

(20) Sef y mod y ystyryawd, dyuynnu kennat [attei ac anuon] at yr amherawdyr ac erchi idaw dyuot yn oet dyd teruynedic y fforest ynyal a oed yn y iarllaeth Giwn yn gyuagos y'r kastell yd **oedynt yn presswylyaw** yndaw a niuer mawr o varchogyon aruawc gyt ac ef. (24–31) 'Thus she devised it, she summoned a messenger to her and sent him to the emperor and asked him to come on an appointed day to the secluded forest which was in Giwn's earldom near the castle in which they were dwelling, and many armed knights together with him.'[23]

(21) Sef yd oydynt yn gwarandaw arnaw y ddeu wr a **oedynt yn y warchadw**. (1091–3) 'Now the two men who were guarding him, were listening to him.'

(22) Yn voredyd glas y dyd hwnnw y gelwis Bratmwnd ar Grandon y nei ac erchi idaw mynet y'r geol a fferi y'r gwyr a **oedynt yn cadw** Bown dyuot y ymwelet

---

21 In the corresponding Anglo-Norman passage the same verbal form is used twice: *Boves recleyme deus, ke ne mentis,* / *Yvori recleyme Mahom e Apolins* (Boeve de Haumtone, l. 3584–5).

22 Compare (23) for a sentence with a similar meaning.

23 See Watkin (YBH 72) for the proposed emendation.

ac ef. (1205–10) 'In the early morning of this day Bradmwnd called Grandon, his nephew, to him and told him to go to the prison and make the men who were guarding Bown come to see him.'

(23) Ac yna yd achubawd Bown vdunt yn gyntaf ar A[r]wndel y varch clotuorus ac yn gyntaf y trewys ef yr hwn a **oed yn dwyn** y maner. (3262–6) 'And then Bown hurried very fast against them on Arwndel, his famous horse, and first he hit the one who was carrying the banner.'[24]

Example (24) is a rare example of auctorial explanation:

(24) ac edrych ar Bown y fford y kerdei kanys y **ledratgaru** ef yd **oed** hi. (442–4) 'and looking at Bown which way he went because she was loving him secretly.'

Here the verbal noun is fronted for explicative emphasis, and the progressive marks the unspecified extension of the verbal event.[25] The instances of the progressive in main clauses with the present of *bot* all occur in direct speech. Since the progressive denotes an extended ongoing process, the present progressive marks this process as extending beyond the immediate present, the point of 'now' on the time axis, i.e., either as moving together with this point along the time axis or as having moved together with it from some unspecified moment in the past to the speaker's 'now'—this is Evans's (GMW 109) 'action continuing up to the present'. The first option may convey an additional nuance of habituality or iterativity. The relevant examples are given as (25–32).

(25) A dydgweith y dywot Bown, 'Oi a Arglwyd Duw, llawer trallawt a gofut yd **wyf** i **yn** y **gael** yn yr eol hon. [...].' (998–1001) 'And one day Bown said: "Alas, Lord God, much sorrow and affliction I am/keep receiving in this prison".'

(26) '[...] Ac yn nawr y **mae yn eiste** ar ddeheu y Tat a dydbrawt a daw y varnu ar vyw a marw [...].' (1323–6) '"And he is sitting now at the Father's right, and he will come on the Day of Judgement to judge the living and the dead."'

(27) 'Oi a Bown, hir a beth yd **wyt yn triciaw**. Yr awr honn y'm lladant y bwystuilet hyn ac ny'm gwely yn gwbyl gwedy hynny.' (1848–52) '"Alas, Bown, you are tarrying long. These wild beasts will kill me now and you will not see me unimpaired after this."'

(28) '[...] A hwnnw yssyd yn ynys yn y mor racco y mywn castell cadarn ac odyno y **mae yn goualu** yn braf. [...]' (2289–92) '"And he [Sabaot] is on an island in

---

24 Compare (18) for a sentence with a similar meaning.
25 But compare the discussion of (10) and (10′) above. Further uses of the progressive with the imperfect of *bot* in direct and indirect speech will be discussed later.

the sea yonder in a strong castle, and from there he is/keeps annoying [us] greatly."'

(29) '[...] ac yn vynych y dwc kyrcheu y'm kyfoeth weitheu hyt dyd weitheu hyt nos. Ac ywelly y **mae yn diffeithaw** yn wastat. [...]' (2300–3) '"and frequently he makes inroads into my realm, sometimes during the day, sometimes during the night. And thus he is/keeps harming [us] constantly."'[26]

(30) [...] a chlybot y meibyon yn germein a ffrystyaw a wnaethant a dywedut: 'Rywyr yd **ym yn kerdet**.' (3147–50) 'and they heard the boys crying and they rushed and said: "We are/have been going too slowly."'

(31) A duhunaw a oruc y wreic a menegi idi a rywelsei, ac y dywawt: 'Arglwyd,' heb hi, 'ryhir yd **wyt yn trigyaw**, y wreic neu y varch a golles.' (3911–4) 'And he woke his wife and told her what he had dreamt, and she said: "Lord", she said, "too long have you been staying, he lost his wife or his horse."'

(32) 'Arglwydi,' heb hi, 'perwch awch holl niueroed gwiscaw arueu y vynet y ganorthwyaw Sabaot, canys Arabyeit yssyd yn chwerwdic yn y ymlit, ac y **mae** ynteu **yn arwein** Arwndel yr hwnn yr oedut yn drist o'e achaws. [...]' (3958–64) '"Lords," she said, "have all your hosts armed to go to help Sabaot, since the Arabs are following him angrily, and he is leading Arwndel because of whom you have been sad."'

In all these examples, with the likely exceptions of (26),[27] from a version of the Creed, and of (32), the progressive's image of processivity appears to signal additionally the speakers' emotional involvement, an emotive focus on the statement. In (29) the adverb *yn wastat* 'constantly' in combination with the marked atelic image of basically telic *diffeithaw* conveys a strong sense of habituality. The basically telic semantics of *cael* and *goualu* are similarly converted in (25) and (28).

In sentences (33–34) the inherent perfective meaning of the verbs involved—*gorchymyn* 'command' and *tybygu* 'think' with object clauses—is difficult to reconcile with the progressive's imperfective meaning. The ensuing transformation of the verb's aspectual image results in highlighting the verbal event—note the fronting of the verbal nouns.

(33) 'Reit vyd ymi mynet ragof kany allaf trigyaw yn y wlat honn; namyn **gorchymyn** yd **wyf** it na ettych heb gof synyeit wrth Sabaot yr hwnn a garaf yn

---

26 Compare (15) for a parallel sequence with the same contrast between non–progressive and progressive forms.

27 The use of the progressive in this sentence of the Creed is also found in another version: *ac y **mae yn eisted** ar deheu y Tat Duw Hollgyuoethauc* (Credo Athanasius Sant, 203).

vawr. [. . .]' (3045–9) '"I will have to leave since I cannot stay in this country, but I command you that you do not forget to look after Sabaot whom I love greatly."'

(34) 'A **thybygu** yd **wyf** y mae y ryuelu a mi y deuth.' (4251–3) '"And I am thinking that he came to fight with me."'

In sentences (35–36) the verbs *colli* 'lose' and *llad* 'kill' have basically telic semantics, but their use in progressive constructions here converts this image to an atelic one. In (35) this conversion effects an emotional focus on the verbal event.[28] The context of (36) indicates that the mortal illness of Bown's wife is one of the causes of his death, and both her illness as well as his death throes extend over a period of time. The use of *llad* with atelic meaning is therefore appropriate here.[29]

(35) 'Mat yn ganet kan **yttym yn colli** y marchawc goreu o gret.' (3074–6) '"Under evil auspices were we born [?], since we are losing the best knight of christendom."'[30]

(36) 'Vy mam,' heb ef, 'yd **wyt yn llad** vynhat, kanys kymeint yw y duchan ac na bu eiroet y gymeint.' (4350–3) '"Mother," he said, "you are killing my father, because his mourning is so great that there never was its equal."'

In subordinate clauses, again all in direct speech, the use of the progressive oscillates between the poles of a predominantly aspectual (37, compare 32, 38–40) and a predominantly pragmatic reading (41, 42, compare 35). In (41–42) the verbs *kymryt yn* and *colli* have basically telic semantics; in (38) the basically telic semantics of *rwystraw* results in an iterative reading.

(37) 'Arglwydi,' heb hi, 'perwch awch holl niueroed gwiscaw arueu y vynet y ganorthwyaw Sabaot, canys Arabyeit **yssyd** yn chwerwdic **yn** y **ymlit**, ac y mae ynteu yn arwein Arwndel yr hwnn yr oedut yn drist o'e achaws. [. . .]' (3958–64) '"Lords," she said, "have all your hosts armed to go to help Sabaot, since the Arabs are following him angrily, and he is leading Arwndel because of whom you have been sad."'

(38) '[. . .] a ffei ym byryut yr eilweith a uei well welly ychydic y gellit dy voli a mi a vwn beth **yssyd yn** y **rwystraw**: ryissel neithwyr y kusseneist dy wreic. [. . .]' (2571–6) '"and if you struck me a second time in a better fashion, you could hardly be praised, and I know what is/keeps preventing it: you kissed your wife

---

28   Compare (42) with the same conversion from telic to atelic semantics and a similar pragmatic result.

29   Compare Nehls's similar Modern English example quoted above (§ 3.1).

30   See Watkin (YBH 145) for the proposed translation.

last night too meanly."'³¹

(39) 'Welwch,' heb y brenhin, 'meint y kam y **mae yn** y **wneuthur** y'r march'. (2903–5) '"Look," the king said, "how much [*literally* the amount of] injury/pace [?] he is/keeps doing to/with the horse."'³²

(40) A phan yttoydynt yvelly yn eu llewenyd, nachaf pedeir kennat yn dyfot rac bronn y brenhin ac yn amouyn Sabaot. Pan gigleu Sabaot y amouyn, 'Mi,' heb ef, 'yw yr neb yd **yttywch yn** y **amouyn**.' (4195–200) 'And when they were thus joyful, four messangers came before the king and looked for Sabaot. When Sabaot heard that he was looked for, he said: "I am the one you are looking for."'³³

(41) 'Pony chlywy di y ryw ryfic ac ynni y **mae** y march **yn** y **gymryt** yndaw o achos clybot enwi Bown vnweith.' (1563–7) '"Do you not perceive the kind of pride and energy that the horse is taking upon itself because of hearing Bown mentioned once."'

(42) 'March, mawr a beth y'th garaf pann **yttwyf yn kolli** vyn dinassoed a'm kestyll o'th achaws [...].' (3034–6) '"Horse, greatly do I love you when I am loosing my towns and my castles because of you."'

It is perhaps not surprising that the uses of the imperfect progressive in direct and indirect speech exhibit a very similar functional range and blend the basic processual image with varying degrees of emotive nuances (43–49):

(43) 'Ynawr y gwn i yn wir y mae tydi yw gwr mwyaf a gereis ac a garaf; ac yd **oedwn** ys llawer o amser **yn damunaw** y welet. [...]' (1577–81) '"Now I know indeed that you are the man I loved most and will love most; and I was wishing to meet him for a long time."'

(44) Heb y brenhin Damascyl: 'Drwc yd **oedem yn credu**, ac yvelly y gwnaeth yn tadeu kyn no ni. [...]' (4164–7) 'The king of Damascus said: "We were believing wrongly, and so did our fathers before us."'

(45) Ar hynny nachaf Copart o'r parth arall yn dyuot ac ymherued y maes yn ymgyuaruot a'r bugeil a gouyn yn vchel idaw pa achos y llo[s]git tan kymeint ac yd **oedit yn** y **losgi**. (2485–91) 'Afterwards Copart came from the other side and met a shepherd in the middle of the field and asked him loudly why there was kindled a fire as big as the one which they were kindling.'

(46) Ac ar hynt hwy a gyrchyssant Ermin ac a dywedyssant wrthaw vot Bown yn

---

31   Compare Watkin (YBH 127) for the translation of the first part of the sentence.

32   Compare Watkin (YBH 138) for a discussion of this sentence and of the homonyms *cam* 'wrong, injury' and *cam* 'stride, pace'.

33   Sabaot's answer is expressed as an identificatory cleft–sentence.

gwneuthur kewilid a sarhaet uawr idaw kan yd **oed** ef **yn kytgyscu** a'e verch ar oleu ac **yn gwneuthur** y ewyllus ohonei. (804–9) 'And at once they approached Ermin and told him that Bown was shaming and disgracing him greatly because he was sleeping with his daughter in open daylight and was satisfying his passion with her.'

(47) Eissoes, ny bu Copart vncam o bedestric wrthaw a rodi tacua idaw a gouyn ystyr a'r achos yd **oedit yn llosgi** tan kymeint a hwnnw. (2494–9) 'However, Copart overtook him by a single pace of walking and gave him a throttling and asked him the meaning and the reason why they were kindling a fire as big as this.'[34]

(48) Ac yna y dywedassant y mae ofer yd **oed yn dywedut**. (3066–7) 'And then they said that he was speaking unreasonably.'

(49) 'Edrychwch,' heb y Bown, 'y py diw yd **oedewch yn credu**.' (4163–4) '"Look," Bown said, "in whom you were believing."'

The combination of pluperfect forms of *bot* and the progressive as in (50–53) causes no conceptual complication, since the pluperfect as a relative tense without an inherent aspectual characterization simply marks the verbal event as anterior to another past event. The functional range of the progressive is the same as in the present and imperfect indicative described above, perhaps with a dominance of the aspectual feature—the contrast between imperfective *y buassei yn gwassanaethu* and perfective *y gwerthyssit* and *y kyhudyssit* in (50) is instructive.

(50) [. . .] a ffa wed y gwerthyssit ynteu y Sarassinieit, a ffa wed y **buassei yn gwassanaethu** y Ermin vrenhin, a ffa wed y kyhudyssit ynteu wrth y brenhin [. . .]. (1437–41) 'and how he had been sold to the Saracens, and how he had been serving king Ermin, and how he had been accused by the king.'

(51) [. . .] ac erchi idaw mynet hyt yn Hamtwn at yr amherawdyr a dywedut idaw y mae Bown oed enw y marchawc a **ryfuassei yn ymddidan** ac ef y nos arall ac a'e [MS ea] twyllwys. (2539–44) 'and asked him to go to Hamtwn to the emperor and to tell him that Bown was the name of the knight who had been talking to him the other night and who deceived him.'[35]

---

34   See Watkin (YBH 125) for the translation, literally: 'was not a single pace of walking from him', and for the suggestion to read *ac* for *a'r*.

35   Alternatively Bown could be the antecedent of *a'e twyllwys* in a co–ordinated cleft: 'that it was Bown that was the name [. . .] and [that it was Bown] who deceived him'. The co–ordination of *a ryfuassei* and *a'e twyllwys* is perhaps the more natural reading, but note that in this case a progressive form and a non–progressive form are co–

(52) Ac mal y harganuu y brenhin ef galw arnaw a oruc a gouyn idaw pa le **buassei yn trigyaw** yn yr hyt y bu. (3094–6) 'When the king recognized him he called him and asked him where he had been staying as long as he had been.'[36]

(53) [...] a medyleit a wnaeth taw hir y **buassei yn llywyaw** y vrenhinyaeth a diolwch a oruc Duw. (3789–91) 'and he thought that he had been ruling his kingdom for a long time, and he thanked God.'

On the other hand, the combination of preterite forms of *bod* and the progressive as in (54–57) creates a conceptual complication, since the preterite conveys a perfective image of a bounded, self–contained past event, where as the progressive conveys an imperfective image of an unbounded process.

(54) Y llythyr a gymerth ac ysgynnu ar y palfrei a wnaeth a mynet racdaw ar dyd hwnnw educher, a thrannoeth a thradwy y **bu** Bown **yn kerdet** heb gael na bwyt na diawt. (853–8) 'He took the letter and mounted the palfrey and travelled that day till evening, and Bown kept travelling the next day and the third day without getting food or drink.'[37]

(55) [...] ac y'r ogof yd aethant. Ynteu Garsi a **fu yn eu keissaw** hwy yn llawer lle ac nys cafas ac ny chyfarfu neb ac ef o'r a wypei dim y wrthunt. Ynteu a'e gedymdeithon yn llidiawc drist a ymhoylyssant dracheuyn. (1794–1800) 'and they went to the cave. But Garsi kept looking for them in many places and did not find them and nobody met him who would know anything about them. And he and his companions went back again angrily and sad.'

(56) 'Arglwyd,' heb ynteu, 'ny chelaf ragot. Mi a **fuum** ys blwydyn **yn keissaw** y palmer a lettyeist ti ac a'e gweleis.' (3096–9) '"Lord," he said, "I shall not hide it from you. I was seeking for years the pilgrim to whom you gave lodgings, and I saw him."'

(57) '[...] Pan uof i y'm gwlat ac ymplith y gwyrda, o dywettwn i neu o bocsachun rydaruot im llad deu lew, titheu a dywedut y mae ti a dalyssei y neill hyt tra **fum** inheu **yn llad** y llall, a hynny nys mynnwn inheu yr yr holl gristonogaeth. [...]' (1899–1906) '"When I am in my realm and among the nobles, if I said or if I boasted that I had killed two lions, you would say that it was you who had hold back the one while I was killing the other, and this I would not wish by all of christendom."'

---

ordinated.

36   For another instance of *trigyaw* [...] *yn yr hyt y bu* see 3848–9.

37   Contrast sentences with the synthetic preterite of *kerdet* such as *yna y kerdawd y genhat racdaw hyny deuth at Sabaot* (3770–2) 'then the messenger travelled until he came to Sabaot'.

In Mittendorf and Poppe (*Celtic Englishes*, 129, 134) we suggested that this apparently contradictory combination of features is used in specific contexts to focus on the temporal duration of bounded processes. This also seems to apply to examples (54–56), in that a beginning and end of the extended verbal event is either stated or at least implied.[38] The contrast in an immediate context between the progressive with a preterite in (54) and with an imperfect (in example (7) above, both repeated as (54')) is instructive with regard to the presentation of the boundedness and unboundedness respectively of the two acts of travelling described here:

(54') Y llythyr a gymerth ac ysgynnu ar y palfrei a wnaeth a mynet racdaw ar dyd hwnnw educher, a thrannoeth a thradwy y **bu** Bown **yn kerdet** heb gael na bwyt na diawt. Y petwyryd dyd yd **yttoed ef yn kerdet** y gwelei palmer yn eisted dan vric pren ac yn kymryt y giniaw. (853–62) 'He took the letter and mounted the palfrey and travelled that day till evening, and Bown kept travelling the next day and the third day without getting food or drink. And on the fourth day he was travelling he saw a pilgrim sitting under a branch of a tree and eating his food.'

In (56) the indefinite temporal adverbial *ys blwydyn* is combined with the statement that the process of seeking the pilgrim came to an end at some specific point in time, namely when the speaker saw him, and this makes it different from sentence (43) with an indefinite temporal adverbial. Less obvious is the use of the preterite in (57), unless it could be connected with the inherent telic/perfective and bounded image of the verb *llad* 'kill'. Even more problematic is (58), with a combination of the particle *ry* and a preterite of *bot*.[39] The particle may simply denote anteriority, but Evans (GMW 168) also notes some examples of synthetic verbal forms 'where *ry* appears to denote customary or repeated action'; and its combination with the progressive may convey the continued repetition of the inherently perfective verbal event *keissaw* 'demand/ask for':

(58) '[...] A Bratmwnd vrenhin gwr arbennic kyfoethawc a **ryfu** y'th **geissaw** ac ny thygawd idaw. [...]' (693–6) '"And king Bradmwnd, a notable powerful man, kept asking for you and it did not avail him."'

---

38   For the use of a preterite of *bot* with an adverbial phrase denoting a definite period of time see *ac o achos hynny mi a fuum ygharchar seith mlyned* (2140–2) 'and for this reason I was in prison for seven years'. For an example from *Peredur* which is parallel to (54) see *dwy nos a deudyd y* **bu yn kerdet** *ynyalwch a diffeithwch, heb uwyt heb diawt* (Peredur, 10.5–7) 'two nights and two days he was travelling the wilderness and the desert, without food, without drink'.

39   Note that *ry* is used here together with the particle *a*.

The example of the progressive with a form of *bot* in the present subjunctive (59) occurs in direct speech in a temporal clause introduced by *pan* which serves as the extended temporal frame for the event of the main clause—the use of the subjunctive is conditioned by the futurity of the planned verbal action (compare CCCG 273).

(59) '[...] a ffan **vo** Garsi y chuinsa **yn swperu** dechreu nos mi a wassanaethaf arnaw a'e getymdeithon o'r gwin hwnnw [...].' (1701–4) '"and when Garsi will be taking supper soon at the beginning of the night, I shall serve him and his companions with this wine."'

The three examples of the progressive with forms of *bot* in the imperfect subjunctive occur in relative clauses (60–62).

(60) Kymryt ofyn mawr y Vradmwnd ac nyt oed aylawt arnaw ny **bei yn krynu**. (942–4) 'Bradmwnd had great fear and he had not a limb that would not be trembling.'

(61) Y gyt ac y gwyl hitheu hynny dechreu lleuein yn vchel a wnaeth ac nyt oed aelawt arnei ny **bei yn crynu** rac ofyn y llewot. (1830–4) 'As soon as she perceived that, she began weeping loudly and she had not a limb that would not be trembling because of fear of the lions.'

(62) a ffwy bynnac a **vei yn edrych** arnadunt truan vydei yn y gallon yr kadarnet vei gwelet eu drycyruerth. (1871–4) 'and whoever would be watching them, he would be sad in his heart, however stout it would be, seeing their lamentation.'

(60) and (61) repeat the same formula. In (62) the relative clause is clearly an indefinite generalizing relative clause which is one of the important domains of the subjunctive (compare CCCG 273). In all instances the progressive marks the temporal extension of a verbal event, possibly with the additional pragmatic nuance of highlighting this event.

3.3. SOME DOUBTFUL EXAMPLES[40]

(63) 'Arglwyd,' heb wynt, 'y Sulgwyn yw hwnn. Ni a dlywn marchogaeth yn meirch a **voont yn swiwrn**.' (2870–3) '"Lord," they said, "This is Whitsunday. We should ride our horses which had been resting."'

Here the precise form of the verb *bot* and the categorial status of *swiwrn* are both problematic: the verbal form in the manuscript is vo|ont (i.e., separated at

---

40 These are not included in the statistics in Table 1 above, but do not affect the results.

the end of the line); Watkin (YBH 136) discusses the possible alternatives *uont* (present subjunctive) and *uuont* (preterite) and suggests that the corresponding phrase *chivals surjornez* 'rested (or recovered) horses' in the Anglo–Norman text (Boeve de Haumtone, l. 2473) supports reading the preterite. He takes *swiwrn* to be a verbal noun 'resting' (YBH 125), and GPC accepts this analysis.[41] If *swiwrn* was indeed understood by speakers of Middle Welsh as functioning as a (pseudo–)verbal noun, then we would have a progressive construction marking the extension of the verbal event, possibly with an additional pragmatic nuance of highlighting it. The semantic nuance intended by the choice of the tense remains difficult to establish; the preterite could convey the idea of an extended duration with a definite end, the speaker's 'now'.

In the next group of examples word order and the collocation with locative adverbs leave the formal syntactic interpretation of *yn* plus verbal noun ambiguous as either part of a progressive construction or as a sub–predicate.

(64) A ffan ytt **oedynt** yn y fforest **yn keissaw** y baed y kyuodes yr amherawdyr o'e llechua. (138–40) 'And when they were looking for the boar in the forest, the emperor rose from his hiding–place', or: 'And when they were in the forest, looking for the boar'.

(65) [..] y gan vab Sabot a **ryfuassei** ymplith Sarassinieit **yn y geissaw** ynteu. (2180–2) 'from Sabaot's son who had been looking for him among the Saracens', or: 'who had been among the Saracens, looking for him'.

(66) A chan y gwanhet hi ny allwys leuein pan doeth Copart a'r Sarassinieit etti a'e chymryt ac adaw y deu uab yn y lle y **buassei** y mywn deil **yn ymgreinaw**. (3139–43) 'And because of her weakness, she could not cry when Copart and the Saracens came upon her and took her and left the two boys where they had been rolling around in the leaves', or: 'where they had been in the leaves, rolling around'.

(67) Ac yna yd **oed** Bown a Therri a Sabaot a Iuor ar veinc **yn eisted**. (3739–41) 'And then Bown and Terri and Sabaot and Ifor were sitting on a bench', or: 'And

---

41   Compare the other two attestations of *swiwrn* in YBH: *yno y tricyssant hwy yn swiwrn* (2528–9) 'there they remained resting' and *gwedy bot yno wers yn swiwrn* (3082–3) 'having been there for a while resting/at rest'—in the last instance *yn swiwrn* seems to function as a sub-predicate. Watkin (YBH cx, 125) takes *swiwrn* to be a loan from Anglo–Norman, with <i> = <dz>. Both Surridge (BBCS xxxii.75) and GPC accept the etymology; GPC remains uncertain about the value of the <i>. The three examples from YBH are the only ones liste in GPC. I wish to thank Andrew Hawke from GPC for supplying me with the draft entry for *swiwrn*.

there were then Bown and Terri and Sabaot and Ifor, sitting on a bench'.[42]

(68) Tewi weithon a wnawn am Bown a dywedut am Sabaot mal yd **yttoed** yn y ystauell **yn kyscu**: Ef a welei breudwyt mal nat oed hof ganthaw. (3162–6) 'We will now be silent about Bown and talk about Sabaot as he was sleeping in his room: he had a dream as it was not pleasant for him', or: 'as he was in his room, sleeping.'[43]

(69) Tewi weithon a wnawn am Bown a dywedut am Sabaot a **oed** gyt a'e wreic yn y ystauell **yn kyscu** a gwelet breidwyt a oruc yny fyd. (3905–8) 'We will now be silent about Bown and talk about Sabaot who was sleeping together with his wife in his room, and he had a dream ... (?)', or: 'Sabaot who was together with his wife in his room, sleeping.'[44]

(70) Ac yn y hol hwynteu yd **yttoed** y teir mil **yn dyuot** wrth yr afwyneu. (1246–8) 'And behind them the three thousand were coming at full tilt', or: 'behind them were the three thousand, coming at full tilt'.

(71) Ac yn y vrwydyr yd **oed** Sabaot a Therri **yn rodi** dyrnodeu diarbet. (3720–2) 'And in the battle Sabaot and Terri were handing out ceaseless blows', or: 'Sabaot and Terri were in the battle, handing out ceaseless blows'.

(72) Ac ar y geir hwnnw y brathassant eu meirch tu a'r llys ac yn gyntaf y barwn penhaf y Mwmbrawnt ac yn y ol ynteu Gi vrenhin a chyt ac ef pymthegmil yn y ganlyn ac ody vaes yd **oed** Bown **yn gwneuthur** marthyrolyaet mawr. (4126–32) 'And with these words they set spurs to their horses towards the castle, first the foremost chief of Mwmbrawnt, after him king Gi with fifteen thousand accompanying him and on the side Bown was making great slaughter', or: 'and on the side was Bown, making great slaughter'.

In these cases a locative adverb may be positioned between the finite verb and *yn* plus verbal noun (64–69) or it may be fronted (70–72). It is not at all clear to me whether two syntactic interpretations were indeed available for native speakers of Middle Welsh in such instances; suprasegmental features which we are unable to recover may have played a role here. Semantically the reading as progressive conveys the idea of an ongoing event or action, whereas the alternative reading conveys the idea of a superordinate state specified by a con-

---

42 See also Williams ('Welsh *yn ei eistedd*', 219) who says that *yn eisted* 'could be described as subjective predicate [...] i.e. ar veinc, yn eisted' here.

43 The punctuation here follows the manuscript, see also (69). Alternatively one could read: *a dywedut am Sabaot: Mal yd* **yttoed** *yn y ystauell* **yn kyscu** *ef a welei breudwyt* 'and talk about Sabaot: As he was sleeping in his room, he had a dream'.

44 See Watkin (YBH 168–9) for a discussion of *yny fyd*.

comitant event or action. The progressive's functional range would fit well the possibilities outlined above. A similar syntactic ambiguity arises in (73–74) in co-ordinated structures.45

(73) Ac edrych yn y gylch a wnaeth a ffan edrych yd **oed** yn nos a ffawb **yn kysgu**. (1150–2) 'And he looked around and when he looked it was night and everybody asleep', or: 'and everybody was sleeping'.

(74) 'Y **may** ef yn y wlat yn iach lawen ac **yn dial** y dat yn ffenedic [. . .].' (1522–3) '"He is in his country well and happy, and revenging his father bravely"', or '"and he is revenging his father bravely"'.

3.4. NON–FINITE EXPRESSIONS OF THE PROGRESSIVE

Contexts in which non–finite expressions of the progressive occur are affirmative object clauses as in (75–81).46

(75) Ac yn oet y dyd y gwydat hi **vot** yr amherawdyr **yn ymdirgelu** yn y fforest honno annoc a wnaeth hitheu yr iarll vynet y hela y baed koet. (45–9) 'And in the course of the day when she knew that the emperor was hiding in this forest she urged the earl to go to hunt the wild boar.'

(76) Ac y gyt ac y guyl ef hihi yn dyuot kymryt idaw ynteu y **vot yn kysgu** a chwrnu yn vchel a wnaeth ef. (770–3) 'And as soon as he saw her coming, he pretended that he was sleeping and he snored loudly.'

(77) '[. . .] a guedy y del Iuor y mywn aet Bown attaw a managet idaw bot y vrawt yn y castell a **bot** brenhin arall a llu praf ganthaw **yn ymlad** ac ef [. . .].' (1636–41) '"and after Ifor comes in, have Bown go to him and tell him that his brother is in the castle and another king with a huge host has been fighting with him."'

(78) 'Arglwydi, chwi a wdawch yn hyspys **bot** Sebawt **yn ryuelu** arnaf ys llawer o amser ac **yn diffeithaw** vyghyfoeth yn braff [. . .].' (2614–8) '"Lords, you know very well that Sabaot has been waging war on me for long time and destroying my realm greatly."'

(79) Ac ar hynt hwy a gyrchyssant Ermin ac a dywedyssant wrthaw **vot** Bown **yn gwneuthur** kewilid a sarhaet uawr idaw kan yd oed ef yn kytgyscu a'e verch ar oleu ac yn gwneuthur y ewyllus ohonei. (804–9) 'And at once they approached

---

45 I take *Yd oed y Bown yspiwr yn gwarandaw arnadunt* (3647–8) to be a possessive construction with a sub–predicate, 'Bown had a spy [who was] listening on them'.

46 For examples of affirmative objective clauses with a finite verb, instead of a verbal noun, compare 107–8, 496–7, 1066, 1413–4, 1690–1; no progressives are attested in these constructions.

Ermin and told him that Bown was shaming and disgracing him greatly because he was sleeping with his daughter in open daylight and was satisfying his passion with her.'

(80) Ac yna seuyll a oruc y march, ac edrych a oruc Bown ar y tir yn y gylch ac adnabot y **vot yn dyuot** y dref y tat. (2921–4) 'And then the horse stopped, and Bown looked at the country around him, and he realized that he was coming to his father's realm.'

(81) '[. . .] ac erchi idaw anuon attaw y da racdywededic a menegi y **vot yn caffel** y rydit a'e vywyt yr hynny o da.' (3767–70) '"and ask him to send him the afore–mentioned goods and say that he would obtain his freedom and his life in return for these goods."'

In (75–76) the progressive marks the temporal extension of the verbal event, and it could be argued that due to the complex subordination in these instances we have rather indirect frames for the superordinate events in the clauses, i.e., *annoc a wnaeth hitheu yr iarll vynet y hela y baed koet* and *kymryt idaw ynteu y vot yn kysgu*. In (77–78) the progressive conveys additional nuances of iterativity and emotive focus on the statement,[47] whereas in (79–80) the emotive focus on the verbal event appears to be the predominant function of the progressive.[48] In (81) the non–finite progressive denotes a posterior verbal event, and although Mittendorf & Poppe (*Celtic Englishes*, 132–133) identified two possible examples of a use of the progressive with a future interpretation in their corpus,[49] it is perhaps more likely that the force of the progressive here is emotive. Finally, in (82) the non–finite progressive is syntactically independent and denotes the temporal extension and iterativity of the verbal event in a statement that is semantically parallel to (28–29) and (77–78):

(82) Bellach y dywedwn am Ermin: **Bot** Iuor vrenhin **yn ryuelu** arnaw, a hynny a gigleu Bown. (3493–5) 'We will talk further about Ermin, that King Ifor was/kept waging war on him and Bown heard this.'

In conclusion it can be said that the non–finite expressions of the progressive parallel the finite expressions with regard to their functional range.

---

47 Compare (15) and (29) for similar sentences with basically telic *diffeithaw* and finite expressions of the progressive.

48 Compare the functionally parallel progressives with a finite form of *bot* in the second part of the clause in example (79), quoted above as (46).

49 These are PKM 14.9–10, 41.9–11; another uncontroversial example is BDe 12:29–31. See also Mac Cana (*Celtica* xxiii.160) and footnote 5 above.

4. CONCLUSIONS

The results of my analysis of the uses of the progressive in *Ystorya Bown de Hamtwn* confirm the earlier findings of Mezger (KZ lviii) and of Mittendorf and Poppe. The progressive construction conveys an image of processivity and marks the temporal extension of a verbal event as a series of identical intervals without defined beginning or end. This processual image added to a verb's meaning may also result in an additional focus on the verbal event as such. There are therefore two features present in the semantic make-up of the progressive, an aspectual feature and a pragmatic feature.[50] The progressive in Middle Welsh thus appears to have a wider functional range than hitherto acknowledged. The relation between the aspectual and the pragmatic feature is more difficult to ascertain. In view of the typological similarity of the Middle Welsh construction to progressive constructions in other languages,[51] it is tempting to assume that the aspectual feature is primary and conveys the core meaning of the construction. In terms of prototype theory, instances in which the pragmatic feature dominates could then be interpreted as less typical, or marginal, uses of the progressive by metaphorization.[52] The frequency of such

---

50   A typologically similar situation seems to obtain in Middle English according to Mossé (*Histoire*), who identified three characteristic features of the periphrastic construction, namely duration, repetition, and insistance. Görlach (*Einführung*, 92) makes the following claim about the development of the 'Expanded Form' [= EF] in English: 'Es ist möglich, daß sich die spezielleren Verwendungen der EF aus allgemeinen Funktionen wie "die Dauer und Intensität der Handlung als solcher betonend" entwickelt haben'. Nehls (*Synchron–diachrone Untersuchungen*, 170) suggests that the Expanded Form had intensifying function 'bei statischen Aussagen und beim Imperativ' from the Old English period to the eighteenth century. Nehls (*Synchron–diachrone Untersuchungen*, 172) explicitly argues against Celtic influence on the English construction. For some further comparative data from other Insular Celtic languages, see Poppe, *Celtic Roots*.

51   Compare Comrie, *Aspect*, 98; Bybee and Dahl, *Studies in Language* xiii.79; and Bybee et al., *The Evolution of Grammar*, 127–133 for typological comparanda, which are, however, only valid if aspectual *yn* is locative in origin, as seems likely.

52   Compare functionally similar cases in Modern English, where the 'use of the progressive with stative verbs (*I'm hating zoology classes*) will shift a State to an Activity, with focus on its dynamic property' (Couper–Kuhlen, *Anglistentag 1994*, 233). See also Nehls (*Synchron–diachrone Untersuchungen*, 117): 'In den Fällen, bei denen die Aussage in der NEF [i.e., non-expanded form] die Aussage in der EF [i.e., expanded form] bezeichnungsmäßig miteinbeziehen kann [. . .], wird bei der Verwendung der EF der imperfektive, dynamische Charakter der Aussage hervorgehoben, oder es wird, wie bei den Aussagen mit *always*, ein anderes Merkmal aus dem Merkmalskomplex des imperfektiven Aspekts realisiert: Die Betonung der Verbalhandlung, die zu

transferred uses in the corpus, as well as the attested uses of the progressive with tenses other than the present and the imperfect, could perhaps be taken as indications that the progressive was a well entrenched and grammaticalized element of the Middle Welsh verbal system.53

---

konnotativen Zwecken genutzt werden kann.'

53 I have not found any examples of a perfect progressive (*gwedy bot yn . . .*) in YBH; in **gwedy bot** *yno wers* **yn swiwrn** *medylyaw a oruc mynet racdaw* (3082–4) 'having been there for a while resting he thought that he would go' *yn swiwrn* functions as sub-predicate—constructions of this type may have provided a springboard for the perfect progressive, in analogy to Wagner's (*Das Verbum*, 238–239) suggestion for the origin of the Irish progressive 'aus der Unterordnung'. The extent to which the progressive was grammaticalised in Middle Welsh and became obligatory in certain contexts, is still a vexed problem; obvious examples in which a progressive would be expected on the basis of the 'rules' outlined above, but in which no progressive is used, appear to be very rare. Evans (GMW 109) gives the following example from *Gereint*: *Ac val y* **kyrchei** *ef y bont, ef a welei vn yn dyuot* [. . .] 'and as he was making for the bridge, he saw someone coming' (Gereint 1061). Potentially contrasting clauses, such as *val yr* **oed** *y brenhin a elwit Sant* **yn kerdet** *ehun* (BDe 2.17–18) 'as the king who was called Sant was journeying alone', use other verbs such as *kerdet* and are therefore not strictly comparable, since *kyrchu* and *kerdet* may differ with regard to inherent aspectuality and Aktionsart, *kyrchu* being probably more telic than *kerdet*. In contrast to synthetic preterite forms of *kyrchu* and to synthetic imperfect forms of *kerdet*, synthetic imperfect forms of *kyrchu* appear to be very rare in actual use. The only example of a progressive of *kyrchu* with the meaning 'to approach' I am aware of is a present tense in *Math uab Mathonwy*: 'Dioer,' *heb hi*, 'ni chawn welet llyw y weilgi gan pob llong ar torr y gilyd. Ac y* **maent yn kyrchu** *y tir yn gyntaf a allont.*' (PKM 82.14–16) '"By God," she said, "we cannot see the colour of the sea for all the ships thronging together. And they are making for the coast as fast as they can."' The force of the progressive is both aspectual and pragmatic here. In the following sentence from YBH, *o lef uchel oedynt kyrchu y cristynogyon* (3692–3), if this indeed to be emended to progressive *oedynt yn kyrchu*, *kyrchu* has the meaning 'to attack'. This semantic development from 'to approach' to 'to attack' involves the shift from a telic image to an atelic one. Thomson (Gereint 98) furthermore draws attention to two examples, one in *Gereint* and the other in *Owein*, where the manuscripts disagree as to the use of progressive and simple tense respectively: *ac o pa le yd* **ywch yn dyuot**? versus *le pan* **deuwch** *chwi* (Owein 560; see also Mac Cana, *Celtica*, 161) 'where are you coming/do you come from?' and *mi a'e managwn yt yr hyn a geissy* versus *hynn yd wyt* **yn y geissaw** (Gereint 99) 'I would tell you what you seek/are seeking'. In both instances the use of the progressive is pragmatically conditioned.

 I am greatly indebted to Ingo Mittendorf M.A. for helpful discussions and advice during the preparation of the original paper for the Oxford meeting and of this final version for publication.

'Marwnad Cunedda' a diwedd y Brydain Rufeinig[1]

John T. Koch

CYFLWYNIAD

MAE'R ailnithio presennol hwn ar y manylion ieithyddol a hanesyddol yn tueddu at y casgliadau a ganlyn. (1) Mae cynnwys *Marwnad Cunedda* yn ymwneud yn ei gyfanrwydd â Gogledd Prydain a digwyddiadau'r 5ed ganrif (neu, mae'n bosibl ond yn llai tebygol, diwedd y 4edd). (2) Mae'n debyg fod y gerdd, fel testun ysgrifenedig, yn perthyn i Ogledd Prydain, yn hytrach nag i Gymru. (3) Yn ieithyddol mae'n perthyn i'r derfynlin gyn-Hen Gymraeg (hynny yw, cyn-*c*. 750). (4) Nid oes modd profi dilysrwydd, hynny yw a gafodd y testun presennol ei gyfansoddi adeg marwolaeth y gwrthrych, ond nid oes unrhyw ffordd i'w wrthbrofi chwaith. Dyma, mae'n debyg, yw'r eglurhad *lleiaf annhebygol* dros gynnwys y gerdd a'r iaith. (5) Felly, gallwn ystyried y posibilrwydd bod terfynlin llenyddiaeth Gymraeg yn ymestyn ymhellach yn ôl ganrif neu fwy nag a gredid gynt, i ddiwedd y cyfnod Brythonaidd-Rufeinig.

I grynhoi, dyma'r prif resymau dros ailagor cwestiwn dilysrwydd posib y *Farwnad*. (1) Yn ieithegol mae'n hynafol. (2) Nid yw'n cynnwys unrhyw gysyniadau

---

1   Golygwyd y testun gyda nodiadau mewn Cymraeg Diweddar gan J. E. Caerwyn Williams, *Astudiaethau ar yr Hengerdd* [AH] 208–233.

Cyflwynwyd fersiynau cynharach o'r bennod hon yn ystod hydref 1997 yn y Ganolfan Uwchefrydiau Cymreig a Cheltaidd yn Aberystwyth, Coleg yr Iesu Rhydychen, ac i grŵp anffurfiol bychan yng Nghaeredin. Dymunaf ddiolch i'r canlynol am eu sylwadau buddiol ar yr achlysuron hyn: Thomas Charles-Edwards, Barry Cunliffe, Iestyn Daniel, Stephen Driscoll, Ellis Evans, Katherine Forsyth, Geraint Gruffydd (a gynigiodd sylwadau manwl ar ddau ddrafft), Barbara Hillers, David Howlett, Ian Hughes, Nicolas Jacobs, Geraint Jenkins, Marion Löffler, William Mahon, Ann Parry Owen, Paul Russell, Britta Schulze-Thulin, Patrick Sims-Williams, Caerwyn Williams, Alex Woolf. Hoffwn roi diolch i Elin ap Hywel a Geraint Gruffydd am eu help gyda'r iaith a'r holl dermau; cyfrifoldeb yr awdur yn unig yw unrhyw wendid a erys yn y Gymraeg.

Cristnogol nac unrhyw eiriau benthyg Cristnogol. (3) Mae'n cynnwys darogan gwleidyddol, ond nid yw'n rhagweld *aduentus Saxonum* neu ddigwyddiadau yng nghyswllt *aduentus* o'r fath.[2] Yr unig ddigwyddiad a ragwelir, fe ymddengys, yn y gerdd ac y mae tystiolaeth amdano o ffynonellau eraill yw chwalfa'r amddiffyniad ôl-Rufeinig ar ffin Hadrian ar ran lluoedd y *ciuitates*, fel a ddisgrifiwyd gan Gildas yn y rhagymadrodd i'w adroddiad ar yr *aduentus*.[3] (4) Nid oes sôn am y Saeson. (5) Ni chyfeirir o gwbl at Chwedl Sefydlu Gwynedd. Yn wir, digon anodd yw cysoni'r *Farwnad* gyda'r Chwedl honno. Nid oes sôn am unrhyw fan i'r de i Cumbria. Mae Cunedda'r gerdd yn marw yn y Gogledd ac nid oes sôn am unrhyw feibion iddo, nac yn wir unrhyw olynydd arall. (6) Anelir unig ergyd uniongyrchol y *Farwnad* o ran propaganda dros *gwŷr Bryneich* (a'r awgrym yw bod hyn cyn dyfodiad yr Eingl-Sacsoniaid). (7) Mae'n synied am y tir i'r de o Fur Hadrian, y taleithiau Rhufeinig gynt, yn un endid unedig, gelyniaethus ond goddefol. (8) Nid y Taliesin chwedlonol mo persona'r bardd, nac yn wir unrhyw fardd arall o fri o'r gorffennol mythopoeig, ond yn hytrach aelod diymhongar a hunanymwybodol o'r urdd broffesiynol draddodiadol. Felly mae modd i ni feddwl yn nhermau rhyw ddilysrwydd yn y berthynas sydd rhwng y bardd, y noddwr a'r *comitatus*.[4] Wrth gyrraedd casgliadau o'r fath, yr wyf yn cymryd na fodolai lefel o ddysg (ac yn benodol lefel o wybodaeth a oedd yn ymwneud â Gogledd Prydain yn y 5ed ganrif) yng Nghymru'r 9fed a'r 10fed ganrif a oedd yn sylweddol fwy na honno sydd i'w gweld yn yr *Historia Brittonum* a ffynonellau eraill y cyfnod.[5] A rhoi'r peth mewn ffordd arall, y mae'n anodd cynnig atebion sy'n argyhoeddi i'r ddau gwestiwn pam na all *Marwnad Cunedda* fod yn ddilys, neu yn wir sut y mae'n bosibl iddi *beidio* â bod.[6]

---

2 Roedd Seisnigeiddio Iseldir Prydain yn broses hir a chymhleth, ond dechreuwyd synio amdani fel un digwyddiad pendant mor gynnar â *De excidio Britanniae* Gildas neu hyd yn oed y *Chronica Gallica ad annum CCCCLII.* Cymerir yn aml fod dyfodiad tri *cyulae* Gildas, rheolaeth y Saconiaid ym Mhrydain o 441 yn y Cronicl Galaidd, a dyfodiad Jiwtiaid i Gaint mewn ffynonellau Seisnig yn cyfeirio at yr un mewnfudiad Ellmynig, ond mae hynny'n bur amheus.

3 *De Excidio Britanniae* [DEB] §19.

4 Ac felly, yn yr un ystyr i bob pwrpas ag y bu Charles-Edwards yn ystyried y ffactorau hyn ar gyfer *Y Gododdin*, yn hytrach na meddwl yn nhermau *ipsissima verba* testun sefydlog. Gweler AH 44–66.

5 Gyda'r pwynt hwn, rwyf yn mynd i'r afael â'r materion a godwyd yn y drafodaeth seminar gan yr Athro Sims-Williams a'r Athro Caerwyn Williams yn Aberystwyth, mis Hydref 1997.

6 Rwy'n bwriadu trafod yn llawn mewn cyhoeddiad arall syniadau ieithyddol Jackson, yn *The Gododdin*, LHEB a'i weithiau eraill, parthed amhosibilrwydd honedig cerdd Gymraeg yn goroesi o'r 5ed ganrif. Yn fyr, rwy'n gweld yn anodd derbyn y syniad hwn am ddau reswm. (1) Mae'r dyddiadau ar gyfer y newidiadau ieithyddol Brythoneg a awgrymwyd gan Jackson

CRYNODEB O'R DEHONGLIAD

Fel yr awgrymodd Geraint Gruffydd, mae tair llinell gyntaf (i–iii) y gerdd yn anghyson â'r gweddill ac felly mae modd eu hepgor. Gellid eu deall yn rhwydd yn nhermau ychwanegiadau sy'n perthyn i gyfnod dwyn ynghyd y *corpus* eclectig ffug-Dalesinaidd.[7] At hynny, ym mhedwaredd linell testun Llyfr Taliesin, llinell 1 yma, mae'r gair cyntaf *cyfrwng* yn ffurfio *dúnad* (neu ddiweddglo adleisiol) gyda'r gair olaf [C]*oelyng*: mae gan y ddau air ddwy sillaf yr un, mae *c-* yn ateb *c-*, *-r-* yn ateb *-l-*, ac *-ng* yn ateb *-ng*. Felly nid yw'r craidd, o'i ddiffinio felly, yn cynnwys unrhyw gyfeiriad at enw'r bardd. Yr unig air benthyg Cristnogol yn y testun yw *bedyð* ('y byd, Gwledydd Cred' < Lat. *ba(p)tizo* 'bedyddio').[8] Digwydd yn llinellau ii a iii. Mae'r deugain a dwy o linellau sy'n dilyn yn un endid tynn ei wead (o ran mydr yn ogystal â thema),[9] ac ynddynt mae persbectif y bardd fel a ganlyn.

Mae'r gwrthrych (y darllenir ei enw, yn ôl y mydr, fel y gair Neo-Frythoneg Hynafol *Cunedag* [kʰunəða:ɣ])[10] wedi marw yn sydyn ac yn ddiweddar iawn (llinellau 12, 26–27, 42). Yr ensyniad yw iddo gael ei ladd gan rai o Ogledd Prydain o'r enw'r Coeling (llinell 42; cymharer llinell 10), hynny yw, grŵp a grybwyllir mewn ffynonellau eraill ac sy'n honni eu bod yn ddisgynyddion i Coїl Hen Guotepauc.[11] Yn llinellau 41–2, mae'r alarnad sy'n gresynu bod diwedd ar haelioni Cunedda ac yn atal cwsg y bardd yn rhoi'r bai ar y Coeling.[12]

---

yn gyffredinol yn rhy gyfyng, yn rhy bendant, a chan amlaf yn rhy hwyr; nid ydynt yn rhoi digon o sylw i ffenomen cyweiriau, hynny yw ffurfiau safonol a datblygedig o'r un iaith yn cyd-fyw yr un adeg mewn amgylchiadau cymdeithasol gwahanol. (2) Meddyliodd Jackson fod barddoniaeth y Cynfeirdd i gyd wedi'i chyfansoddi mewn mydrau sillafog, ac felly yr oedd y testunau i gyd o anghenrhaid yn adlewyrchu'r sefyllfa wedi diflaniad sillafau diacen Brythoneg. Ond nid yw hyn yn wir am lawer o'r testunau cynnar sydd gennym; ac yn achos rhai hen gerddi sy'n ymddangos fel petaent yn rheolaidd, ni fyddai wedi bod yn anodd eu gwneud i gydymffurfio â phatrymau newydd o ran nifer y sillafau yn ystod y broses o'u trosglwyddo, trwy ddewis amrywiadau ac ychwanegu neu hepgor geiriau mân. Mewn gwirionedd, mae'n anodd osgoi newid hen gerddi yn y ffordd hon wrth eu trosglwyddo ar lafar. O safbwynt yr acen a mydrau wedi'u trefnu ar ôl yr acen, ni symudodd y pwyslais o'i safle yn y Frythoneg tan y cyfnod Hen Gymraeg.

7   SC xxiv/xxv.11.

8   Dyma darddiad y gair, ond gweler ymhellach y Nodiadau ar linellau ii–iii.

9   Lleiheir y posibilrwydd fod unrhyw elfen sylweddol wedi ei ollwng o'r testun gan y cymeriadau a'r cyrch-gymeriadau cysylltiol amlwg rhwng yr awdl gyntaf a'r ail, yr ail a'r drydedd, y drydedd a'r bedwaredd, y bedwaredd a'r bumed, gyda'r chweched awdl yn ddiweddglo boddhaol ar y cyfan, gan gynnwys y *dúnad*. Ymddengys yn annhebygol, felly, fod yna gyfeiriadau ar un adeg ym *Marwnad Cunedda* at y chwedl sefydlu, ond i'r rhain lithro o'r testun.

10   Gweler isod, t. 188.

11   Trafodir y Coeling yn fanylach isod.

12   O ystyried statws amwys *h-* yn yr iaith Frythoneg gynnar, sillafiad, a mydrau (yn arbennig

Mae'r bardd yn defnyddio topos marwnadol cyffredin wrth gyfleu canlyniadau marwolaeth y pennaeth fel rhai sy'n effeithio ar yr holl fyd—mae'r cryndod i'w deimlo rhwng yr *hallt* '[y môr]', yr *allt* 'y graig serth', ac *echwyð* 'y dŵr croyw' (llinell 1). Fodd bynnag, o fewn bydolwg oesoedd-tywyll, Gogledd-Brydeinig y gerdd, byddai dau o'r enwau cyffredin hyn yn adleisio enwau mannau pwysig. Felly, byddai *allt* (*alt* yn gynharach) yn dwyn i gof Allt Clud, hynny yw Dumbarton, cadarnle Ystrad Clud.[13] Byddai *Echwyð* yn awgrymu 'y dŵr croyw' sy'n sail i'r enw Erechwyð 'y Tir o flaen y Dŵr Croyw'. Yn y cerddi a gyflwynwyd i Urien Rheged, mae Erechwyð yn ymddangos fel tiriogaeth ganolog i deyrnlin Cynferching Urien. Dyma gangen fwyaf pwerus y Coeling yn rhan olaf y 6ed ganrif. Cysylltwyd yr ardal ag Ardal y Llynnoedd yn Lloegr heddiw, er bod Dyffryndir Swydd Efrog hefyd yn bosibilrwydd llai tebygol.[14] Felly, fel enw priod, mae'n debyg y byddai *Echwyð* yn golygu llynnoedd Cumbria. Er bod y llinell agoriadol yn awgrymu holl diroedd cyfannedd y byd, yng Ngogledd Prydain yn y cyfnod ôl-Rufeinig mae'r ffocws ar ardal rhwng Dumbarton i'r gogledd, Ardal y Llynnoedd i'r de, a'r môr i'r dwyrain a'r gorllewin.

Yn llinell 3, mae'r bardd yn rhagweld ton o drais yn ysgubo tros gaerau Chester-le-Street neu Binchester (y ddwy yn swydd Durham)[15] a Chaerliwelydd (Cumbria). Gorwedd y safleoedd hyn ychydig i'r de o Fur Hadrian, y naill ger y pen dwyreiniol i'r mur a'r llall ger y pen gorllewinol. Gan taw dyma'r ardal y mae'r bardd yn dymuno'n ddrwg iddi, cymerwn taw yn y fan yma y mae'r Coeling bygythiol yn gweithredu. Mae'r caerau hyn yn ffurfio, neu yn rhan o'r, *ky[u]at[a]wt* = **ciuatǫt* (a brofir gan odl fewnol), hynny yw y *ciuitates* 'dinasoedd, tiriogaethau llwythol gweinyddol' Brythonaidd-Rufeinig (llinell 4).[16] Daw'r don o dân, sy'n atgoffa dyn am ddisgrifiad Gildas o 'wrthryfel' y Sacsoniaid yn y 5ed ganrif,[17] tros 'foroedd' (llinellau 5–6). Yn hyn o beth mae'n annhebyg felly i ymgyrchoedd de-gogledd y 6ed ganrif a'r 7fed ganrif, pryd y croeswyd Mur

---

y ffaith fod geiriau sy'n dechrau gydag *h*- yn aml yn ymddangos fel pe baent yn cyflythrennu gyda geiriau sy'n cychwyn gyda llafariaid), credaf fod yna chwarae ar eiriau yn llinell 42 yng nghyswllt *hun* 'cwsg' ac *un* 'yr un', h.y. mae'r Coeling hefyd wedi dinistrio'r gŵr unigryw ac arbennig hwn a fawrygir yn y farwnad.

13   Ar y defnydd o'r ffurf syml *Alt* i olygu *Alt Clut* 'Dumbarton', cymharer CA B2.32.888 *iuð Alt*, 'Iudex o Dumbarton', mae'n debyg, Koch, *Gododdin* 141, hefyd HWydd. *Coirthech rex Aloo* 'Ceredig Frenin Dumbarton' yn Llyfr Armagh.

14   CT xxvi, sy'n cynnig posibiliadau eraill.

15   Ar y cysylltiadau hyn, gweler y nodiadau i linell 3 isod.

16   Mae'r *kyfatwt* ffonolegol amhosibl sydd yn y llawysgrif yn ffurfio odl fewnol gydag *ergrynawt*, nad yw yn cynnig problem. Bwrir bod *kyfatwt* yn foderneiddiad sâl o sillafiad Neo-Frythoneg Hynafol **ciuatǫt* o'r Lladin *ciuitātes*.

17   DEB §24.

Hadrian dros y tir. Ymddengys bod y ffin ger Mur Hadrian yn dal i gael ei hamddiffyn. Roedd *comitatus* Cunedda, a'i ganolfan i'r gogledd o'r Mur, yn cynnwys tir a môr ac yn medru ymosod ar geyrydd y ffin yn y dwyrain a'r gogledd ar yr un pryd. Yn y pen draw, caiff yr arweinwyr eu trechu (llinell 6) yn y gystadleuaeth i ailsefydlu'r oruchafiaeth a fu gynt yn nwylo Cunedda (llinell 7). Mae'r sylw olaf hwn yn awgrymu bod Cunedda yn hawlio, o leiaf, benarglwyddiaeth dros y ddwy blaid a oedd bellach ar fin ymladd, hynny yw y naill ochr a'r llall i'r Mur. Mae'n debyg taw chwarae ar eiriau a wneir eto pan ddywedir i'r benarglwyddiaeth hon ymestyn dros *elfyδ* sef 'tiroedd cyfannedd y byd' o'i ddefnyddio fel enw cyffredin, ond a oedd hefyd wedi golygu 'Albion, Prydain'.[18] Serch hynny, mae'n arwyddocaol taw dim ond y cadarnleoedd hynny sy'n agos at y ffin a dargedir: mae Chester-le-Street rhyw 12 km. i'r de o'r mur, Binchester tua 33 km., a Chaerliwelydd yn union islaw'r Mur. Er enghraifft, nid oes yma fygythiad i Gatraeth a Chaerefrog,[19] ac nid oes sôn o gwbl am unrhyw fan i'r de i Cumbria.

Bydd teulu Cunedda yn gwarchod y ffin. Disgrifir y rhyfelwyr hyn yn ffigurol fel '*cŵn*', sy'n chwarae ar enw'r gwrthrych (llinell 9). Bydd y teulu yn gorfodi cytundeb heddwch parhaol (*kerenhyδ*) ar y Coeling (llinell 10).[20] Yr awgrym yw bod yr heddwch dan orfodaeth hwn yn golygu adfer y *status quo ante* ac yn cyfeirio at yr un ymatal rhag ymladd ag a fynegir yn y ferf *lu[þ]awt* (llinell 6). Bydd y teulu hefyd yn cadw traddodiadau'r bywyd llys Brythonaidd trwy gydnabod ac anrhydeddu beirdd o'r iawn ryw gyda gwisgoedd sy'n cyfleu eu statws (llinell 11).

Yn llinell 12, mae'r bardd yn annerch un goroeswr galarus yn y person unigol. Gan nad oes sôn am olynydd i Gunedda (ac oherwydd hyn, mae'r bardd yn gosod ei obeithion ar y *comitatus* yn ei gyfanrwydd), mae'n bosibl taw annerch gweddw Cunedda y mae yma, neu bennaeth tiriogaethol sy'n teyrnasu dros ryw lys arbennig, neu gapten uchel ei safle yn y teulu.

Yn y folawd gonfensiynol a delir i Gunedda, defnyddir y *topos* o'r arwr fel elfen bensaernïol amddiffynnol sawl tro (llinellau 13, 15, 20, 23). Mae'n debyg

---

18   *Albion*, fel a welir yn *Pliny*, e.e., oedd enw Prydain cyn iddi gael ei galw yn *Pretania* neu *Brittania*, ac mae ffynonellau Lladin o Lydaw yn defnyddio *Albidia* (< Hen Lydaweg *Albɪd*) yn yr ystyr hon. Gweler Koch, *PHCC* vi.1–28; *Emania* ix.17–27

19   Yn *Y Gododdin* A.23.261, mae cyfeiriad a brofir gan yr odl at *Lloegrwys giwet* '*ciuitas* Iseldir Prydain, Lloegr', sydd o bosib yn gyfeiriad at Gatraeth a'i hamddiffynwyr; gweler Koch, *Gododdin* xl–xli.

20   Fe'i profir gan y brifodl. Mae ystyr y gair yma yr un â'r gair cytras HWydd. *cairde* < Celt. **karantiiom* 'cytundeb, cyfamod, heddwch, heddwch lleol, cytundeb rhwng dwy diriogaeth, saib, oedi' (DIL unig. *cairde*); cymharer PT 75–76. Gweler isod ar oblygiadau gwleidyddol cytundeb o'r fath yn y cyfnod hwn.

bod yma chwarae ar eiriau eto, oherwydd cyffelybir Cunedda ddwywaith i gadarnle am ei fod yn *dyfyn-* 'dwfn' (llinell 15).[21] Yn ei achres (y mae'r fersiwn hynaf ohoni sy'n bodoli yn Llundain, BL llsgr. Harley 3859), mae gan Gunedda hynafiad o'r enw Dumn, sy'n golygu 'dwfn'. Fel yr awgrymod Katherine Forsyth i mi, mae'n debyg taw Dumn yw patriarch eponymaidd y Dumnonii, llwyth a leolwyd gan Ptolemy yng Ngogledd-orllewin Prydain ger afon Clyde. Felly, yn y trosiad hwn, mae i Gunedda seiliau mor gadarn â chloddwaith, ac ar yr un pryd, mae cyfeiriad at Dumn, sefydlydd eponymaidd ei lwyth hefyd. Daw amwysedd bwriadol arall yn y defnydd o eiriau cyfystyr gyda'r gair *gweith* yn yr ystyr 'brwydr' a 'tro' yn llinell 20.

Cyfeirir at wŷr Brynaich[22] fel rhan o luoedd Cunedda (llinell 21). Er yr adwaenir y ffurf Brynaich orau fel enw is-deyrnas ogleddol Northumbria'r Angliaid o tua *c.* 600, ni elwir *gwŷr Bryneich* wrth yr enw Saeson yma,[23] ac nid oes ychwaith gyfeiriad at y Saeson, nac at unrhyw garfan ethnig arall. Brythonig, ac nid Eingl-Sacsonaidd, yw tarddiad yr enw Brynaich (HG *Berneich, Bernech´*);[24] felly nid croesddweud fyddai cymryd yma ei fod yn cyfeirio at drigolion Celtaidd deheubarth Gododdin (neu'r ardal rhwng y ddau fur yn fwy cyffredinol) yn y cyfnod cyn dyfodiad yr Eingl-Sacsoniaid.

Mae'r bardd yn dathlu haelioni'r gwrthrych (llinellau 31–35) ac yn ofni bod yr economi *élite* honno a seiliwyd ar gyrchoedd ar fin chwalu (llinellau 28, 42).

---

21   Byddem hefyd, o bosib, am weld diwygio trydydd *dyfyn-* yn rhan o'r testun; gweler y nodyn ar linell 16.

22   Er mwyn gweld odl fewnol sy'n nes yn seinegol at *dy· chluden 't´*, byddai angen adfer **Bernecc´* gyda [-k(k)] di-lais nad yw eto'n sain ffrithiol *-ch* [-χ]. Er yn bosib, nid oes angen adfer HG *Brigeint* yma ac felly gweld cyfeiriad at *Brigantia* neu'r *Brigantes*.

23   Brynaich Northumbraidd oedd cartref teyrnlin Æthelfrith, Oswald, Oswiu, Ecgfrith, ac Aldfrith.

24   Ar hyn o bryd, eiddo Jackson (LHEB 701–5) yw tarddiad sylfaenol yr enw, gyda'r ystyr 'Tir y Bylchau' neu debyg; cymharer HWydd. *bern* 'bwlch'. Os felly, ymddengys na fyddai hwn yn enw arbennig o briodol ar gyfer yr ardal o amgylch Ynys Meddgawd (Lindisfarne) a Bamburgh, sef canolbwynt tebygol y Frynaich Eingl-Sacsonaidd. Efallai i'r Saeson fabwysiadu'r enw ar sail rhyw fan yn bellach i'r mewndir, yng nghyffiniau Yeavering a/neu Melrose. Gellid dyfalu hefyd tybed a yw enw cartref Padrig Sant, a ddiwygiwyd i *Banna Uenta Berniae* (*Confessio* §1), yn cynnwys fersiwn o enw'r un ardal ac yn gosod caer Rufeinig Banna (Birdoswald, Cumbria) yn yr ardal honno; cymharer Thomas, *Christianity in Roman Britain* 312–5; am farn arall, gwelir Higham, *Rome, Britain, and the Anglo-Saxons* 84. Yn y *Farwnad* mae Brynaich y 5ed ganrif yn bygwth caerau yng ngorllewin Cumbria a dwyrain Durham, ac felly ymddengys taw ardal sy'n ymestyn o'r naill arfordir i'r llall sydd yma. Wrth gwrs, gall bwlch fod yn rhywbeth gwahanol, a rhywbeth mwy na bwlch rhwng dau fynydd. Ni wyddom a oedd gan ardal gyfan y ffindir rhwng y ddau fur enw hynafol. Os felly, byddai 'Y Bwlch', *Bernia*, lle'r oedd 'Pobl y Bwlch', **Bernacci*, yn byw, yn llaw-fer naturiol ar ei chyfer.

Roedd pysgod yn gynhaliaeth bwysig i'r bardd (llinell 28). Roedd yr ysbail a rannai Cunedda hefyd yn cynnwys ceffylau (llinellau 31, 33) (roedd ganddo farchoglu (llinellau 24)); buchod godro (llinell 32); nwyddau o ardal Môr y Canoldir, sef gwin (llinellau 34, 42) ac olew (llinell 34)[25]; hefyd gaethweision (llinell 35)—oll yn oll, economi cymysg gydag elfen forwrol gref (gwarchaeoedd ar dir a môr, cyrchoedd, cyfnewid nwyddau moeth yn bell ac yn agos, bwyta bwyd môr yn y llys).

Mae teitlau ac enwau parch Cunedda yn awgrymu swyddogaeth filwrol yn bennaf. Yn llinell 37, mae'n bosib bod y term disgrifiadol neu deitl unigryw hwnnw *gweladur* yn fenthyciad efelychiadol o'r Lladin *speculator*, a olygai yn ei hanfod 'sgowt, ysbïwr, gwyliedydd', swydd yr oedd y Brythoniaid a oedd yn byw rhwng y ddau fur yn ei chyflawni ar ran Rhufain, mae'n debyg. Fodd bynnag, yn ymadrodd Gildas *habet Britannia duces, habet speculatores*, mae'n debyg bod gennym ystyr filwrol fwy arbenigol sy'n dyddio o ddiwedd y cyfnod Rhufeinig neu'r cyfnod ôl-Rufeinig.[26] Yn yr un llinell, mae *pennadur pryt lew* 'y pennaeth llewaidd ei ffurf' yn atgoffa dyn am ddisgrifiad arwrol Gildas o filwyr dewraf ewythr anffodus Maelgwn.[27]

Adwaenir Cunedda, fel y gwneir yn yr achresi, fel mab Edern < Lladin *Aeternus*, a chadarnheir hyn gan ddefnydd mwys arall lle mae'r gair *edyrn* (a ddaw hefyd o *aeternus*) yn golygu 'tragwyddol' (llinell 38).

Nid yw'r diffyg geiriau benthyg Cristnogol neu gyfeiriadau Cristnogol yn golygu o angenrheidrwydd nad oedd hyd yr adeg honno unrhyw Gristnogion i'r gogledd o Fur Hadrian. Golyga yn hytrach nad oedd dysg Gristnogol, Ladin yr eglwys a diwylliant brodorol llafar y llys wedi cydymdreiddio yn y cyfnod hwn. Yn ôl Gildas—a oedd yn gyfoes ag ef—roedd sefyllfa o'r fath yn dal i fod yn llys gor-ŵyr honedig Cunedda, Maelgwn.[28] Eto nid yw'n amhosibl nad oedd Cunedda a'i ddilynwyr yn Gristnogion.

Mae'r bardd hefyd yn ymboeni am statws y dosbarth barddol yn gyffredinol—dymunai iddynt gael eu cydnabod yn deilwng gan y teulu (llinell 11) ac roedd yn awyddus i lynu at eu dull traddodiadol o ddod â chais ger bron y llys (llinell 29).

---

25   Ar olew a fewnforid yn y cyfnod is-Rufeinig cymharer Dark, *Civitas to Kingdom* 211.

26   DEB §1.14; gweler trafodaeth Higham, *English Conquest* 87 n. 51, 117 n. 88, sy'n awgrymu'r ystyr 'capten milwrol' yn 155. Ni fyddai'r awgrym amgen, sef 'esgob', yn tycio yn y cyd-destun presennol.

27   DEB §33; cymharer Sims-Williams, *Gildas* 185.

28   DEB §34. Gweler ymhellach Koch, *Gododdin* lxxxviii a n. 2. Cf. Breatnach, *Ériu* xxxii. Ó Corráin, *Proc. VIIth Intl. Congress of Celtic Studies* 142 a 156 n. 3.

Y CYD-DESTUN HANESYDDOL

Mae'r sefyllfa a amlinellwyd uchod yn cydweddu â'r cyfnod 383×490, ac yn ymsefydlu orau o bosib o fewn y cyfnod 409×454. Mae'r fasnach ag ardal Môr y Canoldir yn parhau, ond mae'r safon economaidd Rufeinedig ar sail metalau gwerthfawr yn amlwg absennol.[29] Nid oes unrhyw sôn am rym Rhufeinig canoledig yng Ngogledd Prydain. Mae *tyrannus* is-Rufeinig o'r enw Cunedda wedi esgyn a disgyn, ac mae hyn yn cyfateb i'r cyfnod wedi gwrthryfel Cystennin III (407–411), fel y'i disgrifiwyd gan yr hanesydd Bysantaidd o'r 6ed ganrif, Procopius.[30]

Serch hynny, i raddau deil ffin Hadrian o hyd: os am ymosod, rhaid gwneud hynny o'r môr;[31] ni ragwelir ymosodiadau i'r de o Cumbria a Durham. Yn ddiweddar casglodd Kenneth Dark dystiolaeth archaeolegol dros ail-amddiffyniad ôl-Rufeinig ar Fur Hadrian. Gan fod pob un namyn un o'r safleoedd dan sylw dan reolaeth *Dux Britanniarum* yn y *Notitia Dignitatum*, gwêl Dark adfywio rheolaeth filwrol o'r cyfnod Rhufeinig Diweddar yn hytrach na gwawr llywodraeth frodorol ar raddfa sylweddol. Dyma'r safleoedd a nodir gan Dark sy'n dangos tystiolaeth iddynt gael eu hail-ddefnyddio yn y 5ed/6ed ganrif:

ceyrydd

    (1)   Benwell/Condercum
    (2)   Binchester/Uinouia
    (3)   Birdoswald/Banna
    (4)   Castlesteads/Camboglanna
    (5)   Carvoran/Magnis
    (6)   Chesterholm/Uindolanda
    (7)   Housesteads/Uercouicium
    (8)   Manchester/Mamucium
    (9)   Maryport/Alauna
    (10)   Old Carlisle/Olenacum
    (11)   Piercebridge/Magis
    (12)   Ribchester/Bremetennacum
    (13)   South Shields/Arbeia

---

29   Cyn *c.* 420 a fyddid wedi rhestru aur ac arian Rhufeinig ymhlith y rhoddion a gyflwynid gan bennaeth i'w ddilynwyr yn yr ardal rhwng y ddau fur?

30   Mae Procopius, *Vandal Wars* iii.2.31–38 (gol. Dewing ii.18–21) yn disgrifio sut y bu i'r Rhufeiniaid golli eu gafael ar Brydain wedi'r cyfnod hwn a sut yr aeth y grym o hynny allan i ddwylo'r *tyranni* 'teyrnedd'. Cf. Thompson, *Britannia* viii.316–7; Wright, *Gildas* 2–3.

31   Mae hyn yn gyson â disgrifiad Gildas o ymosodiadau o'r môr ar Brydain yn y cyfnod ôl-Rufeinig cynnar o amgylch Mur Hadrian o'r gogledd, DEB §19.

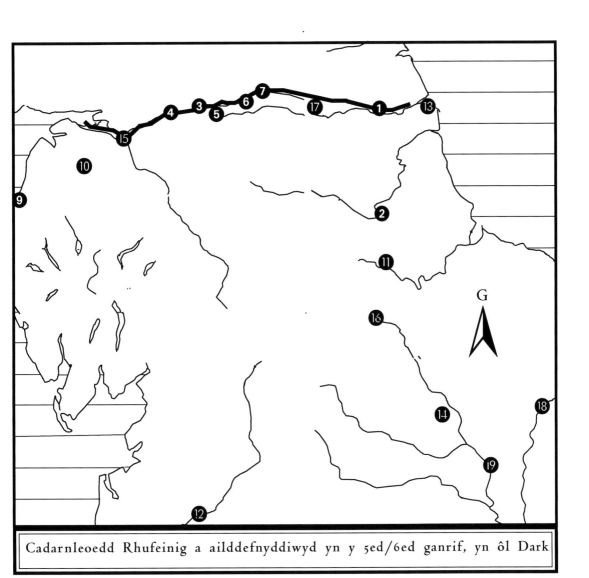

Cadarnleoedd Rhufeinig a ailddefnyddiwyd yn y 5ed/6ed ganrif, yn ôl Dark

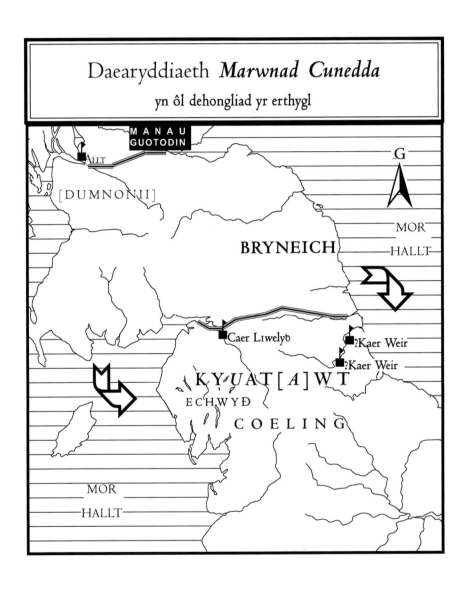

Daearyddiaeth *Marwnad Cunedda*

yn ôl dehongliad yr erthygl

trefi caerog

(14)   Aldborough/Isurium

(15)   Caerliwelydd/Luguualium

(16)   Catraeth/Cataracta[32]

(17)   Corbridge[33]

(18)   Malton/Deruentio

(19)   Caerefrog/Eburacum.[34]

Yn gyfansoddiadol, gelwir y Brydain Rufeinig gynt yn *ciuatọt* < *ciuitātes* yn y *Farwnad*. Mae hynny o bosibl yn adlewyrchu llythyrau'r Ymerawdwr Honorius at *ciuitates* Prydain yn 410[35], yn dweud wrthynt am drefnu i'w hamddiffyn eu hunain, gyda'r goblygiad nad oedd lefel o awdurdod uwch na'r *ciuitates* yn hen daleithiau'r *Britanniae* wedyn. Yn adeg bresennol y gerdd, nid yw trefi caerog cyfnod y Rhufeiniaid (*ciuitates* eto) wedi eu chwalu a'u diboblogi fel y mae Gildas yn eu disgrifio yn ei gyfnod ef ei hun (hanner cyntaf y 6ed ganrif mae'n debyg), gan olrhain y sefyllfa honno yn ôl i'r hyn a eilw yn 'Wrthryfel y Sacsoniaid' wedi 446.[36] Fel y soniwyd, mae Gildas yn disgrifio cyfnod pryd yr oedd *ciues* Brythonaidd y *ciuitates* (a defnyddio ei dermau ef) yn gwarchod y mur deheuol wedi i'r Rhufeiniaid ymadael. Cefnwyd ar ffin Hadrian wedyn yn sgil pwysau milwrol dinistriol o'r newydd o'r Gogledd, ac arweiniodd hyn at chwalu'r drefn sifil Rufeinedig yn gyffredinol.[37] O fewn ei gronoleg ef, digwyddodd yr ymgiliad hwn wedi i'r garfan olaf o'r lluoedd Rhufeinig parhaol ymadael (a hynny heb fod yn hwyrach na chamfeddiant Cystennin III yn 407), ond cyn yr apêl a wnaed i

---

32   Ar gymeriad cymysg is-Rufeinig/Brythonaidd ac Ellmynig Catraeth yn y 6ed ganrif, gweler Wilson *et al.*, *Medieval Archaeology* xl.1–61.

33   Fel arfer rhoddir enw Brythonaidd-Rufeinig Corbridge fel *Corstopitum*, ond mae **Corioritum* 'Rhyd y Fyddin' yn fwy tebygol; gweler Hind, *Britannia* xi.165–71.

34   Dark, *Britannia* xxiii.111–20; Dark & Dark, *Archaeologia Aeliana* (5th Series) xxiv.57–72.

35   Ar lythyrau Honorius i'r *ciuitates*, gweler Thompson, *Britannia* viii.315-6; *Britannia* x.207; *Classical Quarterly* lxxvi [NS xxxii] 445-62; Wood, *Gildas* 5-6; Dumville, *Gildas* 61, 64-65; Higham, *Rome, Britain and the Anglo-Saxons* 73, 82; Jones, *End of Roman Britain* 249. Am y farn taw camgymeriad ar ran y copïydd yw 'ateb Honorius' i *ciuitates* Prydain, gweler Bartholomew, *Britannia* xiii.261–70; cymharer Matthews, *Western Aristocracies* 320-1; Sims-Williams, CMCS vi.17.

35   Zosimus iv.10. Fodd bynnag, tynnodd Molly Miller (BBCS xxvii.515–532) sylw at ein diffyg gwybodaeth am y trefniadau diogelwch yn y Gogledd yn ystod degawdau olaf y cyfnod Rhufeinig. Felly mae'n bosibl fod y grym ymerodrol wedi cilio tua'r de, gan adael Mur Hadrian yn nwylo lluoedd y cynghreiriaid Brythonig erbyn, dyweder, 383 × *c.* 400.

36   DEB §26.

37   DEB §19.

'Agitius'[38] yn ei drydydd cyfnod fel conswl (mis Ionawr 446–mis Rhagfyr 453).[39]

Roedd yr ail-arsiynu ôl-Rufeinig ar Fur Hadrian, a drafodwyd gan Dark, yn cynnwys milwyr cyflog Eingl-Sacsonaidd a lluoedd Brythonaidd/is-Rufeinig *élite*, a gallai fod wedi digwydd (neu ddigwydd am yr eildro) mor hwyr â'r 6ed ganrif.[40] O safbwynt y *Farwnad*, hyd yn hyn nid yw'r Eingl-Sacsoniaid yn bresenoldeb gwleidyddol a milwrol annibynnol pwysig yn yr ardal i'r gogledd o afon Tees ac i'r gorllewin o fynyddoedd y Penwynion. Mae Dumville wedi awgrymu dyddiad eithriadol o hwyr ar gyfer *aduentus Saxonum* Gildas, sef *c.* 490.[41] Yn y pegwn arall, ym marn Higham byddai lluoedd Sacsonaidd 'cyfunol' Gildas yn gynharach na'r sôn am reolaeth y Sacsoniaid dros ryw ran o Brydain yn OC 441 yn y *Chronica Gallica ad annum CCCCLII.*[42] Beth bynnag fo'r dyddiad, gan i gynghreiriaid Sacsonaidd Gildas gael eu recriwtio i ymladd y Pictiaid, mae hi'n annhebygol y byddent wedi dod i gysylltiad, wedi iddynt gyrraedd, â Brythoniaid y Gogledd.[43] Fodd bynnag, ni fyddai gan y bardd unrhyw reswm penodol dros grybwyll Ellmynwyr a oedd yn gwasanaethu fel milwyr cyflog i'r *ciuitates* dan arwein-

---

38   Methodd sawl hanesydd â sylweddoli bod sillafiad Gildas *Agitius* yn cyfateb yn well i'r Lladin *Aëtius* nag i enw'r cadfridog arall hwnnw o'r 5ed ganrif, *Aegidius*. Yngenid y ddau, *Agitius* ac *Aëtius*, fel y Lladin Prydeinig [ajɪdjəs], ond *Aegidius* ar y llaw arall fel [ɛjɪ̄bjəs].

39   DEB §19. Ni fyddai rhai awduron yn cymryd bod sylw Gildas am y 'drydedd gonswliaeth' yn un wedi'i seilio ar wybodaeth sicr nac yn un i'w gymryd yn llythrennol o anghenraid. Felly gellid gwthio apêl y Brythoniaid at Aëtius yn ôl i'r 420au neu'r 430au. Gweler, e.e., Higham, *English Conquest* 118–45. Fodd bynnag, os ydym am wrthod yr un dyddiad pendant 5ed-ganrif a rydd DEB, gedy hyn y fath lanast cronolegol fel bod ceisio adeiladu unrhyw amserlin 5ed-ganrif ar sail DEB yn mynd yn ddrwg anobeithiol.

40   Dark, *Britannia* xxiii.111–20; Dark & Dark, *Archaeologia Aeliana* (5th Series) xxiv.57–72.

41   DEB §23; cymharer Dumville, *Gildas* 83, lle y mae'n caniatáu hyd at *c.* 480×490 ar gyfer y digwyddiad hwn.

42   Higham, *English Conquest* 118–45. Ymhlith ymgeisiau eraill i sefydlu cronolegau ceir, e.e., eiddo O'Sullivan (*De Excidio of Gildas* 176–7 *et passim*) a fyddai hefyd am weld *aduentus Saxonum* Gildas yn dyddio o gyfnod cyn 441, ond sy'n gadael yr apêl i 'Agitius' yn 446×454. Bu Cronicl 452 a'i gofnodion Prydeinig yn destun dadlau dwys dros y ddau ddegawd diwethaf. Credai Miller (*Britannia* ix.315–8) taw rhyngysgrifeniadau Carolingaidd oedd y cofnodion Prydeinig, a ddeilliai yn wreiddiol o *Chronica Maiora* Beda, y mae ei ddyddiad ar gyfer yr *aduentus* yntau'n seiliedig ar ddarlleniad (gwallus mae'n debyg) o Gildas. Mae Bartholomew, *Britannia* xiii.268–70 yn cymryd agwedd debyg. Daw Muhlberger (*Britannia* xiv.23–33; at 33) i'r casgliad '[t]he Chronicler [of 452]'s date for the fall of Britain may well be approximate; nevertheless it is the approximation of a contemporary and not to be lightly dismissed.' Mae Jones a Casey (*Britannia* xix.367–98) yn dadlau bod 441 yn ddyddiad cyfoes, ac yn fanwl gywir hefyd. Dadleuodd Burgess (*Britannia* xxi.185–95) ar y llaw arall y gallai cwymp Prydain i'r Sacsoniaid yn 441, er ei bod yn wir ei fod yn gofnod o'r 5ed ganrif ac yn adlewyrchu digwyddiad go iawn, fod yn anghywir o rai blynyddoedd ac mae'n debyg felly i'r copïydd gamddeall arwyddocâd yr hyn a gofnododd.

43   Cf. Thompson, *Britannia* x.217; Sims-Williams, *CMCS* vi.20.

yddiaeth y Coeling, oni bai eu bod wedi gwrthryfela.

Ymddengys taw cyd-destun cyfoes y *Farwnad* yw cyfnod o ryfel a chynnwrf gwleidyddol mawr yn ardal y ffin Rufeinig gynt. Yr hyn sydd wedi methu, a'r hyn y mae olynwyr Cunedda yn awyddus i'w ailsefydlu, yw cyflwr o *kerenhyδ* neu 'gytundeb'. Yn y cyfnod hwn, byddai ffynhonnell Ladin yn galw *foedus* ar hwn, h.y. cytundeb lle byddai'r awdurdodau Rhufeinig neu is-Rufeinig yn recriwtio aelodau arfog o'r llwythau i ymsefydlu ger rhyw ffin a'i hamddiffyn yn gyfnewid am fwyd a nwyddau. Roedd teulu Cunedda, a oedd yn hanu o Frynaich, felly yn *foederati* neu'n lluoedd 'cyfunol' ac yn awyddus i ailsefydlu *foedus* a fyddai o fantais iddynt gyda Coeling y *ciuitates*. Dyma'r un math o drefniant a ddisgrifiwyd gan Gildas *vis-à-vis* y Sacsoniaid: recriwtiodd *ciues* Prydain filwyr cyflog o farbariaid trwy wahoddiad y *superbus tyrannus* a'i gyngor. *Foedus* yw un o'r termau technegol a ddefnyddir gan Gildas yn y darn hwn, ynghyd â *hospites* ar gyfer y 'gwesteiwyr' y lluestwyd y Sacsoniaid arnynt, *annonae* ar gyfer cymorthdaliadau bwyd, ac *epimenia* ar gyfer y dognau misol.[44] Fel y digwyddodd yn enghraifft Gildas o roi tir i'r Sacsoniaid a'r gwrthryfel a gododd o ganlyniad, yn aml iawn y milwyr cyflog a reolai eu 'gwesteiwyr' is-Rufeinig yn hytrach nag fel arall. Mewn geiriau eraill, tueddai cynghreiriaid i godi i fod yn fechdeyrnedd milwrol yn y bwlch a adawyd yn sgil ymadawiad y Rhufeiniaid.

Mae'n bosibl taw'r un ymosodiad yw'r don o dân a oedd am ysgubo tua'r *ciuitates* yn y *Farwnad* (407×454) â honno a arweiniodd, yn ôl Gildas, at ymadael â'r Mur a'r *ciuitates*. Er mwyn tynnu'r gyfatebiaeth hon, byddai gofyn credu bod Gildas yn sôn am Frythoniaid i'r gogledd i Fur Hadrian fel *Picti*.[45] Mae'r ffaith bod Gildas hefyd yn dweud wrthym fod y Pictiaid (ar y cyd â'r Sgotiaid o bosib) wedi cipio rhan ogleddol yr ynys yn ei chyfanrwydd hyd at y Mur (Mur Hadrian)[46] yn awgrymu nad yw'n gwahaniaethu'n benodol rhwng Brythoniaid rhydd (a militareiddiedig a gelyniaethus) y Gogledd, a'r Pictiaid.[47] Mae Padrig Sant, ar y llaw arall, yn gwahaniaethu rhwng *milites* Brythonaidd is-Rufeinig

---

44   DEB §§22–3. Gweler Thompson, *Britannia* x.217–9; Dumville, *Gildas* 72–82. Cymharer Sims-Williams, CMCS xxii.55 a n. 92.

45   Defnyddir y termau *Britanni*, *Picti*, a *Romani* gan Gildas yn bennaf i wahaniaethu rhwng pobloedd ar sail gwleidyddiaeth a chrefydd. Felly, mae'n debyg fod Miller yn anghywir wrth dybio bod adroddiad Gildas, sy'n sôn i'r Pictiaid (a'r Sgotiaid) feddiannu hyd at Fur Hadrian erbyn rhyw bwynt rhwng ymgyrch Stilicho (398×400) a'r apêl i 'Agitius' (446×453), yn awgrymu unrhyw beth tebyg i goncwest neu wladychu ar raddfa eang. Yn hytrach, roedd y teuluoedd Brythonaidd rhwng y muriau wedi dod yn gyfeillgar gyda'r Pictiaid a'r Sgotiaid ac yn elyniaethus i'r *ciuitates* i'r de i ffin Hadrian. Ar y broses o 'ddad-Rufeineiddio' cymharer M. Jones, *End of Roman Britain, passim.*

46   DEB §19: *muro tenus.*

47   Cf. Koch, *Gododdin* xxix.

Ceredig (Coroticus) a'r Pictiaid a'r Sgotiaid, ond mae'n ystyried iddynt wrth-
ryfela yn erbyn y Gristnogaeth Rufeinig a'u bod wedi cynghreirio gyda'r
barbariaid gogleddol.[48]

Nid yw'r *Farwnad* yn sôn yn benodol pam y bu i'r *kerenhyb/foedus* rhwng teulu
Cunedda a'r *ciuitates* chwalu, ond ceir ambell i awgrym, rhai yn y gerdd ei hun a
rhai mewn mannau eraill. Mae llinell 42 yn uniaethu'r alarnad i Gunedda gydag
atal gwin y llys. Mae'n bosibl nad oedd yr awdurdodau is-Rufeinig yn medru
dygymod â'r baich o dalu'r *annonae* a'r *epimenia*. Mae'n bosibl felly fod y
Prydeinwyr yn y cyfnod wedi ymadawiad y Rhufeiniaid yn yr un sefyllfa parthed
eu cynghreiriaid o blith Brythoniaid y Gogledd ag a ddigwyddodd yn achos y
Sacsoniaid yn hanes Gildas. Nid oedd yr *hospites* yn fodlon cwrdd â'r taliadau
cynyddol, a gwrthryfelodd cadluoedd y milwyr cyflog gan anrheithio'r *ciuitates*.

Awgrym arall i'r un cyfeiriad yw nad ydyw'r gerdd yn cyfeirio o gwbl at
ddarnau arian, na metalau gwerthfawr, yn y rhestr o roddion Cunedda i'w
ddilynwyr (llinell 31–35). Mae'r rhestr debyg sydd i'w gweld yn *Trawsganu Kynan
Garwyn* yn cynnwys addurniadau harnais arian ar gyfer cant o geffylau (llinell 6),
100 o freichdlysau (llinell 9), cleddyf ac iddo wain wedi ei mewnosod â meini
(gwerthfawr) (llinell 11). Mae absenoldeb unrhyw sôn yn y *Farwnad* am waith
metel gwerthfawr yn drawiadol hefyd yng ngoleuni dau fanylyn o'r 5ed ganrif. Yn
y lle cyntaf, mae Padrig Sant yn sôn am bridwerthoedd o filoedd lawer o *solidi*
(darnau arian Rhufeinig) pan geisiodd drefnu i garcharorion o Gristnogion gael
eu rhyddhau.[49] Roedd y rhain yn nwylo cadlywydd o Frython oedd â'i bencadlys
mae'n debyg yn y gogledd, y tu hwnt i'r mur, ac felly'n agos i Gunedda o ran
gofod ac amser. Mae hefyd yn cyferbynnu â'r celc mawr o arian o'r cyfnod
Rhufeinig Diweddar a gafwyd ym mryngaer y Gododdin yn Traprain Law,
Dwyrain Lothian. Roedd llawer o'r celc hwnnw o ryw 110 o ddarnau o lestri ac
ingotiau arian Rhufeinig (gyda chwe darn o leiaf yn dwyn symbolau Cristnogol)
wedi cael eu morthwylio'n fflat a'u torri'n ddarnau er mwyn eu rhannu rhwng
aelodau o'r teulu.[50] Mae'n debyg taw taliadau a wnaed i gynghreiriaid Brythonaidd (neu ysbail a gipiwyd gan gyn-gynghreiriaid a oedd wedi gwrthryfela) wedi
i'r ffynhonnell o ddarnau arian ddod i ben (407 × c. 425) oedd y trysor hwn.[51]

---

48 *Epistola* §2; gweler ymhellach isod.
49 *Epistola* §14.
50 H.y., yr hyn y mae'r *Farwnad* yn ei alw yn *kymun* (llinell 31).
51 Ar y dyddiad terfynol ar gyfer cylchredeg darnau arian, gweler Burnett, *Britannia* xv.163–8;
    Higham, *Rome, Britain and the Anglo-Saxons* 85–6. Ar y ddadl sy'n parhau parthed y
    cwestiwn ai tâl ai ysbail yw Traprain a chelciau tebyg, gweler Painter, *Antiquaries Journal*
    lii.84–92; Alcock, *Arthur's Britain* 254; Mytum, *Roman West* 445–9; Todd, *Proc. Society of
    Antiquaries of Scotland* cxv.229–32; Esmonde-Cleary, *Ending of Roman Britain* 99; Raftery,

Mae modd dyddio'r celc ei hun ar sail tystiolaeth y darnau arian i ddiwedd teyrnasiad Honorius (t. 395–423).[52] Os yw llestri arian Traprain yn cynrychioli cyfnod pan oedd y *ciuitates* is-Rufeinig yn mynd yn brin o ddarnau arian Rhufeinig, mae'n bosibl fod y *Farwnad* yn cynrychioli'r cam nesaf pan nad oedd arian Rhufeinig o unrhyw fath ar ôl i dalu'r cynghreiriaid. Mewn geiriau eraill, mae'n bosibl fod distawrwydd annifyr y *Farwnad* ar bwnc metalau gwerthfawr yn awgrymu bod y *kerenhyb/foedus* wedi chwalu'n rhyfela rhwng gwahanol garfanau ethnig oherwydd i economi y *ciuitates* ei hun chwalu.

Rhydd y gronoleg betrus a ganlyn grynodeb o'r uchod:

383—Magnus Maximus yn gorchymyn i'r lluoedd Rhufeinig parhaol ymgilio unwaith ac am byth o Fur Hadrian neu, yn fwy tebygol;

407/9—Cystennin III yn gorchymyn i'r lluoedd Rhufeinig parhaol ymgilio unwaith ac am byth o Fur Hadrian;

407×411—Yn ôl Procopius, *tyranni* bellach yn cymryd lle llywodraeth Rhufain ar Brydain;

410—Llythyr Honorius yn ateb *ciuitates* Prydain, gan ddweud wrthynt am drefnu i'w hamddiffyn eu hunain;

c. 407 × *c.* 430—Diwedd ar gylchredeg arian Rhufeinig yng Ngogledd Prydain a chyflenwadau amgen o ingotiau a llestri yn cael eu dihysbyddu;

MARWNAD CUNEDDA

c. 425 × 454—amddiffyniad y *ciues* ar Fur Hadrian yn chwalu a'r *ciuitates* yn wynebu ymosodiad o'r gogledd;

446×454—yr apêl ar 'Agitius, conswl deirgwaith' gan y (*ciuitates* sy'n dal i fodoli ymhlith y) Brythoniaid;

446 × *c.* 470—yn ôl Gildas, y Brythoniaid i'r de o Fur Hadrian yn adennill eu nerth milwrol.[53]

(*c.* 435–) 446 × *c.* 490—y *superbus tyrannus* [Gwrtheyrn] yn recriwtio ac yn defnyddio milwyr cyflog o Sacsoniaid i ymladd pobloedd y gogledd: Mur Hadrian yn cael ei ail-arsiynu, a hynny'n rhannol ag Eingl-Sacsoniaid.

Pagan Celtic Ireland 216–7; Swift, *Ogam Stones* 4–6 (sydd oll yn dadlau dros dâl); (hefyd, gan ddadlau dros ysbail) Thomas, *Christianity in Roman Britain* 102–3; Smyth, *Warlords and Holy Men* 15; Salway, *Oxford Illustrated History of Roman Britain* 270–4; (ac yn fwy amhendant) Higham, *Northumbria* 56–7.

52 Ar fryngaer Traprain Law, ei chelc arian, a sut i'w dehongli: gweler Curle, *Treasure of Traprain*; Alcock, *Arthur's Britain* 180–1, 236, 254, 261, 347

53 DEB §§20–1.

PENIARTH 2, 69.9–70.15

Y TESTUN WEDI'I OLYGU A CHYFIEITHIAD CYMRAEG DIWEDDAR

i Myꝺỽyf Taliessin deryꝺ.
   [*Myfi yw Taliesin frwd.*

ii Gỽaỽt goꝺolaf vedyꝺ,
   Rhoddaf i'r byd gân ysbrydoledig,

iii bedyꝺ rỽyꝺ rifeꝺeu eidolyꝺ.
   fel un sy'n adrodd hynt rhyfeddodau'r byd.]

1 Kyfrỽnc [h]allt ac·Allt ac Echỽyꝺ,
   Rhwng yr hallt [fôr] a'r garreg serth [Clud] a llynnoedd dŵr croyw [?Cumbria],

2 ergrynaỽr Cuneꝺaf creisseryꝺ.
   [bydd y tir] yn crynu er Cunedda, yr ysbeiliwr didostur.

3 Yg̃·Kaer Weir a·Chaer Liwelyꝺ,
   Yn y dref gaerog ar Afon Uedra a thref gaerog Luguualium,

4 ergrynaỽt kyfatỽt kyfergyr—   [*r.* kiuataỽt]
   bydd ymladdfa yn ysgwyd y ciuitates—

5 kyfan-wanec tân, tra·myr
   ton orchuddiol o dân, ton fydd yn croesi'r moroedd.

6 ton; llupaỽt gleỽ y·gilyꝺ,   [*r.* lluþaỽt]
   Bydd pennaeth yn gorfodi pennaeth i ildio,

7 kan kafas y whel uch eluyꝺ,   [*r.* uhel]
   oherwydd yr uchel radd a gipiodd [Cunedda] dros y byd hwn (yn Albion),

8 mal vcheneit gỽynt ỽrth onwyꝺ.
   fel ochenaid y gwynt yn y coed ynn.

9 Kefyn-ꝺerchyn' y·gỽn y·gyfyl.
   Bydd ei gŵn [h.y. ei deulu] yn cadw gwyliadwraeth dros ei ffin.

10 Kyfachetwyn' â·Choelyn kerenhyꝺ.
   Byddant yn cyfyngu'r Coeling mewn cytundeb heddwch (foedus).

11 Gỽiscant veirꝺ kywrein kanonhyꝺ
   Byddant yn arwisgo'r beirdd cymwys teilwng sydd yn canu

12 marỽ Cuneꝺaf a·gỽynaf a·gỽynit.
   am farwolaeth Cunedda, yr wyf innau yn galaru o'i herwydd fel y gwnei dithau.

13 Cƀynitor teƀor teƀdun,
Mae yna alaru dros y drws amddiffynnol trwchus yn y bwlch llydan,

14 diarchar; dȳchyfal, dȳchyfun,
didostur, di-ail, neb dyfnach ei sail nag ef,

15 dyfyn-veis, dyfyn-gleis, dȳchyfun.
dwfn ei sail (?fel ei hynafiad llwythol Dumn), a gloddiwyd yn ddwfn (?fel Dumn),
ag iddo seiliau dwfn

16 Ymadraƀo cƀdëdaƀo caletlƀm.
Roedd y geiriau a lefarai yn galed ac yn gynnil.

17 Kaletach ƀrth elyn noc ascƀrn.
Roedd yn galetach nag asgwrn yn erbyn y gelyn.

18 Ys=kynyal Cuneɗaf: kyn kywys â·thytwet,
Ymchwydd Cunedda: cyn [mynd i'w] wely pridd,

19 y·ƀyneb a gatwet.
cadwodd ei anrhydedd.

20 Kan·weith cyn bu lleith yn· dorglƀyt,
Ganwaith (mewn can brwydr) cyn cwymp cilbost ein porth amddiffynnol,

21 dy· chluden´t´ wŷr Bryneich ym· pymlƀyt.   [r. plymlƀyt]
cynullwyd gwŷr Brynaich (Bernicia) a'u dwyn i flaen plwm llwyd [y gad].

22 Ef canet rac-y·ofyn a-e arsƀyt
Roedd canu yn wyneb ofn a dychryn [y frwydr]

23 oer-gerɗet. Kyn bu dayr dogyn y·dƀet,
[wrth gamu ymlaen] ar yr orymdaith oer. Cyn cael clwt o bridd yn wely iddo,

24 heit haual am=ƀyɗwal gwnebrƀyt.   [?r. gwrebrƀyt]
bu haid fel clawdd amddiffynnol o ddynion a meirch.

25 Gƀeinaƀ gƀaeth llyfreɗ noc aɗƀyt.
Gwyddai fod llwfrdra yn waeth nag angau.

26 Aɗoet hun dimyaƀ a·gƀynaf:
Oherwydd y farwolaeth hon yr wyf yn galaru mewn arswyd—

27 amlys, am grys Cuneɗaf.   [r. aml-grys]
dros Gunedda aml ei lysoedd, aml ei gyrchoedd.

28 Am ryaflaƀ hallt, am hydyruer môr, am breiɗ a·fƀrn aballaf.
Dros eog toreithiog yr heli, dros gnwd bywiol y môr, dros ysbail y ffwrn
byddaf farw.

29 Gßaƀt veirð a·ogon' a·ogaf,
   Datganaf yr un farddoniaeth ysbrydoledig ag a ddatganai'r beirdd [?],

30 ac ereill a·refon' a·rifaf.   [r. rifon']
   a chyfrifaf yr hyn a gyfrifwyd gan eraill:

31 Rȳfedaƀr yn erulaƀö: 'Anaƀ cant gorƀyð kyn kymun Cuneða[γ]:
   cymerir cyfrif ein rhyfela—'rhodd o gant o feirch cyn [mynnu] cyfran Cunedda;

32 ry-m·afei biƀ blith yr· haf;   [= ry-m·auei]
   arferai ganiatáu gwartheg godro i mi yn yr haf;

33 ry-m·afei edystraƀt y·g̃ayaf;   [= ry-m·auei]
   arferai ganiatáu ceffylau i mi yn y gaeaf;

34 ry-m·afei win gloyƀ ac·oleƀ;   [= ry-m·auei]
   arferai ganiatáu gwin ac olew gloyw i mi;

35 ry-m·afei torof keith rac vn treƀ.' [= ry-m·auei]
   arferai ganiatáu llond tyddyn o gaethweision i mi.'

36 Ef dyfal, o·gressur, o·gyfleƀ,
   Ef oedd yr ysbeiliwr ffyrnig a dinistriol,

37 gßeladur, pennadur pryt lleƀ.
   y gwyliwr (*speculator*), y pennaeth ag iddo wyneb llew.

38 Lludƀ//y ueðei gywlat rac mab Edern, kyn edyrn anaeleƀ.
   Roedd y ffin yn lludw erioed o flaen mab Edern, cyn y tristwch tragwyddol.

39 Ef dywal, diarchar, diedig̃.
   Roedd yn wyliadwrus, yn ddidostur, yn ddi-ildio,

40 Am=ryfreu ag̃heu dȳchyfyg̃.
   yn rhyferthwy o angau di-ben-draw.

41 Ef goborthi aes y·man//regoraƀl. | Gßir gßraƀl | oeð y vnbyn.
   Arferai ddwyn ei darian yn y safle ym mlaen y gad. Roedd dynion dewr yn
   arglwyddi iddo.

42 Dȳ-m·hun | â·chyfatcun | athal gßin |
   kamða./ Diua/ hun | o·Goelig̃.   [r. Kunıða[γ]]
   Fe'm deffroir gan yr alarnad, yr atal ar win Cunedda;
   mae'r Coeling wedi lladd cwsg [felly hefyd y gŵr unigryw].

Y TESTUN WEDI EI ADFER

i   [Mɪtûɪu Taliessin derɪd.

ii   Guaut guodolaf betɪd,

iii   betɪd ruɪd rɪfedeu eitolɪd.]

1   Cubrung halt | hac·Alt | hac Echuɪd,

2   er-crɪnọr Cunedag crësërɪd;

3   ɪn·Caɪr | Gueir ha·Chaɪr | Lɪṿelɪd,

4   er-crɪnọt | Cɪuatọt | cumercɪr—

5   cumann-guan|ec tan, | tra·mɪr

6   tonn; ludọt gleu r·cilɪd,   [> luþaut]

7   cant· cabas ɪ· uchel | uch el|bɪd,

8   hamal· uchenet′ guɪnt guurth onn-guɪd.

9   Cemn-derchɪn′ ɪ·cun ɪ· cumɪl.

10   Cumachetuɪn′ | hâ· Choɪlin | cerentɪd.

11   Guiscant | ber′d′ cubrɪgän′t′ | cänönt|ɪd

12   marṵ Cunedag | har·cuɪnam | har·<u>cuɪn</u>ɪd.

13   <u>Cuɪn</u>itor | teu-dor | teu-tunn

14   diarchar, | dihamal, | dichufunn

15   dumn-bes′, | dumn-cles′, | dichufunn;   [?< dumn-funn]

16   ɪmmatrọd | cum-ɪd-uọd | calet-lumm;

17   caletach guurth·gelɪn noc <u>ascurn</u>.

18   Äscɪnn-gal Cunedag: cɪnt cuṵɪs[t] (hâ·)tɪtṵet,

19   ɪ· enep <ha· >catṵet.

20   Cant· gueith | cɪnt bu leith | ɪnn·dorcluɪt,

21   du·chluten′t′ | guɪr Bernech′ | ɪmm·plummluɪt. [< Bernecc′]

22   Canet rac ɪ·omn ha-ɪ arsûɪt

23   oɪr-cerdet. Cɪnt bu daɪr docn r·cluët,

24   het′ hamal | amm-guɪdṵal | guur-ep-ret.

25   Gueinau guoɪth lubred noc·<u>adûɪt</u>.

26 A̲d̂u̲ı̲t̲ hᴜnn dimmi̯o̯ᴜ haı·cᴜınam:

27 ampl-lıs | ampl-crıs | Cᴜnedag.

28 Amm·rë-gablaᴜ halt, amm hıtr-ber mor, amm pred′
     ha·fᴜrn apallam.

29 Gᴜo̯t ber′d′ haı·gᴜocon‘ haı·gᴜocam,

30 hac erell′ haı·rimon‘ haı·rimam.

31 Rimeto̯r | ınn erblo̯d: | ‘Anaᴜ cant gᴜorûıd cınt cᴜmmun
     Cᴜnedag;

32 rı-mm·aᴜe biᴜ blith ın·ham;

33 r̲ı̲-̲m̲m̲·̲a̲ᴜ̲e̲ edıstro̯r ın·gaıam;

34 r̲ı-mm·aᴜe gᴜin gloıᴜ hac oleᴜ;

35 rı-mm·aᴜe torm ceith rac ᴜn treb.′

36 (Bᴜ·)em diᴜ̯al gᴜocrëssur, gᴜocᴜbleg,

37 gᴜelatur, | pennatur | prıt le̯ᴜ.

38 Lᴜtᴜ̯ ı bıde cᴜ̯ᴜ̯lat rac map Ætern | cınt etırn |
     annaıl̲e̲m̲.

39 (Bᴜ·)e̲m̲ diᴜ̯al, | diarchar, | diedıng,

40 Ammrofroᴜ | ancoᴜ | dichᴜbıng.

41 Em gᴜo-porthi aıs ım· man raco̯ro̯l. | Gᴜ̯ır gᴜ̯ᴜro̯l |
     oıd ı· ᴜnpınn.

42 Di-mm· hᴜn hâ· chᴜmatcan, attalg (|) gᴜin Cᴜnıdag. |
     Dibag | hᴜn o· COILING◆

CRYNODEB IEITHYDDOL

NODWEDDION CYN-HEN GYMRAEG. ℭ Llinell 2 llsgr. *cunedaf* y ffordd orau o
ddeall hwn yw fel diweddariad gwael ar y ffurf hynafol *Cunedag* [kʰunəðaɣ], yn gywir
HG *Cında* [kʰənɓa], < Bryth. *Cunodagos* (h.y. ‘dyn sydd ganddo gŵn [h.y. milwyr]
da’). Sillafiad 7fed- neu 6ed-ganrif yw *Cunedag* a gellid ei gymharu agosaf â ffurf
gyfarchol Ladinedig Gildas, *Cuneglase*. Mae’r gerdd yn cadarnhau ffurf yr enw, sy’n
ymddangos bum tro ynddi. Mewn tair enghraifft (llinellau 12, 27, 31), mae’r enw yn
odli gyda geiriau a fyddai’n diweddu [-aμ] mewn Hen Gymraeg a Neo-Frythoneg
Hynafol, ac yn galw felly am y sain ffrithiol leisiol yn yr [-aɣ] terfynol. Yn llinell 42,

ceir odl rhwng *Cunıdag* a Hynaf. *dibag (llsgr. *diua*); cymharer Gwydd.C. *dîbaigim* 'Dinistriaf' (GPC dan y cofnod *difâf*). Yn llinellau 18, 31, a 42, ceir cyseinedd sy'n cysylltu *Cunedag* a chymeriadau geiriol â'r Neo-Frythoneg Hynafol **cu-*, gwreiddyn [kʰœ-], > CCanol *ky-* (y sain *y*-'dywyll'). Ni cheir yr un enghraifft o'r llafariad gyfansawdd ganol yn cael ei thrin fel /*e*/. Eto, tystiolaeth sillafiad y gerdd ar yr enw yw bod ei chopïwyr Cymraeg unwaith yn rhagor wedi camddeall yn llwyr y sillafiad *Cunedag*. Maent wedi camddeall tarddiad a chyfundrefn lafariaid y sillaf gyntaf, natur dywyll y llafariad gyfansawdd ganolog ddiacen (y maent wedi rhoi iddi ansawdd sefydlog glir ac, mae'n ddiau, acen CCanol), ac maent wedi camddeall nodweddion odlol y ~*g* lleisiol terfynol, a foderneiddiwyd ganddynt felly yn -*f*. Gweler Isaac, BBCS xxxviii.100–101; Koch, *Gododdin* cxxii.   ❦ Yn llinell 4, mae llsgr. *kyfatwt* sy'n ffurfio odl fewnol cydag *ergrynawt* yn adlewyrchu diweddariad gwael ar *ciuatut, yn gynharach *ciuatọt < Lladin *ciuitātēs*. Ar yr *w* [u] Gymraeg acennog o'r Frythoneg [aː], cymharer HG *Morcanhuc* < *Mārocantācon. Mae'r camddehongli ar yr hen *u* [w] fel CCanol *f* yn nodwedd gyffredin yn orgraff y gerdd; cymharer yr *afei* ar gyfer HG *aue* sy'n cael ei ailadrodd yn llinellau 31–35.   ❦ Mae'n bosib bod llinell 5 llsgr. *myr* yn ffurf dderbyniol unedig ffurfdroëdig ar *môr* 'sea', yn hytrach na ffurf luos.   ❦ Hapax yw *llupawt* yn llinell 6 llsgr. a eglurir gan enghraifft ogleddol lle y defnyddiwyd y llythyren Eingl-Sacsonaidd *þ* ar gyfer y sain ffrithiol leisiol ddeintiol [ð]. Gwelir y nodwedd hon hefyd yn yr achres Harleaidd HG ar gyfer Ystrad Clud, lle mae'r sillafiad *Guipno* yn sefyll am *Guıþno*. Yn y ddwy enghraifft gellir cymryd y *p* hwn ar gyfer *þ* ar gyfer *ð* yn dystiolaeth dros drosglwyddo'r llsgr. yn y gogledd mewn cyfnod cynnar. Mae'n rhaid i ni dybio i'r testun aros yn y Gogledd yn ddigon hir i'r Angliaid ddod yn llythrennog a dod i arfer peth dylanwad deallusol ar y Brythoniaid a oedd yn y rhanbarth. Gwelir yr un nodwedd gyda gair cysylltiedig, Hen Lydaweg *arlup* gl. 'pedicam' 'rhwym, llyffethair, rhwystr' (Orléans llsgr. 221), Cernyweg *arludd*; mae'r Hen Lydaweg yn adlewyrchu cam-ddarlleniad ar *arluþ* cynharach.   ❦ Yn llinell 11, mae llsgr. *gwiscant . . . kywrein* yn mynd yn ôl i gyfuniad hynafol **guiscant . . . cobrıgän´t´* sy'n adlewyrchu cyfansoddiad sy'n dyddio o gyfnod cyn cwblhau'r affeithiad-*i* terfynol.   ❦ Yn llinell 11, er nad oes modd dyddio'r nodwedd hon yn fanwl, mae'r rhagenw perthynol lluosog *ôl* *cänöntıd (llsgr. *kanonhyd* yn cael ei brofi gan yr odl) < Celteg *kanonti-ịo 'a ganant' yn hynafol iawn; dyma gystrawen na lwyddodd, ar y cyfan, i oroesi hyd y cyfnod HG. Gyda'r un ffurf, byddem yn disgwyl datblygiad i Gymraeg Canol *kenynhyð yn ôl ffonoleg reolaidd; felly, cymerwn fod gennym enghraifft ysgrifenedig sy'n dyddio o'r cyfnod cyn i affeithiad mewnol gael ei gwblhau.   ❦ Dylid darllen llinell 18 llsgr. *ys=kyn=yal* is fel *äscınn-gal hynafol (heb affeithiad mewnol llwyr ar yr *i*) os ydym am weld y cyrch-gymeriad sy'n cydio'r *awdl* gydag *ascwrn* ar ddiwedd un llinell 17.   ❦ Cymerir taw hen ffurf dderbyniol ffurfdroëdig ar *kywes(t)* yw *kywys* yn llinell 18 o'r llsgr.; cymharer Caerwyn Williams, AH 223.   ❦ Is-frawddeg berthynol uniongyrchol gyda geiryn perthynol enclitig yw llinell 26, lle mae'r geiryn perthynol uniongyrchol *a*ᴸ < HG *haı* yn sefyll yn yr ail safle o fewn ei gymal.   ❡ Yn llinell 29 mae *gu̯o̯t ber'd' haɪ·guocon' haɪ·guocam 'datganaf yr un farddoniaeth ysbrydoledig ag a ddatgenid gan y beirdd' hefyd yn is-frawddeg berthynol uniongyrchol, gyda geiryn perthynol enclitig (gweler yr eitem flaenorol). Enghraifft o gystrawen fwy modern fyddai *gwawd a ganasont beirdd a ganaf.*   ❡ Yn llinell 38, cymerir taw ffurf dderbyniol ffurfdroëdig *edern* o'r Lladin. *aeternus* 'tragwyddol, ayb,' yw *edyrn.*

NODWEDDION HEN GYMRAEG. ❡ Mae cyflythreniad yn llinell ii llsgr. *gwawt goɓolaf* yn awgrymu enghraifft sy'n dyddio o gyfnod cyn y symudiad o HG *guo-* i CCanol *go-*. ❡ Mae llinell iii llsgr. *rifedeu* 'rhyfeddodau' yn dangos ôl drysu *i* ac *y*; felly hefyd llinell 3 gyda llsgr. *liwelyd* am *Lywelyɓ*. ❡ *h-* heb ei ysgrifennu yn llinell 1 *allt* am *hallt*.   ❡ Yn llinell 7, os yw llsgr. *whel* yn sefyll am *uhel* yn y testun hwn, fel yr awgrymir, yna bydd y copïwyr yn disgwyl *u* am yr *w* ddiweddarach ac roedd gan y gwreiddiol *h* am [χ] fel a ddigwyddai weithiau yn y cyfnod HG a hynafol. ❡ Yn llinell 8, llsgr. mae *gwynt wrth onwyd* yn cyflythrennu fel HG *gu̯ɪnt gu̯urth onn-gu̯id.*   ❡ Yn llinell 9, mae cyseinedd *cun* a *cumɪl* yn awgrymu bod gan yr ail air sain /u/ o hyd, ac nid, hyd yma, y llafariad dywyll HG. ❡ Yn llinell 10, mae'n debyg bod y sillafiad *Choelyn* am y *C(h)oeling* mwy cyffredin yn adlewyrchu enghraifft lle nad oedd *y* eto yn cael ei defnyddio yn ôl ei gwerthoedd CCanol confensiynol. ❡ Llinell 12, mae'n debyg taw rhyw fath o ffurf hynafol yw'r ffurf ferfol broblemataidd *cwynɪɓ*, a brofir gan yr odl.   ❡ Llinell 13 llsgr. mae *cwynitor* yn dangos y defnydd cywir ar ffurf ddiamod berf syml gysefin.   ❡ Yn llinell 21 llsgr. *dychludent*, dylid darllen y terfyniad fel y goddefol lluosog *-eint* gyda methiant rheolaidd HG i ddangos epenthesis-*i*; gweler Caerwyn Williams, AH 224.   ❡ Dengys llinell 23 llsgr. *dayr* ar gyfer *daear* yr ymdriniaeth ograffyddol HG gyffredin â'r deirsain hon; cymharer *Talhaern (Historia Brittonum §63).* ❡ Mae'n debyg fod llinell 24 llsgr. *gwnebrwyt* yn dangos drysu rhwng hen ffurfiau'r llythrennau *r* ac *n*, *gu̯ur-epret* neu *-eprûit.*   ❡ Llinell 28 llsgr. mae [*p*]*reiɓ a·fwrn* 'praidd, ysbail o'r ffwrn' yn dangos *a* HG am *o* CCanol 'o, oddi wrth'; cymharer *Ha, a* yn yr ystyr CCanol a Modern. Mae *o* yn nodwedd HG, e.e. *a· guïrdou* 'o wyrthiau' yn Naw Englyn y Juvencus; gweler ymhellach Koch, *Gododdin* 219, 231. ❡ Llinell *i* am *y* CCanol yn *gwɪr*.   ❡ Llinell 42 llsgr. mae *athal* am *at(t)aly* 'atal' yn awgrymu enghraifft lle gellid ysgrifennu seiniau ffrithiol di-lais mewn safle annechreuol fel y ffrwydrolion cyfatebol, fel y gwneir, er enghraifft, yn englynion y Juvencus.

CRYNODEB MYDRYDDOL

Mae nifer y sillafau yn hynod o afreolaidd. Mae modd darllen y rhan fwyaf o'r llinellau (fel y'u dynodir gan y brifodl) yn rhwydd mewn tri ymadrodd. Yn y cyswllt hwn mae modd cymharu'r mydr â llawer o awdlau llinell-hir *Y Gododdin*, yn arbennig y rhai hynny yn y Testunau B sydd yn llai rheolaidd eu sillafau. Trafodwyd y *dúnad* a'r cymeriadau

cysylltiol uchod. Digwydd toddaid (ymadroddion sy'n ymestyn y tu hwnt i'r brifodl)
yn llinellau 5/6 a 22/23. Mae odlau generig o'r math 'Gwyddelig' (yr un llafariaid gyda
chytseiniaid terfynol sy'n debyg ac eto'n wahanol) i'w gweld yn aml, yn fewnol ac ar
ddiwedd llinellau. Mewn sawl man, mae patrymau ailadrodd y cytseiniaid yn amrywio
dros fwy nag un o linellau olynol, a geiriau allweddol (fel *hallt* a *môr*) yn ailymddangos
mewn gwahanol gyd-destunau, gan wau'r gerdd wrth ei gilydd. Mae'r rhagddodiad *kyf-*
< hynafol **cum-* yn cael ei ddefnyddio dro ar ôl tro (ac yn aml nid oes ganddo fawr
ddim gwerth semantig), gan adleisio elfen gyntaf enw'r gwrthrych.

CYSEINEDD. ii *Gυaut gυodolaf*... iii *rυid rïfedeu* . . . 1 *ha·halt hac* . . .
2 *crinor Cunedag crëserïd.* 3 *Cair Gueir ha·Chair* . . . 4 -*crinot Ciυatot*
cυmercir. 5 . . .*tan,* tra·mir 6   *tonn;* . . . *gleu r·ïlïd.* 7 *cant· cabas i· uchel uch*
. . . 8 *hamal· uchenet' gυmt gυurth onn-gυïd.* 9 *Cemn-derchin' rcυn i· cυmïl.* 10
Cυmachetυin' hâ· Choïlïn cerentïd. 11 . . . *ber'd' cυbrïgän't' canontïd* 12 . . .
Cunedag ^*har·cυïnam har·cυïnïd.* 13 *Cυïnïtor teυ-dor teυ-tunn,* 14 *diarchar,*
dihamal, dichufunn, 15 *dυmn-bes', dυmn-cles' dichufunn.*   16 *cυm-ïd-υod caletl-*
lumm; 17 *caletach gυurth·gelïn noc ascυrn.* 18 *Äscïnn-gal Cunedag: cïnt cυυïs[t]*
. . . 20 *Cant· gueith cïnt* . . . *dorclυït,* 21 *dυ·chblυten't'* . . . 22 . . . *r·omn ha- ï*
arsûït 23 *oïr-cerdet. Cïnt bu daïr docn* . . . 24 *het' hamal amm-gυïdυal*
gυur- . . . 25 *Gυeinau gυoïth* . . . *adûït.* 26 *Adûït* . . .   27 *ampl-lïs ampl-crïs*
Cunedag. 28 *Amm· rë-gablau halt, amm* hïtr-ber mor, *amm* pred' *ha·*furn
apallam. 29 *Gυot ber'd' har·gυocon' har·gυocam,* 30 . . . *har·rimon' har·rimam.* 31
Rïmetor . . . *cant gυorûïd cïnt cυmmun Cunedag;* 32 *rï-mm·aυe iυ* blith . . . 33
rï-mm·aυe . . . 34 *rï-mm·aυe gυïn gloïυ hac oleυ;* 35 *rï-mm·aυe* torm . . . treb. 36
. . . *gυocrëssur, gυocυbleg,* 37 *gυelatur, pennatur* prït *leu.* 38 *Lutυ* ^ . . . *Ætern cïnt*
etïrn annaïlem. 39 *diυal, diarchar, diedïng,* 40 *ammrofrou* ^*ancou* . . .   41
Gυïr gυυrol oïd ï· *unpïnn.* 42 *Di-mm· hun hâ· chumatcan* . . . *Cunïdag. Dïbag*
hun ^o· *Coïlïng.*

ODL FEWNOL 1 . . . *Alt ha·halt hac Echυïd* . . . 4 *er-crïnot Ciυatot* . . .
5 -*gυanec tan* . . . 7 *uchel uch* elbïd. . . . 10 *Cυmachetυïn' hâ· Choïlïn* . . .
11 *Guiscant ber'd' cυbrïgän't' canontïd.* 12 . . . *Cunedag* ^*har·cυïnam* . . .
13 *Cυïnïtor teυ-dor* . . . 14 *diarchar, dihamal* . . . 15 *dumn-bes' dumn-cles'* . . .
16 *Ïmmatrod cυm-ïd-υod* . . . 20 *Cant· gueith* cïnt bu *leith* . . . 24 . . . *hamal*
amm-gυïdυal . . . 27 *ampl-lïs ampl-crïs* . . . 31 *Rïmetor* ïnn *erblod* . . .
37 *gυelatur, pennatur* . . . 39 *diυal, diarchar* . . . 40 *Ammrofrou ancou* . . .
41 . . . *racorol. Gυïr gυυrol* . . . 42 *Di-mm· hun hâ· chumatcan,* attalg *gυïn*
Cunïdag. Dïbag | *hun* o· *Coïlïng.* . .

NODIADAU

Yr arfer a ddefnyddir yma, fel y gwnaed yn fy astudiaeth ar y *Gododdin*, fydd ymatal rhag cynnig sylwadau oni fônt yn wahanol i eiddo'r golygiad safonol, neu'n ymhelaethu'n sylweddol arno, sef ar hyn o bryd Caerwyn Williams, AH 208–33.

ii. **rwyd** < **ruɪd*. O ran ei darddiad, mae Celteg **rēdo-* ym ymwneud â marchogaeth, fel yn e.e. y gair cyfansawdd *gorwyϑ* 'march'; felly cymeraf taw ystyr **betɪd ruɪd rɪmedeu* 'yw hynt rhyfeddodau'r byd'.

ii–iii. ***betɪd** < Lladin *baptizo* 'bedydd'. Mae'n werth nodi nad yw *betɪd*, ayb yn y farddoniaeth gynnar yn galw bob amser am yr ystyr 'bedydd', neu hyd yn oed, trwy estyniad, 'Gwledydd Cred' neu debyg; bydd 'byd' yn yr ystyr seciwlar bur yn tycio. Mae'n debyg i debygrwydd y gair brodorol *bɪt* 'byd' a hefyd *elfyϑ* effeithio'n gynnar ar yr ystyr ar lefel boblogaidd.

2 **ergrynaϭr** < **er-crɪnọr*. Grym dyfodol amhersonol sydd i hwn: 'a gryn ger bron/oherwydd'.

creisseryd < ?**crēsẽrɪd*. Mae hwn yn broblemataidd. Mae Caerwyn Williams yn dilyn Lloyd-Jones, *Geirfa* trwy ei ddiwygio i *treisryd* 'o rym rhydd', ac felly 'grymus'. Heb fwrw bod yma gamddarllen ar hen ffurfiau llythrennau, fodd bynnag, mae HG *crɪs* 'cyrch', ayb, yn debygol, ac felly 'yn ymosod yn rhydd, yr ymosodwr mawr, ayb'. Os nad yw hwn yn wall gan y copïydd, gallai'r sillaf fewnol fod yn hen lafariad gyfansawdd yn yr ansoddair cyfansawdd.

3 **kaer weir** < **Caɪr Gueir*. Yn ôl Syr Ifor Williams, Durham yw hwn; gwelir *Beirniad* vi.208, er iddo ddechrau mynegi peth amheuaeth ynglŷn â hyn yn *Armes Prydein* 20. Dylid dwyn mewn cof bod yno geyrydd Rhufeinig, Chester-le-Street/Concangis a Binchester/Uinouia ar Afon Wear, a'r enw Rhufeinig-Frythonig ar yr afon oedd *Uedra*.

4 **kyfatϭt** < **ciʋatọt* (sy'n corfannu fel *-awt*) < Lladin *ciuitates*; gweler uchod.

6 ***ludọt** [> **luþaut*] **gleu** ɪ·cilɪd 'bydd pennaeth yn ffrwyno ei wrthwynebydd'; cymharer LlC *lluzyaff* 'emrouiller, mêler', ac yn ieithwedd y Gogynfeirdd ... *werthfawr wyrthau newydd* | *a ludd i'r gelyn ladd ei gilydd* 'y gwyrthiau gwerthfawr newydd sy'n atal y gelyn rhag lladd ei wrthwynebydd' CBT, *Llywelyn Fardd* I.ii. Yn *Gweith Gwen Ystrat* (CT ii; Ch. IV), darllenwn am wrthwynebwyr Uryen: *vn-ynt tanc gan aethant golluϭyon* 'unasant mewn hedd oherwydd iddynt ddiffygio/gael eu ffrwyno'. Felly, mae'r gwreiddyn *-luϭ* yn disgrifio'r weithred o atal ymladdfa cyn dod at gytundeb heddwch *tanc*/*kerenhyϭ*.

7 Cefnogir y darlleniad **ɪ·uhel* 'ei uchel', a chadarnheir 'ei uchel fan' gan gyseinedd gydag *uch* yn yr un llinell (odl gudd lawnach gyda *uch el* | *bɪd*), ac adleisir hefyd yn llsgr. *vcheneit* yn y nesaf.

9 **kefynderchyn** < **cemn-derchɪn*. Mae yna demtasiwn naturiol i ddymuno

diwygio hwn i *Kynferchyn*, teyrnlin Urien Rheged, fel y gwnaeth Lloyd-Jones, *Geirfa*, unig. *kefynderchyn*. Byddai hyn yn creu anachroniaeth gan fod y patriarch Kynvarch, ac o reidrwydd ei ddisgynyddion, yn byw ymhell wedi Cunedda (yn ôl unrhyw gronoleg bosibl). Byddai'r datganiad yn y llinell hefyd yn rhedeg yn groes i'r athrawiaeth achresol safonol, yn ogystal â thystiolaeth *Gwaith Argoed Llwyfain*, bod teulu Urien (y Cynferching) mewn gwirionedd yn gangen gydnabyddedig o'r Coeling. Ond nid yw'r testun yn dweud *Kynferchyn*, felly nid yw'r problemau hyn yn codi. Rwy'n cymryd taw 'cefn', yn syml, yw *kefyn-*, a ddefnyddir yn gyffredin yn adferfol yn yr ymadrodd *trachefyn*. Yn yr ail elfen, gwelaf yr hyn sy'n cyfateb i'r gwreiddyn berfol a gawn yn y ffurf berffaith gyflenwadol HWydd. *ad·con-darc* 'gwelodd'. Mae'n debyg bod y gwreiddyn hwnnw yr un â'r Gernyweg *derch* ac yn *ar-dderch-og*, *gor-dderch*, *Rhy-dderch*, &c.; gweler Caerwyn Williams, AH 218. Rwy'n cymryd taw 3 lluos. terfyniad berfol ac iddo rym dyfodol yw'r sillaf olaf; ac felly, o'u cymryd gyda'i gilydd ac yn llythrennol, 'edrychant drachefn (ar)'. Yn yr achos yma, gyda chŵn (*cŵn*) yn oddrych a ffin Cunedda yn wrthrych, mae 'edrych drachefn' yn golygu 'amddiffyn, cadw gwyliadwraeth'.

11 kywrein < **cubrɪgän´t´* 'cymwysedig, awdudordedig, breintiedig' < Bryth. **co-brigantī*. Gweler Koch, *Gododdin* 150.

kanonhyd < **cänöntɪd* 'a ganant' < Celteg **kanonti-i̯o* = HWydd. *cétae*; cymharer Galeg DVGIIONTIIO a *toncsiiontio*, a gweler uchlaw.

12 Mae llsgr. **agwynit** yn corfannu fel **har·cuɪnɪd*, a chymerir felly bod yma'r ffurf reolaidd 2il berson unigol 'yr hyn a alarwch o'i herwydd, ayb', er gwaethaf syniad Morris Jones (WG 333) y gallai hon fod yn ferf person 1af unigol gydag ystyr dyfodol.

14–15 dychyfun < **dichufunn* < **di-(e)χs-com-* + Lladin *fundus* 'heb sail gydradd'. *Dichyffwn* fyddai'r Gymraeg Modern cywir.

15 dyfynveis dyfyngleis < **dumn-bes´ dumn-cles´*; cymharer Caerwyn Williams, AH 221; hefyd 'Crynodeb Dehongliadol' uchod.

I osgoi gweld **dichufunn*, llsgr. **dychyfun**, yn odli gydag ef ei hun, adfered **dumn-funn* 'dwfn ei sail', gan barhau â'r gyfres. Rwy'n ddyledus i William Mahon am yr awgrym hwn.

16 cƀdedaƀd < ?**cum-ɪd-u̯ọd*. Petrus iawn yw'r awgrym, ond yn y fan hon mae'r cyd-destun yn awgrymu bod gennym ferf sy'n golygu yn ei hanfod 'dywedodd'. I gael odl fewnol gydag llsgr. **ymadrawƀ**, byddem am weld yr ail air yn diweddu gydag *-awƀ*, sydd yn dwyn ein sylw i'r gorffennol cyflenwadol (yr hen amser perffaith) *amkawƀ* yn *Culhwch ac Olwen*, felly hefyd y gorff. HG *ɪm-guod-ant* yn Memorandwm 'Surexit'. Rwyf yn meddwl bod y *-kawƀ* (= *-gawƀ*) hwn yn tarddu o'r amser gorffennol perffeithiol Hen Gelteg (< amser perffaith Indo-Ewropeeg) **ko(m)-wāde*; cymharer HWydd. *ad· cu(a)id* < Celt. **ad-kom-wāde*, y ffurf berffaith ar *ad·fét*, *in·fét* 'edrydd'; gweler Thurneysen, GOI §533. Cymerir bod un o'r tri *d* yn llsgr. **cwdedawd** yn perthyn i eiryn perthynol enclitig, ac felly 'yr hyn a ddywedodd, y soniodd amdano'.

17 *gelın 'gelyn'. Mae'r gwreiddyn *gal-* yn rhagfynegi ail elfen y gair cyfansawdd sy'n cychwyn y llinell nesaf ac yn adlewyrchu ffurf ddiaffeithiad sylfaenol.

18 ys kynyal < *ǟscınn-gal, a gymerir yma fel pe bai'n tarddu o'r Lladin *ascendo* + *gal* brodorol, ac felly 'ymchwydd, ymosodiad'.

24 gwnebr6yt < ?*gu̯ur-ep-ret. Mae'r darlleniad yn broblemataidd ac yn gofyn am *-t* ar gyfer y brifodl. Felly, ni fydd y gair profedig *ebrwydd* yn corfannu. Yn HWydd., mae'n bosibl fod *echrad* 'ceffylau' yn tarddu o enw torfol Hen Gelteg *ekʷo-retom, gan olygu 'haid o geffylau (yn rhedeg)'; gweler Thurneysen, GOI §§263–264. Os felly, mae'r moderneiddiad *ebrwyt* yn anghywir a chafodd ei effeithio arno gan yr odl lawn gyda'r llinellau blaenorol. Awgrymaf yn betrus adferiad ar ddelw gair cyfansawdd *dvandva*, Brythoneg tybiannol *wiro-epo-reton 'rhediad o wŷr a cheffylau'.

25 Mae *gu̯einau fel y'i dehonglwyd yn cynrychioli ffurf syml hen ferf berffaith heb y geiryn rhagferfol a welir fel arfer yn y Gymraeg a'r Hen Wyddeleg, ac felly Celteg *gegnāwe < Indo-Ewropeeg *ǵ'eǵ'nōwe 'gwyddai', Sanscrit *jajñáu*; cymharer *ad-waen* 'roedd yn adnabod, mae'n gwybod, roedd yn gwybod', HWydd. *ad·géuin* < *-gegn-e, HG *hep amgnaubot* gl. 'sine mente'. Ar y ffurfiant cymharer HG *guoreu* 'gwnaeth' < Celteg *weurāge.

26 dimyaw < *dimmıǫu. Mae GPC (unig. *dimiaw*) yn cymharu Gwydd.C. *dimbáig, dimbág;* sail hwn yw HWydd. *ág* 'ofn'.

27 amlys am grys < *ampl-lıs ampl-crıs 'aml ei lys, aml ei gyrchoedd', gweler Caerwyn Williams, AH 226.

29 *har·gu̯ocon' har·gu̯ocam, dengys y llinell yn BT yr *aogon aogaf* anodd, felly tybiadol yw'r dehongliad. Mae'n amlwg, fodd bynnag, bod gennym ffurf 3rd lluos. a 1af unigol ar yr un ferf ac y dylai gweithred y ferf hon fod yn rhywbeth y mae'n briodol i'n bardd ni ac i feirdd eraill ei wneud gyda *gwawt* 'barddoniaeth ysbrydoledig'. Heb newid y testun mae'n bosib awgrymu gair Cymraeg *gogaf cytras â Lladin *voco* 'galwaf, dywedaf' neu air benthyg ohono.

29–30. Lle dywed y bardd y bydd yn llefaru, neu yn deisyf, yr hyn a lefarodd y beirdd ac yn enwi yr hyn a enwid gan eraill, gellid cymryd bod hyn yn golygu nad yw hon yn farwnad gyfoes, a bod y bardd yn cydnabod taw adroddiad sy'n cyfleu cyfansoddiad hŷn yw ef. Fodd bynnag, byddai hyn yn annodweddiadol ac yn anarferol, felly mae fy nealltwriaeth i o'r llinellau hyn yn wahanol. Mae bardd y farwnad yn tynnu ar y mawl a dderbyniodd Cunedda gan feirdd a dilynwyr eraill yn ystod ei fywyd. Mewn geiriau eraill, bydd y bardd yn siarad yn y person cyntaf fel pe bai'n wrthrych holl haelioni Cunedda, ond mewn gwirionedd ailrestru ar gerdd y mae yr holl roddion a dderbyniwyd a'r diolchgarwch a fynegwyd gan wahanol aelodau o'r llys. Mae'r bardd yn cydnabod yr hyn y byddai'r gynulleidfa yr awgymir ei bodolaeth h.y. teulu Cunedda ac aelodau eraill o'r llys, yn gwybod ei fod yn wir. Mae'n llefaru ar ran y gymuned ac yn ailadrodd yn ffurfiol yr hyn a glywodd.

31 **kymun**, nid y cymundeb Cristonogol yma ond 'rhannu' yr ysbail, o ystyr hŷn y Lladin *commūniō*. Gweler Koch, *Gododdin* 152.

32–35 **ry-m· afei** < **rɪ-mm· aṵe* 'arferai ganiatáu i mi, rhoddodd i mi'. Mae copïydd Llyfr Taliesin neu ei ffynhonnell yn aml yn camddehongli'r *u* HG yn ei destun. Yma golygai [w], nid [v]. Mae'n debyg bod y ferf *aw-* 'rhoi' wedi darfod â bod erbyn dyddiad ein copi ni. Mae'n bosibl bod yma'r un gair â'r elfen fformwlaig Galeg gyffredin *auot*, y gellir ei dehongli'n rhwydd fel 'rhoddodd'.

34 **oleϭ** 'olew (olewydd)'. Mewnforid hwn yn gyffredin yn ystod y cyfnod Rhufeinig ac mae'n debyg y byddai'n dal i fod yn un o'r nwyddau moeth a fasnechid o Fôr y Canoldir i Ynysoedd Prydain yn y cyfnod ôl-Rufeinig, fel y dengys y crochenwaith a fewnforiwyd yn y cyfnod hwn. Nid yw'r cyfosodiad 'gwin ac olew' yn gyffredin yn y farddoniaeth lys gynnar. Mae'n debyg bod hyn yn arwyddocaol. Fodd bynnag mae'n codi eto mewn ffynhonnell CCanol ddiweddarach, Hengwrt llsgr. 202, bellach Peniarth 12: *amlder o win ac olew* (*Cymmrodor* vii.136).

37 **dyfal** < **dɪṵal* 'ffyrnig' (gweler Caerwyn Williams, AH 229), enghraifft arall o'r copïydd yn camddeall *u* yn y testun.

38 **anaeleϭ** < **annaɪlem*, 'tristwch, galar, &c.' < **ande-ad-lem-*; cymharer *llef-ain*.

ABBREVIATIONS OF LANGUAGE NAMES

Av.	Avestan
B	Breton
CCanol	Cymraeg Canol (Middle Welsh)
EMod.B	Early Modern Breton
EMod.Ir.	Early Modern Irish
EMod.W	Early Modern Welsh
Gm.	Germanic
Goth.	Gothic
Gr.	Greek
HG	Hen Gymraeg (Old Welsh)
HWydd.	Hen Wyddeleg (Old Irish)
IE	Indo-European
I-Ir.	Indo-Iranian
EWS	Early West Saxon
Lat.	Latin
LWS	Late West Saxon
MB	Middle Breton
MCo.	Middle Cornish
MDutch	Middle Dutch
ME	Midde English
MHG	Middle High German
MIr.	Middle Irish
MLG	Middle Low German
Mod.B	Modern Breton
Mod.Ir.	Modern Irish
MW	Middle Welsh
OB	Old Breton
OCSl.	Old Church Slavonic

ODan.	Old Danish
OE	Old English
OFris.	Old Frisian
OHG	Old High German
OIc.	Old Icelandic
OIr.	Old Irish
OMB	Old and Middle Breton
ONorw.	Old Norwegian
ORuss.	Old Russian
OSax.	Old Saxon
OScand.	Old Scandinavian
OW	Old Welsh
PBr.	Proto-Brittonic
PGm.	Proto-Germanic
PIE	Proto-Indo-European
PIr.	Proto-Irish
Pol.	Polish
PSl.	Proto-Slavonic
Russ.	Russian
Sc.G	Scottish Gaelic
SCr.	Serbo-Croat
Skt.	Sanskrit
V	Vannetais dialect of Breton
Ved.	Vedic
W	Welsh

ABBREVIATIONS OF PERIODICALS

BBCS   Bulletin of the Board of Celtic Studies

CMCS   Cambridge Medieval Celtic Studies (vols. 1–25), Cambrian Medieval Celtic Studies (vols. 26–)

ÉC   Études celtiques

IF   Indogermanische Forschungen

JCL   Journal of Celtic Lingusitics

JIES   Journal of Indo-European Studies

KZ   Zeitschrift für vergleichende Sprachforschung auf dem Gebiete der indogermanischen Sprachen

MSS   Münchener Studien zur Sprachwissenschaft

NLWJ   National Library of Wales Journal

PBA   Proceedings of the British Academy

PHCC   Proceedings of the Harvard Celtic Colloquium

RC   Revue celtique

SC   Studia Celtica

TPhS   Transactions of the Philological Society

ZCP   Zeitschrift für celtische Philologie

REFERENCES

PRIMARY SOURCES

AC   *Annales Cambriae*: A Version, ed. E. Phillimore, 'The *Annales Cambriae* and
            the Old Welsh Genealogies from Harleian MS. 3859', *Y Cymmrodor* 9
            (1888) 141–83; A, B, C Version, ed. J. Williams ab Ithel, Rolls Ser.
            (London, 1860); *Annales Cambriae, A. D. 682–954: Texts A-C in Parallel*, ed.
            and transl. D. N. Dumville (ASNC, Cambridge, 2002).

AS Charters *Anglo-Saxon charters*, ed. A.J. Robertson (CUP, Cambridge, 1956).

Boeve de Haumtone *Der anglonormannische Boeve de Haumtone*, ed. A. Stimming (Max
            Niemeyer, Halle, 1899).

AP   *Armes Prydein*, ed. I. Williams (transl. R. Bromwich) (DIAS, Dublin, 1972).

Asser   *Asser's Life of King Alfred*, ed. W. H. Stevenson (Clarendon, Oxford, 1904).

BA   Cardiff, South Glamorgan Library, MS 2.81, 'The Book of Aneirin',
            facsimile, D. Huws, *Llyfr Aneirin* (South Glamorgan County Council,
            National Library of Wales, 1989). See CA for details of edition.

BB   *Brut y Brenhinedd. Llanstephan MS 1 Version*, ed. B. F. Roberts (DIAS, Dublin,
            1971).

BBC   Black Book of Carmarthen (Aberystwyth, NLW, Peniarth MS 1); facsimile,
            J. G. Evans, *Facsimile of the Black Book of Carmarthen* (Clarendon Press,
            Oxford, 1888). See LlDC for details of the edition.

BDe   *The Welsh Life of St David*, ed. D. S. Evans (UWP, Cardiff, 1988).

Bethu Phátraic *Bethu Phátraic*, ed. K. Mulchrone (RIA, Dublin, 1939).

BM   'Die Freilassungsurkunden des Bodmin-evangeliars', ed. M.T.W. Förster, in
            A grammatical miscellany presented to Otto Jespersen on his seventieth birthday, ed. N.
            Bøgholm, C.A. Bødelsen, A. Brusendorff (Lein and Munksgaard, Copen-
            hagen; Allen and Unwin, London, 1930), 77–99.

Branwen   *Branwen Uerch Lyr*, ed. D. S. Thomson, Medieval and Modern Welsh Series
            II (DIAS, Dublin, 1961).

Braint Teilo 'Braint Teilo', ed. W. Davies, BBCS xxvi (1975) 123–37.

BRh   Breudwyt Ronabwy, ed. M. Richards (UWP, Cardiff, 1948).

BT   Book of Taliesin (National Library of Wales, Peniarth MS 2); facsimile
            and text: J. G. Evans, *Facsimile and Text of the Book of Taliesin* (private press,
            Llanbedrog, 1910).

BT(Pen. 20) *Brut y Tywysogion, Peniarth MS. 20*, ed. T. Jones (UWP, Cardiff, 1941).

BT(RB) *Brut y Tywysogion, or the Chronicle of the Princes, Red Book of Hergest Version*, ed. and tr. T. Jones (UWP, Cardiff, 1955).

ByS *Brenhinedd y Saeson*, ed. and tr. T. Jones (UWP, Cardiff, 1971).

CA Canu Aneirin, gol. I. Williams (UWP, Cardiff, 1938); see also *The Gododdin of Aneirin: Text and Context from Dark-Age North Britain*, ed. J. T. Koch (UWP, Cardiff & Celtic Studies Publications, Andover, MA, 1997).

Cal of Ch Roll Var *Calendar of Various Charter Rolls: Supplementry Close Roll, Welsh Rolls, Scutage Rolls, 1277–1326* (PRO, London, 1912).

Cambridge Psalter *Der Cambridger Psalter*, ed. K. Wildhagen, Bibliothek der angelsächsischen Prosa vii (Grand, Hamburg, 1910; repr. Darmstadt: Wissenschaftliche Buchgesellschaft, 1964).

CBT *Cyfres Beirdd y Tywysogion*, gen. ed. R. G. Gruffydd (UWP, Cardiff, 1991–96).

CBT I *Gwaith Meilyr Brydydd a'i Ddisgynyddion*, ed. J. E. C. Williams with P. I. Lynch and R. G. Gruffydd (UWP, Cardiff, 1994).

CBT II *Gwaih Llywelyn Fardd I ac Eraill o Feirdd y Ddeuddegfed Ganrif*, ed. M. E. Owen et al. (UWP, Cardiff, 1994).

CBT III *Gwaith Cynddelw Brydydd Mawr*, i, ed. N. A. Jones and A. Parry Owen (UWP, Cardiff, 1991).

CBT IV *Gwaith Cynddelw Brydydd Mawr*, ii, ed. N. A. Jones and A. Parry Owen (UWP, Cardiff, 1995).

CBT V *Gwaith Llywarch ap Llywelyn 'Prydydd y Moch'*, ed. E. M. Jones with N. A. Jones (UWP, Cardiff, 1991).

CBT VI *Gwaith Dafydd Benfras ac Eraill o Feirdd Hanner Cyntaf y Drydedd Ganrif ar Ddeg*, ed. N. G. Costigan et al. (UWP, Cardiff, 1995).

CBT VII *Gwaith Bleddyn Fardd ac Eraill o Feirdd Ail Hanner y Drydedd Ganrif ar Ddeg*, ed. R. M. Andrews et al. (UWP, Cardiff, 1996).

CG *Críth Gablach*, ed. D. A. Binchy (DIAS, Dublin, 1941).

CIH *Corpus Iuris Hibernici*, ed. D. A. Binchy(DIAS, Dublin, 1978).

CLlH Canu Llywarch Hen, ed. I. Williams (UWP, Cardiff, 1935)

CO *Culhwch ac Olwen*, gol. R. Bromwich, D. S. Evans (UWP, Cardiff, 1988); *Culhwch and Olwen: An Edition and Study of the Oldest Arthurian Tale*, ed. R. Bromwich, D. S. Evans (UWP, Cardiff, 1992).

Cóic conara fugill *Cóic conara fugill, Die Fünf Wege zum Urteil, ein altirischer Rechstext*, ed. R. Thurneysen, *Abhandlungen der preussischen Akademie der Wissenschaften, Phil.-Hist.*

Klasse, Jahrgang 1925 (Berlin, 1926).

Computus   'The computus fragment', ed. I. Williams, BBCS iii (1927) 245–272.

Credo Athanasius Sant   'Credo Athanasius Sant', ed. H. Lewis, BBCS v (1929–31) 93–203.

CT   *Canu Taliesin*, ed. I. Williams (UWP, Cardiff, 1960), English version by J. E. Caerwyn Williams, *The Poems of Taliesin* [abbr. PT], Mediaeval and Modern Welsh Series III (DIAS, Dublin, 1968).

DEB   Gildas, *De excidio Britanniae*, ed. M. Winterbottom (Phillimore, Chichester, 1978).

EWGT   *Early Welsh Genealogical Tracts*, ed. P. C. Bartrum (UWP, Cardiff, 1966).

Gereint   *Ystorya Gereint uab Erbin*, ed. R. L. Thomson, Medieval and Modern Welsh Series X (DIAS, Dublin, 1997).

GM   Gwarchan Maelderw; see '*Gwarchan Maeldderw*: a "lost" medieval Welsh classic', ed. G. R. Isaac, CMCS xliv (2002) 73–96.

GP   *Gramadegau'r Penceirddiaid*, ed. G.J. Williams, E.J. Jones (UWP, Cardiff, 1934).

Gwaith Casnodyn *Gwaith Casnodyn*, ed. R. I. Daniel, Cyfres Beirdd yr Uchelwyr (University of Wales Centre for Advanced Welsh and Celtic Studies, Aberystwyth, 1999).

Gwaith Gruffydd ap Dafydd ap Tudur *et al. Gwaith Gruffydd ap Dafydd ap Tudur, Gwilym Du o Arfon, Trahaearn Brydydd Mawr ac Iorwerth Beli*, ed. N. G. Costigan (Bosco) *et al.*, Cyfres Beirdd yr Uchelwyr (University of Wales Centre for Advanced Welsh and Celtic Studies, Aberystwyth, 1995).

H   Llawysgrif Hendregradredd (NLW MS 6680B).

HB   'Nennius', *Historia Brittonum*, ed. T. Mommsen, *Monumenta Germaniae Historica, Chronica Minora*, vol. iii (Weidmann, Berlin, 1894), 111–222; translated by J. Morris, *Nennius: British History and the Welsh Annals* (Phillimore, Chichester, 1980); *The* Historia Brittonum *3: The 'Vatican' Recension*, ed. D. N. Dumville (Boydell and Brewer, Woodbridge, 1985).

Liber Landavensis The Text of the Book of Llan Dâv, ed. J. G. Evans, J. Rhŷs (Clarendon, Oxford, 1893).

Litt. Wall.   *Littere Wallie*, ed. J. G. Edwards (UWP, Cardiff, 1940).

LlDC   *Llyfr Du Caerfyrddin*, ed. A. O. H. Jarman (UWP, Cardiff, 1982).

Marwnad Cunedda   '"Marwnad Cunedda" o Lyfr Taliesin', ed. J. E. C. Williams, in *Astudiaethau ar yr Hengerdd*, 208–33; see J. T. Koch above, pp. 171–197.

Owein   *Owein or Chwedyl Iarlles y Ffynnawn*, ed. R. L. Thomson, Medieval and Modern Welsh Series IV (DIAS, Dublin, 1968).

Ox. 1   Oxford, Bodley MS, Auct. F.4.32 (Liber Commonei); facsimile: *Saint Dunstan's Classbook from Glastonbury*, ed. R. W. Hunt (North-Holland Publishing Co., Amsterdam, 1961).

Patrick, *Epistola* 'Liber epistolarum Sancti Patricii episcopi: Introduction, Text' and Commentary', ed. L. Bieler, *Classica et Mediaevalia* xi (1950), 1–150; xii (1952), 81–214. Translated by E. B. Hood, *Saint Patrick: His Writings and Muirchu's Life* (Phillimore, Chichester, 1978).

Peredur   *Historia Peredur vab Efrawc*, ed. G. W. Goetinck (UWP, Cardiff, 1976).

PKM   *Pedeir Keinc y Mabinogi*, gol. I. Williams (UWP, Cardiff, 1930).

Procopius   Procopius, *History of the Vandal Wars*, ed. H. B. Dewing, 7 vols. (Loeb, Cambridge, Mass., 1914–40)

PT   See CT.

Pwyll   *Pwyll Pendeuic Dyuet* ed. R. L. Thomson, Medieval and Modern Welsh Series I (DIAS, Dublin, 1957).

RV   Rig Veda: *Der Rig-Veda* I-IV, ed. K. Geldner (Harvard UP, Cambridge, Mass., 1951–57).

Salisbury Psalter *The Salisbury Psalter*, ed. K. Sisam and C. Sisam, Early English Text Society original series 242 (OUP, Oxford, 1959).

SHD   *Survey of the Honour of Denbigh*, ed. P. Vinogradoff, F. Morgan (British Academy, London, 1914).

TN   *Testament Newydd ein Arglwydd Jesu Christ*, gol. W. Salesbury (Denham, London, 1567)

TYP²   *Trioedd Ynys Prydein*, ed. R. Bromwich, 2nd edn. (UWP, Cardiff, 1978).

Valuation of Norwich   *Valuation of Norwich*, ed. W. E. Lunt (Clarendon, Oxford, 1926).

VSB   *Vitae Sanctorum Britanniae et Genealogiae*, ed. A. W. Wade-Evans (UWP, Cardiff, 1944).

YBH   *Ystorya Bown de Hamtwn*, gol. M. Watkin (UWP, Cardiff, 1958).

YT   *Ystoria Taliesin*, ed. P. K. Ford (UWP, Cardiff, 1992).

Zosimus   Zosimus, *Historia Nova*, ed. L. Mendelssohn (Teubner, Leipzig, 1887).

SECONDARY SOURCES

V. I. Abaev, *Istoriko-etimologiċeskij slovar' osetinskogo jazyka* IV (Izdvo Akademii Nauk SSSR. Leningrad, 1989).

Akten des 2. deutschen Keltologensymposium (Bonn, 2.4. April 1997) hrsg. S. Zimmer, R. Ködderitzsch, A. Wigger; Buchreihe der Zeitschrift für celtische Philologie, Bd. 17 (Niemeyer, Tübingen, 1999).

L. Alcock, *Arthur's Britain. History and Archaeology AD 367–634* (Penguin, Harmondsworth, 1989)

R. M. Andrews, 'Y Rhagenwau ôl yng ngherddi'r Gogynfeirdd' BBCS xxxvi (1989) 12–29.

Astudiaethau ar yr Hengerdd: Studies in Old Welsh Poetry cyflwynedig i Syr Idris Foster, ed. Rachel Bromwich and R. Brinley Jones (UWP, Cardiff, 1978).

G. Awbery, *Pembrokeshire Welsh. A Phonological Study* (Welsh Folk Museum, St. Fagan's, 1986).

G. Awbery, A. E. Jones, R. Suggett, 'Slander and defamation: a new source for historical dialectology' *Cardiff Working Papers in Linguistics* iv (1985) 1–24.

C. Bartholomae, *Altiranisches Wörterbuch* (Trübner, Strassburg, 1904).

P. Bartholomew, 'Fifth-century facts', *Britannia* xiii (1982) 261–70.

E. Benveniste, *Études sur la langue ossète* (Klincksieck, Paris, 1959).

H. Bohman, *Studies in the Middle English dialects of Devon and London* (Pehrsson, Göteborg, 1944).

L. Breatnach, 'Some remarks on the relative in Old Irish', *Ériu* xxxi (1980) 1–9.

L. Breatnach, '"The Caldron of Poesy"', *Ériu* xxxii (1981) 45–93.

A. Breen, 'The liturgical materials in MS. Oxford, Bodleian Library, Auct. F.4/32', *Archiv für Liturgiewissenschaft*, xxxiv (1992) 121–53.

G. Broderick, 'Manx' in *The Celtic Languages*, ed. M. J. Ball with J. Fife (Routledge, London and New York, 1993) 228–85.

M. Budny, '"St Dunstan's Classbook" and its frontispiece: Dunstan's portrait and autograph', in *St Dunstan. His Life, Times and Cult*, ed. N. Ramsey, M. Sparks, T. Tatton-Brown (Boydell, Woodbridge, 1992), 103–42.

R. W. Burgess, 'The dark ages return to fifth-century Britain: the "restored" Gallic Chronicle exploded', *Britannia*, xxi (1990) 185–95.

A. Burnett, 'Clipped siliquae and the end of Roman Britain', *Britannia* xv (1984) 163–8.

P. Busse, *Cynddelw Brydydd Mawr (fl. 1155–95)—Archaismus und Innovation: Sprache und Metrik eines kymrischen Hofdichters des 12. Jahrhunderts* (Nodus, Münster, 2002).

P. Busse, 'Die 3. Sg. Prät. im Mittelkymrischen—ein Wechsel im Paradigma', ZCP lii (2001) 154–99.

J. T. Bybee, Ö. Dahl, 'The creation of tense and aspect systems in the languages of the world', *Studies in Language*, xiii (1989) 51–103.

J. T. Bybee, R. Perkins, W. Pagliuca, *The Evolution of Grammar. Tense, Aspect, and Modality in the Languages of the World* (University of Chicago Press, Chicago, 1994).

E. Campanile, *Profilo etimologico del cornico antico* (Pacini, Pisa, 1974).

A. Campbell, *Old English Grammar* (OUP, Oxford, 1959).

CCCG = H. Lewis, H. Pedersen, *A Concise Comparative Celtic Grammar* (Vandenhoeck & Ruprecht, Göttingen, 1961).

G. Charles-Edwards, 'The scribes of the Red Book of Hergest', NLWJ xxi (1979/80) 246–56.

T. M. Charles-Edwards, 'The authenticity of the *Gododdin*: an historian's view' in *Astudiaethau ar yr Hengerdd*, 44–71.

T. M. Charles-Edwards, 'The Uses of the Book in Wales, *c.* 400–1100', in *The Cambridge History of the Book*, vol. I (CUP, Cambridge, forthcoming).

T. M. Charles-Edwards, *The Welsh Laws* (UWP, Cardiff, 1989).

T. M. Charles-Edwards, P. Russell, 'The Hendregadredd Manuscript and the Orthography and Phonology of Welsh in the early fourteenth century', NLWJ xxviii (1993/94) 419–62.

R. Cleasby, G. Vigfusson, W. Craigie, *An Icelandic—English Dictionary* (Clarendon, Oxford 1957).

B. Comrie, *Aspect* (CUP, Cambridge, 1976).

B. Čop, 'Beiträge zur indogermanischen Wortforschung', *Zeitschrift für vergleichende Sprachforschung* lxxiv (1956) 225–32.

E. Couper-Kuhlen, 'On the foregrounded progressive in American conversational narrative: a new development', in *Anglistentag 1994 Graz*, ed. W. Riehle, H. Keiper (Max Niemeyer, Tübingen, 1995) 229–245.

W. Cowgill, 'The etymology of Irish *guidid* and the outcome of *$gʷh$ in Celtic' in *Lautgeschichte und Etymologie. Akten der Vi. Fachtagung der Indogermanischen Gesellschaft. Wien*, ed. M. Mayrhofer, M. Peters, O. E. Pfeiffer (Reichert, Wiesbaden, 1980) 49–78.

H. H. E. Craster, 'The Glosses of the Codex Oxoniensis posterior', RC xl (1923) 135–6.

A. O. Curle, *The Treasure of Traprain* (Maclehose, Jackson & Co., Glasgow, 1923).

K. Dark, 'A Sub-Roman re-defence of Hadrian's Wall?', *Britannia* xxiii (1992) 111–20.

K. Dark, *From Civitas to Kingdom. British Political Continuity 300–800* (Leicester UP, Leicester, 1994).

K. Dark and S. P. Dark, 'New archaeological and palynological evidence for a sub-Roman occupation of Hadrian's Wall', *Archaeologia Aeliana* xxiv (5th series) (1996) 57–72.

J. R. Davies, '*Liber Landavensis*: its date and the identity of its editor', CMCS xxxv (Summer 1998) 1–11.

P. W. Davies, R. Saunders, *A Grammar of Bella Coola*, University of Montana Occasional Papers in Linguistics no. 13 (University of Montana, Missoula, Montana, 1997).

W. Davies, *The Llandaff Charters* (NLW, Aberystwyth, 1979).

W. Davies, *An Early Welsh Microcosm. Studies in the Llandaff Charters* (RHS, London, 1978).

W. Davies, 'The orthography of the personal names in the charters of the *Liber Landavensis*', BBCS xxviii (1979/80) 553–7.

D. De Bruyne, 'Une abréviation inconnue', *Palaeographia latina* v (1927) 48–49.

D. De Bruyne, 'Encore l'abréviation de *haeret*', *Palaeographia latina* vi (1929) 67–68.

A. Deissmann, *Licht vom Osten. Das neue Testament und die neuentdeckten Texte der hellenistich-nomischen Welt*. 3rd edn. (Mohr, Tübingen, 1909).

R. Delaporte (= R. ar Porzh), *Geriadur brezhoneg-saozneg / Breton-English dictionary* (s.l. 1989).

R. Derksen, *Metatony in Baltic* (Rodopi, Amsterdam/Atlanta, 1996).

R. Derolez, *Runica manuscripta* (De Tempel, Bruges, 1954).

B. Dickins, *Runic and heroic poems* (CUP, Cambridge, 1915).

D. N. Dumville, *English Caroline Script and Monastic History: Studies in Benedictinism, AD 950–1030* (Boydell, Woodbridge, 1993).

D. N. Dumville, 'The chronology of *De Excidio Britanniae*, Book i', in *Gildas. New Approaches*, 61–84.

D. N. Dumville, 'A Thesaurus Paleoanglicus? The Celtic experience', in *Anglo-Saxon Glossography*, ed. R. Derolez (Koninklijke Academie voor Wetenschappen, Letteren en Schone Kunsten, Brussells, 1992), 61–76.

Early Welsh Poetry: Studies in the Book of Aneirin, ed. B. F. Roberts et al. (NLW, Aberystwyth, 1988).

Ekwall, ERN = E. Ekwall, *English River-Names* (OUP, Oxford, 1928).

E. Ekwall, *Etymological notes on English place-names* (Gleerup, Lund, 1959).

R. W. V. Elliott, *Runes: an introduction* (Manchester UP, Manchester, 1963).

L. P. Elwell-Sutton, *Colloquial Persian* (Kegan Paul, Trench, Trubner & Co., London, 1941).

E. Ernault, *Dictionnaire étymologique du breton moyen* (= second part of *Le Mystère de Sainte Barbe*) (Thorin, Paris, 1888).

E. Ernault, *Glossaire moyen-breton* I-II (Bouillon, Paris, 1895).

A. S. Esmonde-Cleary, *The Ending of Roman Britain* (Batsford, London, 1989)

Evans, GMW = D. S. Evans, *A Grammar of Middle Welsh* (DIAS, Dublin, 1964).

F. Falc'hun, *L'histoire de la langue bretonne d'après la géographie linguistique* (Presse universitaire, Rennes, 1949; new enlarged edition: *Perspectives nouvelles sur l'histoire de la langue bretonne*, Union générale d'Editions, Paris, 1981).

F. Favereau, *Geriadur ar brezhoneg a-vremañ / Dictionnaire du breton contemporain* (Skol Vreizh, Morlaix, 1993).

G. G. Findlay, 'The worth of sparrows, Matthew X.29–31, Luke XII,6–7', *The Expositor* vii (second series) (1884) 103–16.

J. Firbas, 'Scene and Perspective', *Brno Studies in English* 14 (1981) 37–79.

L. Fleuriot, C. Evans, *A Dictionary of Old Breton / Dictionnaire du vieux-breton* I–II (Prepcorp, Toronto, 1985).

M. Förster, *Der Flussname Themse und seine Sippe* (Sitzungberichte der Bayerischen Akademie der Wissenschaften. Philosoph-Historische Abteilung 1941, Band I, Munich, 1941).

W. Foy, 'Die indogermanischen s-Laute (s und z) im Keltischen', IF vi (1896) 313–39.

G. Friedlein, 'Victori Calculus e codice Vaticano editus', *Bolletino di bibliografia e di storia degli scienze matematiche e fisiche*, iv (1871) 443–463.

G. Friedlein, 'Der Calculus des Victorius', *Zeitschrift für Mathematik und Physik*, xvi (1871) 42–79.

H. Frisk, *Zur indoiranischen und griechischen Nominalbildung* (Elandes, Göteborg 1934).

O. Fynes-Clinton, *The Welsh vocabulary of the Bangor district* (Clarendon, Oxford 1913; reprint Llanerch Press, Felinfach 1995).

GA: B. Griffiths, D. Glyn Jones, *The Welsh Academy English-Welsh Dictionary / Geiriadur yr Academi* (UWP, Cardiff, 1995).

H. B. Garey, 'Verbal aspect in French', *Language* xxxiii (1957) 91–110.

Geirfa = J. Lloyd-Jones, J., *Geirfa Barddoniaeth Gynnar Gymraeg* (UWP, Cardiff, 1931–63).

K. Geldner, *Der Rig-Veda* I-IV (Harvard Univerity Press, Cambridge, Mass., 1951–57).

O. D. Gensler, 'Why should a demonstrative turn into a preposition? The evolution of Welsh predicative *yn*', *Language* lxxviii (2002) 710–64.

Gildas. New Approaches, ed. M. Lapidge, D. N. Dumville (Boydell and Brewer, Woodbridge, 1984).

W. Gillies, 'Scottish Gaelic' in *The Celtic Languages*, ed. M. J. Ball with J. Fife (Routledge, London and New York) 145–227.

M. Görlach, *Einführung ins Frühneuenglische* (Winter, Heidelberg, 1994).

GOI = R. Thurneysen, *A Grammar of Old Irish* (DIAS, Dublin, 1946).

GPC = *Geiriadur Prifysgol Cymru: A Dictionary of the Welsh Language*, ed. R. J. Thomas, *et al.* (UWP, Cardiff, 1950–2002).

H. Grassmann, *Wörterbuch zum Rig-Veda* (Harrassowitz, Wiesbaden 1875, reprint with additions 1996).

R. G. Gruffydd. 'Canu Cadwallon ap Cadfan', in *Astudiaethau ar yr Hengerdd*, 25–43.

R. G. Gruffydd, 'Wales's second grammarian: Dafydd Ddu of Hiraddug', PBA xc (1996) 1–28.

R. G. Gruffydd, 'From Gododdin to Gwynedd: reflections on the story of Cunedda', SC xxiv/xxv (1989/90) 1–14.

A. Guerreau-Jalabert, *Questiones grammaticales, Abbon de Fleury* (Belles Lettres, Paris, 1982).

A Guide to Welsh Literature, vol. 1, ed. A. O. H. Jarman, G. R. Hughes, 2nd edition (Christopher Davies, Swansea, 1992).

S. Gwara (ed.), *Latin Colloquies from Pre-Conquest Britain*, Toronto Medieval Latin Texts, 22, (Centre for Medieval Studies, Toronto, 1996).

S. Gwara, D. W. Porter, *Anglo-Saxon Conversations. The Colloquies of Aelfric Bata* (Boydell, Woodbridge, 1997).

J. Hajek, *Universals of Sound Change in Nasalization*, Publications of the Philological Society, 31 (Blackwell, Oxford, 1997).

E. P. Hamp. 'Varia etymologica. I. Welsh *ffriw, ewin, tafod* and labiovelars', EC xiv (1975) 461–6.

E. P. Hamp, 'Varia. 3. OW *enep* and the imperfect 3 sg.', *Ériu*, xxv (1974) 268–70.

E. P. Hamp, 'Miscellanea Celtica', SC x/xi (1975/76) 54–73.

Haycock, BBGCC = M. Haycock, gol., *Blodeugerdd Barddas o Ganu Crefyddol Cynnar* (Cyhoeddiadau Barddas, Llandybïe, 1994).

M. Haycock, 'Metrical models for the poems in the Book of Taliesin' in *Early Welsh Poetry*, 155–77.

F. Heidermanns, *Etymologisches Wörterbuch der germanischen Primäradjektive* (de Gruyter, Berlin/New York, 1993).

V. Henry, *Lexique Étymologique des termes les plus usuels du breton moderne* (Bibliothèque bretonne armoricaine, Rennes, 1900).

A. Heubeck, 'Mykenisch *qi-si-po* = ξίφος', Minos vi/1 (1958) 55–60.

N. J. Higham, *The English Conquest. Gildas and Britain in the Fifth Century* (Manchester UP, Manchester/New York, 1994)

N. J. Higham, *The Kingdom of Northumbria, AD 350–1100* (Sutton, Stroud, 1993).

N. J. Higham, *Rome, Britain and the Angle-Saxons* (Seaby, London, 1992).

J. G. F. Hind, 'The Romano-British name for Corbridge' Britannia xi (1980) 165–71.

Hispano-Gallo-Brittonica. Essays in honour of Professor D. Ellis Evans on the occasion of his sixty-fifth birthday. ed. J. Eska, R. G. Gruffydd, N. Jacobs (UWP, Cardiff, 1995).

A. Holder, *Alt-Celtischer Sprachschatz* (Teubner, Leipzig, 1896–1910).

R. M. Hogg, *A Grammar of Old English, volume I: Phonology* (Blackwell, Oxford, 1992).

H. Hübschmann, 'Iranica', KZ xxvii (1885) 103–112.

F. Hultsch, *Metrologicorum Scriptorum Reliquiae*, 2 vol. (Teubner, Leipzig, 1864–66).

R. W. Hunt, *Saint Dunstan's Classbook from Glastonbury, Codex Biblioth. Bodleianae Oxon. Auct. F. 4/32*, (A Facsimile), Umbrae Codicum Occidentalium, IV (North Holland Publishing Co., Amsterdam, 1961).

D. Huws, 'Llyfr Gwyn Rhgydderch', CMCS xxi (1991) 1–37 (= Huws, MWM 227–68).

D. Huws, *Five Ancient Books of Wales* (ASNC, Cambridge, 1995) (= Huws, MWM 65–83).

D. Huws, 'The Manuscripts', in *Lawyers and Laymen* ed. T. M. Charles-Edwards, M. E. Owen, D. Walters (UWP, Cardiff, 1986), 119–36 (= MWM 177–92).

Huws, MWM = D. Huws, *Medieval Welsh Manuscripts* (UWP, Cardiff/NLW, Aberystwyth, 2000).

D. Huws, 'Llawysgrif Hendregadredd', NLWJ xxii (1981–82) 1–26 (= Huws, MWM 193–226).

G. R. Isaac, 'Cunedag', BBCS xxxviii (1991) 100–101.

G. R. Isaac, 'Readings in the history and transmission of the *Gododdin*', CMCS xxxvii (Summer 1999) 55–78.

G. R. Isaac, '*Canu Aneirin* awdl LI', JCL ii (1993) 65–91.

G. R. Isaac, 'The progressive aspect marker: W. *yn*/OIr. *oc*', JCL iii (1994) 33–39.

G. R. Isaac, *The Verb in the Book of Aneirin: Studies in Syntax, Morphology and Etymology* (Niemeyer, Tübingen, 1996).

G. R. Isaac, 'Zwei kymrischen etymologien', ZCP xlvi (1994) 200–2.

K. H. Jackson, *The Gododdin: the Oldest Scottish Poem* (Edinburgh UP, Edinburgh, 1969).

Jackson, HPB = K. H. Jackson, *A Historical Phonology of Breton* (DIAS, Dublin, 1967).

K. H. Jackson, 'Brittonica', *Journal of Celtic Studies* i (1949) 69–79.

Jackson, LHEB = K. H. Jackson, *Language and History in Early Britain* (Edinburgh UP, Edinburgh, 1953).

K. H. Jackson, 'The date of the Old Welsh accent shift', SC x (1975) 40–53.

D. Jenkins, M. E. Owen, 'The Welsh marginalia in the Lichfield Gospels. Part II: the "Surexit" Memorandum', CMCS vii (Summer 1984) 91–120.

G. P. Jones, 'A list of epithets from Welsh pedigrees', BBCS iii (1926) 31–48.

T. G. Jones, 'Catraeth a Hirlas Owain', *Y Cymmrodor* xxxii (1922) 1–57.

M. E. Jones, *The End of Roman Britain* (Cornell UP, Ithaca/London, 1996).

M. E. Jones, J. Casey, 'The Gallic Chronicle restored: a chronology for the Anglo-Saxon invasions and the end of Roman Britain', *Britannia* xix (1988) 367–98.

R. M. Jones, 'Rhagymadrodd', in *Llyfr Gwyn Rhydderch. Y chwedlau a'r Rhamantau*, ed. J. G. Evans, repr. with new introduction by R. M. Jones (UWP, Cardiff, 1993), i–xix.

R. Jordan, *Handbuch der mittelenglischen Grammatik* (Winter, Heidelberg, 1925); English version updated with distribution-maps by E.J. Crook, *Handbook of Middle English grammar: phonology* (Mouton, The Hague, 1974).

J. Kellens, 'Vibration and twinkling', JIES v/3 (1977) 197–201.

N.R. Ker, *Catalogue of manuscripts containing Anglo-Saxon* (OUP, Oxford, 1957).

P. R. Kitson, 'On Old English nouns of more than one gender', *English Studies* lxxi (1990) 185–221.

P. R. Kitson, 'Topography, dialect, and the relation of Old English psalter-glosses', *English Studies* lxxxiii (2002) 474–503; lxxxiv (2003) 9–32.

P. R. Kitson, 'Geographical variation in Old English prepositions and the location of Ælfric's and other literary dialects', *English Studies* lxxiv (1993) 1–50.

P. R. Kitson, 'The nature of Old English dialect distributions, mainly as exhibited in charter boundaries. Part I: Vocabulary' in *Mediaeval dialectology* ed. J. Fisiak (Mouton de Gruyter, Berlin, 1995), 43–135.

P. R. Kitson, 'The dialect position of the Old English Orosius', *Studia Anglica Posnaniensia* xxx (1996) 3–35.

P. R. Kitson, 'British and European river-names', *Transactions of the Philological Society* xciv (1996) 73–118.

P. R. Kitson, forthcoming (a), *A new foundation for Old English dialect study*.

P. R. Kitson, forthcoming (b), *A guide to Anglo-Saxon charter boundaries* (English Place-Name Society, Nottingham).

P. R. Kitson, 'Natural dialects and literary dialects in Old and early Middle English', paper delivered at *Third International Conference of Middle English Language and Text*, University College, Dublin, 1.vii.1999.

J. T. Koch, 'The Cynfeirdd Poetry and the language of the sixth century' in *Early Welsh Poetry*, 17–43.

J. T. Koch, 'Ériu, Alba, Letha: when was a language ancestral to Gaelic first spoken in Ireland?', *Emania* ix (1991), 17–27.

J. T. Koch, *The Gododdin of Aneirin: Text and Context from Dark-Age North Britain* (UWP, Cardiff/Celtic Studies Publications, Andover, 1997).

J. T. Koch, *A Grammar of Old Welsh* (forthcoming).

J. T. Koch, 'Further to Indo-European *gwh in Celtic', in Eska, *et al.*, *Hispano-Gallo-Brittonica*, 79–95.

J. T. Koch, 'Gallo-Brittonic Tasc(i)ouanos "Badger-slayer" and the Reflex of Indo-European gwh', JCL i (1992) 101–18.

J. T. Koch, 'New thoughts on *Albion, Ierné*, and the "Pretanic" Isles', PHCC vi (1986) 1–28.

J. T. Koch, 'When was Welsh literature first written down?' SC xx/xxi (1985/86) 43–66.

J. T. Koch in collaboration with J. Carey, eds., *The Celtic Heroic Age: Literary Sources for Ancient Celtic Europe and Early Ireland and Wales*, 3rd edn. (Celtic Studies Publications, Oakville Connecticut & Aberystwyth, 2000).

R. Künzel, D. Blok, J. Verhoeff, *Lexicon van Nederlandse toponiemen tot 1200*, (P. J. Meertens-Institute voor Dialectologie, Volkskunde en Naamkunde, Amsterdam, 1988).

M-J. Lagrange, *Evangile selon saint Luc* (Gabalde, Paris, 1921).

P.-Y. Lambert, 'Welsh *Caswallawn*: the Fate of British **au*', in *Britain 400–600: Language and History*, ed. A. Bammesberger, A. Wollmann, Anglistische Forschungen, 205 (Winter, Heidelberg, 1990) 203–15.

P.-Y. Lambert, '"Thirty" and "Sixty" in Brittonic', CMCS viii (Winter 1984) 29–43.

P.-Y. Lambert, 'Les gloses du manuscrit BN Lat. 10290', ÉC xix (1982) 173–213.

P.-Y. Lambert, 'Les gloses grammaticales brittoniques', ÉC xxiv (1987) 285–308.

P.-Y. Lambert, 'La tuile gauloise de Châteaubleau (Seine-et-Marne)', ÉC xxxiv (1998–2000) 57–115.

P.-Y. Lambert, 'Varia VI.1 Celtic Latin *uigilare* "to wait for"', *Ériu* xxxvi (1985) 188–9.

M. Lapidge, 'Abbot Germanus, Winchcombe, Ramsey and the Cambridge Psalter', in *Words, texts and manuscripts: studies in Anglo-Saxon culture presented to Helmut Gneuss*, ed. M. Korhammer (Brewer, Cambridge, 1992) 99–129.

W. Lehmann, *A Gothic etymological dictionary* (Brill, Leiden 1986).

L. Létoublon, Ch. de Lamberterie, 'La roue tourne', *Revue de Philologie* liv (1980) 305–26.

C. M. Lewis, 'The court poets: their function, status and craft', in *A Guide to Welsh Literature*, Vol. 1, 123–56.

H. Lewis, *Yr Elfen Ladin yn yr Iaith Gymraeg* (UWP, Cardiff, 1943).

H. Lewis, '*Ene, eny*', BBCS i (1921–23) 9–12.

H. Lewis, 'Glosau Rhydychen', BBCS iii (1926–27) 1–4.

Lewis, LlCC = H. Lewis, *Llawlyfr Cernyweg Canol*, argraffiad newydd (UWP, Cardiff, 1946).

Lewis and Piette, LlLlC = H. Lewis, J. R. F. Piette, *Llawlyfr Llydaweg Canol*, diwygiedig (UWP, Cardiff, 1966).

M. Lewis, 'Disgrifiad o orgraff Hen Gymraeg gan ei chymharu ag orgraff Hen Wyddeleg', MA dissertation, University of Wales (Aberystwyth, 1961).

E. Lhuyd, *Archaeologia Britannica* (Clarendon, Oxford, 1707; repr. Irish University Press, Dublin, 1971).

W. M. Lindsay, *Early Welsh Script* (Clarendon, Oxford, 1912).

J. E. Lloyd, *A History of Wales*, 2 vol. (Longman, London, 1911).

C. Lloyd-Morgan, 'Late Medieval Welsh Grail traditions', in *The Changing Face of Arthurian Romance*, ed. A. Adams et al. (Boydell, Woodbridge, 1986) 78–91.

A. Loprieno, *Ancient Egyptian, A Linguistic Introduction* (CUP, Cambridge, 1995).

J. Loth, Review of H. d'Arbois de Jubainville, *Études sur le droit celtique* (Thorin, Paris, 1895–96), in *Revue de l'Histoire des Réligions* xxxiii (1896) 368–88.

J. Loth, *Vocabulaire vieux-breton* (Champion, Paris, 1884; repr. Champion, Paris / Slatkine, Geneva, 1970, 1982).

R. Lühr, *Expressivität und Lautgesetz im Germanischen* (Heidelberg, 1988).

R. Lühr, 'Fälle von Doppelkonsonanz im Keltischen, zur Frage ihrer Genese', *Sprachwissenschaft* 10 (1985) 274–346.

Macalister, CIIC = R. A. S. Macalister, *Corpus Inscriptionum Insularum Celticarum*, 2 vols. (The Stationery Office, Dublin, 1945–9).

P. Mac Cana, 'Syntax and style in Middle Welsh prose: notes on periphrasis and epitaxis', *Celtica* xxiii (1999) 157–168.

K. R. McCone, 'Some remarks on the relative in Old Irish', *Ériu* xxxi (1980) 10–27.

K. R. McCone, 'The Würzburg and Milan glosses: our earliest sources of "Middle Irish"', *Ériu* xxxvi (1985) 85–106.

K. R. McCone, *Indo-European Origins of the Old Irish Nasal Presents, Subjunctives and Futures* (Institut für Sprachwissenschaft der Universität Innsbruck, Innsbruck, 1991).

K. R. McCone, 'OIr *aub* "river" and *amnair* "maternal uncle"', MSS liii (1992) 101–11.

K. R. McCone, 'An tSean-Gaeilge agus a réamhstair', in *Stair na Gaeilge*, 61–219.

K. R. McCone, *Towards a Relative Chronology of Ancient and Medieval Celtic Sound Change*, Maynooth Studies in Celtic Linguistics I (Dept. of Old and Middle Irish, St. Patrick's College, Maynooth, 1996).

F. Madan, H. Craster, *A Summary Catalogue of Western Manuscripts in the Bodleian Library at Oxford*, 2 vols. (Clarendon, Oxford, 1922).

I. Maddieson, *The Patterns of Sound* (CUP, Cambridge, 1984).

M. Manitius, *Geschichte der lateinischen Literatur des Mittelalters*, 3 vols. (Beck, Munich, 1911–31).

J. F. Matthews, *Western Aristocracies and the Imperial Court* (OUP, Oxford, 1975).

A.T.E. Matonis, 'The Welsh bardic grammars and western grammatical tradition', *Modern Philology* lxxix (1981) 121–45.

W. Mayerthaler, 'Markiertheit in der Phonologie', in *Silben, Segmente, Akzent*, ed. T. Venneman (Niemeyer, Tübingen, 1982) 205–46.

Mayrhofer EWAia = M. Mayrhofer, *Etymologisches Wörterbuch des Altindoarischen* (Winter, Heidelberg, 1989–).

M. Mayrhofer, *Die iranischen Namen*. Iranisches Personennamenbuch Bd. 1 (Österreichische Akademie der Wisenschaften, Vienna, 1979).

H. D. Meritt, *Old English Glosses* (Modern Language Association of America, New York, 1945).

F. Mezger, 'yn + Verbalnomen in den Zweigen des Mabinogi', KZ lviii (1931) 238–47.

F. Miklosich, *Lexicon palaeoslovenico-graeco-latinum* (Braumüller, Vienna, 1862–64).

M. Miller, 'The foundation legend of Gwynedd in the Latin texts', BBCS xxvii (1976–8) 515–32.

M. Miller, 'The last British entry in the "Gallic Chronicles"', *Britannia* ix (1978) 315–18.

I. Mittendorf, 'Sprachliche und orthographische Besonderheiten eines mittelkymrischen Textes aus dem 13. Jahrhundert (*Gwyrthyeu e Wynvededic Veir*)', in *Akten des 2. deutschen Keltologensymposium*, 127–48.

I. Mittendorf, E. Poppe, 'Celtic contacts of the English progressive?', in *Celtic Englishes II*, ed. L. C. H. Tristram (Winter, Heidelberg, 2000) 117–145.

M. Monier-Williams, *A Sanskrit-English dictionary* (Clarendon, Oxford, 1899).

J. Morris, *Nennius: British History and the Welsh Annals* (Phillimore, London, 1980).

J. Morris-Jones, 'Taliesin', *Y Cymmrodor* xxviii (1918).

Morris-Jones WG = J. Morris-Jones, *A Welsh Grammar: Phonology and Accidence* (OUP, Oxford, 1913).

W. M. Morris, *A Glossary of the Demetian dialect of North Pembrokeshire* (Evans and Short, Tonypandy 1910; reprint Llanerch Press, Felinfach, 1991).

F. Mossé, Fernand, *Histoire de la forme périphrastique être + participe présent en germanique. Deuxième partie: Moyen-anglais et anglais moderne* (Klincksieck, Paris, 1938).

Muhlberger, 'The Gallic Chronicle of 452 and its authority for British events', *Britannia* xiv (1983) 23–33.

H. Mytum, 'Ireland and Rome: the maritime frontier', in *The Roman West in the Third Century. Contributions from archaeology and history*, ed. A. King, M. Henig. British Archaeological Reports, International Series, 109 (BAR, Oxford, 1981).

D. Nehls, 'Kontrastive Anmerkungen—Deutsch, Französisch, Italienisch, Spanisch, (Russisch)—zur Expanded Form im Gegenwartsenglischen', in *Papers from the International Symposium on Applied Contrastive Linguistics, Stuttgart, October 11–13, 1971*, ed. G. Nickel (Cornelsen-Velhagen & Klasing, Bielefeld, 1972) 175–200.

D. Nehls, *Synchron-diachrone Untersuchungen zur Expanded Form im Englischen. Eine strukturalfunktionale Analyse* (Max Hueber, München, 1974).

J. Nichols 'Chechen', 'Ingush' in *The Indigenous Languages of the Caucasus*, vol. iv, part 2, ed. R. Smeets (Caravan Books, Delmar, New York, 1994) 1–77, 79–145.

A. Noreen, *Altnordische Grammatik* 4th edn. (Niemeyer, Tübingen, 1923).

M. A. O'Brien, 'Short notes. *Uchtlach* 'lapful'. *Littiu* 'porridge'', *Celtica* ii (1952–54) 353.

D. Ó Corráin, 'Historical need and literary narrative', in *Proceedings of the Seventh*

International Congress of Celtic Studies, Oxford 1983, ed. D. E. Evans, J. G. Griffith, E. M. Jope (Oxbow, Oxford, 1986), 141–58.

S. Ó hEinirí, *Scéalta Chois Cladaigh—Stories of Sea and Shore*, Collected, Translated and Annotated by Séamas Ó Cathain (Comhairle Bhéaloideas Éireann, University College, Dublin, 1983).

R. Ó hUiginn, 'The Old Irish nasalizing relative clause', *Ériu* xxxvii (1986) 33–88.

P. Ó Néill, 'The earliest dry-point glosses in Codex Usserianus Primus', in *A Miracle of Learning. Studies in Manuscripts and Irish Learning. Essays in honour of William O'Sullivan*, ed. T. Barnard, D. Ó Cróinín, K. Simms (Ashgate, Aldershot, 1998), 1–28.

M. Ó Siadhail, *Modern Irish: Grammatical Structure and Dialectal Variation* (CUP, Cambridge, 1989).

T. D. O'Sullivan, *The 'De Excidio' of Gildas. Its authenticity and date* (Brill, Leiden, 1978).

H. Owen, *The Desription of Penbrokeshire by George Owen of Henllys*, 4 vol. Cymmrodor Record Series, 1 (Society of the Cymmrodorion, London, 1902–36).

R. I. Page, *An introduction to English runes* (Methuen, London, 1973).

R. I. Page, 'More Old English Scratched Glosses', *Anglia* xcvii (1979) 27–45.

K. S. Painter, 'A late-Roman silver ingot from Kent', *Antiquaries' Journal* lii (1972) 84–92.

T. H. Parry-Williams, *The English Element in Welsh* (The Honourable Society of Cymmrodorion, London, 1923).

T. H. Parry-Williams, 'Some points of similarity in the phonology of Welsh and Breton (contd.)', RC xxxv (1914) 317–56.

H. Pedersen, 'Die Nasalpräsentia und der slavische Akzent', KZ xxxviii (1905) 297–421.

Pedersen, VKG = H. Pedersen, *Vergleichende Grammatik der keltishen Sprachen*. 2 vols (Vandenhoeck & Ruprecht, Göttingen, 1909–13).

W. Pfeiffer, *Etymologisches Wörterbuch des Deutschen* (Akademie Verlag, Berlin, 1989).

W. J. T. Pijnenburg, *Bijdragen tot de etymologie van het oudste Nederlands* (Lumo-Zet/Gema, Eindhoven, 1980).

Pokorny IEW: J. Pokorny, *Indogermanisches etymologisches Wörterbuch* (Francke, Bern, 1949–59).

E. Poppe, 'The "expanded form" in Insular Celtic and English: some historical and comparative considerations, with special emphasis on Middle Irish' in *The Celtic Roots of English*, ed. M. Filpulla, J. Klemola, H. Pitkänen, Studies in Language 37 (University of Joensuu, Faculty of Humanities, Joensuu, 2002) 237–70.

E. Poppe, 'The position of temporal adverbials with *nos* as core in MW sentences. A functional approach', SC xxiv/xxv (1989/90) 117–129.

E. Poppe, *Untersuchungen zur Wortstellung im Mittelkymrischen. Temporalbestimmungen und funktionale Satzperspektive* (Helmut Buske Verlag, Hamburg, 1991).

P. Pulsiano, 'The originality of the gloss of the *Vespasian Psalter* and its relation to the gloss of the *Junius Psalter*', *Anglo-Saxon England* xxv (1996) 37–62.

M. Raftery, *Pagan Celtic Ireland. The Engima of the Irish Iron Age* (Thames and Hudson, London, 1994).

M. Reichardt, S. Reichert, *Grammatik des Modernen Chinesisch* (Verlag Enzyklopädie, Leipzig, 1990).

M. Richards, *Cystrawen y Frawddeg Gymraeg* (UWP, Cardiff, 1938)

M. Richards, *Enwau Tir a Gwlad* (Gwasg Gwynedd, Caernarfon, 1998).

M. Richards, 'Early Welsh territorial suffixes', *Journal of the Royal Society of Antiquaries of Ireland* xcv (1965) 205–12.

B. F. Roberts, 'Tales and Romances', in *A Guide to Welsh Literature*, I, 203–43.

J. R. Roberts, *Amele* (Croom Helm, London/New York/Sydney, 1987).

E. Risch, *Wortbildung der homerischen Sprache* (de Gruyter, Berlin/New York, 1974).

A. J. Roderick, 'The four cantreds: a study in administration', BBCS x (1939–41) 246–55.

S. Rodway, 'A datable development in Medieval Literary Welsh', CMCS xxxvi (1998) 71–94.

J. Rowland, '*allan, ymaes*', BBCS xxxvii (1990), 118–19.

J. Rowland, *Early Welsh Saga Poetry* (Brewer, Woodbridge, 1990).

P. Russell, *Celtic Word-Formation. The Velar Suffixes* (DIAS, Dublin, 1990).

P. Russell, 'Orthography as a key to codicology: innovation in the work of a thirteenth-century Welsh scribe', CMCS xxv (Summer 1993) 77–85.

P. Russell, 'What did medieval Welsh scribes do? The scribe of the Dingestow Court MS', CMCS xxxvii (1999) 79–96.

P. Russell, 'Some neglected sources for Middle Welsh phonology', ÉC xxix (1992) 383–90.

P. Russell, 'The Celtic preverb *uss and related matters', *Ériu* xxxix (1988) 95–126.

P. Russell, *Introduction to the Celtic Languages* (Longman, London/New York, 1995).

P. Russell, 'Scribal (in)competence in thirteenth-century North Wales: the orthography of the Black Book of Chirk (Peniarth MS 29)', NLWJ xxix (1995/96) 129–76.

P. Russell, 'Preverbs, prepositions and adverbs: sigmatic and asigmatic,' TPhS lxxxvi (1988) 144–72.

S = Charter numbered as in Sawyer, *Anglo-Saxon Charters*.

P. Salway, *The Oxford Illustrated History of Roman Britain* (OUP, Oxford, 1993).

P. H. Sawyer, *Anglo-Saxon Charters: an annotated list and bibliography* (RHS, London, 1968).

P. Schrijver, 'The development of PIE *sk in British', BBCS xxxix (1992) 1–15.

P. Schrijver, 'The Châteaubleau tile as a link between Latin and French and between Gaulish and Brittonic', ÉC xxxiv (1998–2000), 135–41.

Schrijver, SBCHP = P. Schrijver, *Studies in British Celtic Historical Phonology* (Rodopi, Amsterdam, 1995).

P. Schrijver, *Studies in the History of Celtic Pronouns and Particles*, Maynooth Studies in Celtic Linguistics II (The Department of Old Irish, National University of Ireland, Maynooth, 1997).

S. Schumacher, 'Archaische Verbalformen im Buch von Aneirin und in anderen frühen Texten des Kymrischen' in *Akten des 2. deutschen Keltologensymposium*, 202–35.

K. von See, (Hrsg.), *Europäisches Frühmittelalter*. Neues Handbuch der Literaturwissenschaft, 6 (Harrassowitz, Wiesbaden, 1985).

E. Seebold, *Vergleichendes und etymologisches Wörterbuch der germanischen starken Verben* (Mouton, Den Haag, 1970).

P. Sims-Williams, 'The development of the Indo-European voiced labio-velars in Celtic', BBCS xxix (1982) 201–29.

P. Sims-Williams, 'The emergence of Old Welsh, Cornish and Breton orthography, 600–800: the evidence of Archaic Old Welsh', BBCS xxxviii (1991) 20–86.

P. Sims-Williams, *The Celtic Inscriptions of Britain: Phonology and Chronology, c. 400–1200*, Publication of the Philological Society, 37 (Blackwell, Oxford, 2003).

P. Sims-Williams, 'Gildas and the Anglo-Saxons', CMCS vi (Winter 1983), 1–30.

P. Sims-Williams, 'The submission of Irish kings in fact and fiction: Henry II, Bendigeidfran, and the dating of *The Four Branches of the Mabinogi*', CMCS xxii (Winter 1991) 31–61.

P. Sims-Williams, 'Gildas and vernacular poetry', in *Gildas. New Approaches*, 169–90.

P. Sims-Williams, 'Indo-European *g^wh in Celtic, 1894–1994', in *Hispano-Gallo-Brittonica*, 196–218.

A. H. Smith, *The place-names of the West Riding of Yorkshire*, 8 vols., English Place-Name Society xxx–xxxvii (EPNS, Nottingham, 1958–63).

A. P. Smyth, *Warlords and Holy Men. Scotland A.D. 80–1000* (Edward Arnold, London, 1984; repr. Edinburgh UP, Edinburgh, 1989).

A. Sommerfelt, *Studies in Cyfeiliog Welsh. A contribution to Welsh dialectology* (Dybwald, Oslo, 1935).

Stair na Gaeilge in ómós do Pádraig Ó Fiannachta, ed. K. McCone, D. McManus, C. Ó Háinle, N. Williams, L. Breatnach (Roinn na Sean-Ghaeilge, Coláiste Phádraig, Maigh Nuad, 1994).

W. H. Stevenson (ed.), *Early Scholastic Colloquies* (Clarendon, Oxford, 1929).

W. Stokes, 'The Irish verses, notes and glosses in Harl. 1802', RC viii (1887) 346–69.

W. Stokes, 'Cambrica', TPhS 1860–1, 232–88.

W. Stokes, A Bezzenberger, *Wortschatz der keltischen Spracheinheit* (Vandenhoeck and

Ruprecht, Göttingen 1979, repr. of *Urkeltischer Sprachschatz*, 1894).

A. Stolz, 'Christi de passeribus parabola', *Verbum Domini* xiv (1934) 56.

M. E. Surridge, 'The number and status of Romance words attested in *Ystorya Bown de Hamtwn*', BBCS xxxii (1985) 68–78.

C. Swift, *Ogam Stones and the Earliest Irish Christians*. Maynooth Monograph, Series Minor, 2. (Dept. of Old and Middle Irish, Maynooth, 1997).

O. Szemerényi, 'Greek γάλα and the Indo-European term for 'milk', KZ lxxv (1958) 170–90.

O. Szemerényi, 'The labiovelars in Mycenaean and historical Greek', *Studi micenei ed egeo-anatolici* i (1966) 29–52.

Thes. ii = W. Stokes, J. Strachan, ed., *Thesaurus Palaeohibernicus*, vol. ii (CUP, Cambridge, 1903).

B. Thomas, P. W. Thomas, *Cymraeg, Cymrâg, Cymrêg. . . Cyflwyno'r Tafodieithoedd* (Gwasg Taf, Cardiff, 1989).

C. Thomas, *Christianity in Roman Britain to AD 500* (Batsford, London, 1981).

P. W. Thomas, 'Middle Welsh dialects: problems and perspectives', BBCS xl (1993) 17–50.

P. W. Thomas, 'In search of Middle Welsh dialects' in *Celtic Languages and Celtic Peoples, Proceedings of the Second North American Congress on Celtic Studies, held in Halifax August 16–19 1989* ed. C. J. Byrne, M. Harry, P. Ó Siadhail (D'Arcy McGhee Chair of Irish Studies, Saint Mary's University, Halifax, 1992 [1989]) 287–303.

E. A. Thompson, 'Zosimus 6.10.2 and the letters of Honorius', *Classical Quarterly* 32 (1982) 445–62.

E. A. Thompson, 'Britain, A.D. 406–410', *Britannia* viii (1977) 303–18.

E. A. Thompson, 'Gildas and the History of Britain', *Britannia* x (1979) 203–26; xi (1980) 344.

D. A. Thorne, *A Comprehensive Welsh Grammar* (Blackwell, Oxford, 1993).

R. Thurneysen, 'Notes sur quelques gloses galloises', RC xi (1890) 203–6.

W. C. Till, *Koptische Dialektgrammatik* (Verlag C. H. Beck, München, 1961).

M. Todd, 'The Falkirk hoard of denarii: trade or subsidy?', *Proceeding of the Society of Antiquaries of Scotland* cxv (1985) 229–32.

A. N. Tucker, J. T. O. Mpaayei, *A Maasai Grammar with Vocabulary* (Longmans, Green & Co., London, New York, Toronto, 1955).

E. van Tassel Graves, *The Old Cornish Vocabulary* (University Microfilms: Ann Arbor, 1962).

J. Vendryes, 'Questions étymologiques', EC iv (1948) 55–66.

J. Vendryes, 'Le bétail numéraire', RC xlii (1925) 391–4.

Vendryes, LEIA: *Lexique Étymologique de l'irlandais ancien*, ed. J. Vendryes, E. Bachellery, P.-Y. Lambert (DIAS, Dublin/CNRS, Paris: *A* 1981, *B* 1980, *C* 1987, *D* 1996, *MNOP* 1961, *RS* 1974, *TU* 1978).

R. L. Venezky and A. di P. Healey, *Microfiche Concordance to Old English* (Pontifical Institute for Medieval Studies, Toronto, 1980 [original], 1985 [high-frequency words]).

H. de la Villemarqué, 'Rapport présenté à S. Exc. M. le Ministre de l'instruction publique et des cultes . . ., sur une mission littéraire accompli en Angleterre—Seconde partie: Notices des principaux manuscrits de l'Angleterre concernant la langue, la littéraire et l'histoire des anciens Bretons', *Archives des missions scientifiques et littéraires* v (1856) 234–72.

W. von Christ, 'Über das Argumentum Calculandi des Victorius und dessen Commentar', *Sitzungberichte der königlichen bayerischen Akademie der Wissenschaften zu München*, Jahrgang 1863, vol. I, 100–152.

J. de Vries, *Altnordisches etymologisches Wörterbuch*, 2nd edn. (Brill, Leyden, 1962).

H. Wagner, *Das Verbum in den Sprachen der britischen Inseln. Ein Beitrag zur geographischen Typologie des Verbums* (Niemeyer, Tübingen, 1959).

A. Walde, J. Pokorny, *Vergleichendes Wörterbuch der indogermanischen Sprachen* I–III (de Gruyter, Berlin/Leipzig, 1927–32).

C. Watkins, 'Preliminaries to a historical and comparative analysis of the syntax of the Old Irish verb' *Celtica* vi (1963) 1–49.

T. A. Watkins, 'CC *y/yn* berfenwol', BBCS xviii (1960) 362–372.

T. A. Watkins, 'Points of similarity between Old Welsh and Irish orthography', BBCS xxi (1964–66) 135–41.

T. A. Watkins, 'Dulliau orgraffyddol Cymraeg Canol o ddynodi'r treiglad trwynol', BBCS xxiii (1968–70) 7–13.

S. Watson, 'Gaeilge na hAlban' in *Stair na Gaeilge*, 661–702.

WDS = *The Welsh Dialect Survey*, ed. A. R. Thomas et al. (UWP, Cardiff, 2000).

G. Williams, *An Introduction to Welsh Poetry* (Faber and Faber, London 1951).

G. A. Williams, 'Owain Cyfeiliog: bardd-dywysog?' in *Beirdd a Thywysogion, Barddoniaeth Llys yng Nghymru, Iwerddon a'r Alban cyflwynedig i R. Geraint Gruffydd*, ed. M. E. Owen and B. F. Roberts (UWP, Cardiff, 1996) 180–201.

I. Williams, 'The Towyn inscribed stone', *Archaeologia Cambrensis* c (1949) 160–72 [repr. Williams BWP 25–40].

I. Williams, 'The Computus fragment', BBCS iii (1927) 245–72.

I. Williams, 'Glosau Rhydychen: mesurau a phwysau', BBCS v (1929–31) 226–48.

I. Williams, 'Notes on Nennius', BBCS vii (1935) 380–94.

Williams BWP = I. Williams, *The Beginnings of Welsh Poetry*, 2nd edn. (UWP, Cardiff, 1980).

I. Williams, '*Gregynog*', *Y Llenor* ix (1930) 225–32.

I. Williams, 'An Old Welsh verse', NLWJ ii (1941) 69–75 [reprinted Williams BWP 181–9].

J. E. C. Williams, *The Court Poet in Medieval Wales: an Essay* (Edwin Mellen, Lewiston/ Lampeter, 1997).

J. E. C. Williams, '*difod, diw, pyddiw*', BBCS xxiii (1968–70) 217–33.

J. E. C. Williams, 'Meilyr Brydydd and Gruffudd ap Cynan' in *Gruffudd ap Cynan, A Collaborative Biography* ed. K.L. Maund (Boydell, Woodbridge, 1996) 165–86.

J. E. C. Williams, 'Welsh *yn ei eistedd, yn ei orwedd, yn ei sefyll*', in *Indo-Celtica. Gedächtnisschrift für Alf Sommerfelt*, ed. H. Pilch, J. Thurow (Max Hüber, München, 1972) 206–18.

J. E. C. Williams, *The Poets of the Welsh Princes*, 2nd edn. (UWP, Cardiff, 1994).

M. Williams, *Diawl y Wenallt* (Y Lolfa, Talybont, 1990).

N. Williams, 'An Mhanainnis' in *Stair na Gaeilge*, 703–44.

P. R. Wilson, P. Carwell, R. J. Cramp, J. Evans, R. H. Taylor-Wilson, A. Thompson, J. S. Wacher, 'Early Anglian Catterick and Catraeth', *Medieval Archaeology* xl (1996) 1–61.

I. Wood, 'The end of Roman Britain: continental evidence and parallels', in *Gildas. New Approaches*, 1–25.

N. Wright, 'Gildas's geographical perspective: some problems', in *Gildas. New Approaches*, 85–105.

D. Yerkes, 'The provenance of the unique copy of the Old English translation of Bili, Vita Sancti Machuti', *Manuscripta* xxx (1986) 108–11.

D. Yerkes, *The Old English Life of Machutus* (Toronto University Press, Toronto, 1984).

J. C. Zeuss, *Grammatica Celtica*, 2nd edn. (Weidmann, Leipzig, 1871).

S. Zimmer, *Studies in Welsh Word-formation* (DIAS, Dublin, 2000).

E. Zupitza, 'Etymologien', *Beiträge zur Kunde der indogermanischen Sprachen* xxv (1899) 89–105.

CELTIC STUDIES PUBLICATIONS I

The Celtic Heroic Age: Literary Sources for Ancient Celtic Europe and Early Ireland and Wales, ed. John T. Koch with John Carey (Fourth Edition, revised and expanded, 2003) Pp. x + 440

ISBN 1–891271–04–0

CELTIC STUDIES PUBLICATIONS II

A Celtic Florilegium: Studies in Memory of Brendan O Hehir, ed. Kathryn Klar, Eve Sweetser, and †Claire Thomas (1996) Pp. xxxvi + 227

ISBN *hc* 0–9642446–3–2 *pb* 0–9642446–6–7

CELTIC STUDIES PUBLICATIONS III

A Single Ray of the Sun: Religious Speculation in Early Ireland—three essays by John Carey (Second Edition, revised 2003) Pp. viii + 123

ISBN 1–891271–03–2

CELTIC STUDIES PUBLICATIONS IV

Ildánach Ildírech. A Festschrift for Proinsias Mac Cana, ed. John Carey, John T. Koch, and Pierre-Yves Lambert (1999) Pp. xvii + 312

ISBN 1–891271–01–6

CELTIC STUDIES PUBLICATIONS V

The Instcriptions of Early Medieval Brittany / Les inscriptions de la Bretagne du Haut Moyen Âge, Wendy Davies, James Graham-Campbell, Mark Handley, Paul Kershaw, John T. Koch, Gwenaël Le Duc, Kris Lockyear (2000) Pp. xviii + 340

ISBN 1–891271–05–9

CELTIC STUDIES PUBLICATIONS VI

The Saints of Wales:An Inventory of their Cults and Dedications, Graham Jones (in preparation)

ISBN 1–891271–06–7

CELTIC STUDIES PUBLICATIONS VII

Yr Hen Iaith: Studies in early Welsh, ed. Paul Russell (2003) Pp. viii + 224

ISBN 1–891271–10–5